STUDY GUIDE

Douglas A. Johnson
Western Michigan University

INVITATION TO PSYCHOLOGY
FIFTH EDITION

Carole Wade
Dominican University of California

Carol Tavris

Prentice Hall

Boston   Columbus   Indianapolis   New York   San Francisco   Upper Saddle River

Amsterdam   Cape Town   Dubai   London   Madrid   Milan   Munich   Paris   Montreal   Toronto

Delhi   Mexico City   Sao Paulo   Sydney   Hong Kong   Seoul   Singapore   Taipei   Tokyo

Prentice Hall
is an imprint of

© 2012 by PEARSON EDUCATION, INC.
Upper Saddle River, New Jersey 07458

10 9 8 7 6 5 4 3 2 1

ISBN 10: 0-205-06635-6
ISBN 13: 978-0-205-06635-3

Contents

To the Student

This Study Guide is designed for use with *Invitation to Psychology,* Fifth Edition, by Carole Wade and Carol Tavris. It does not serve as a substitute for the textbook but rather as a supplement to help you comprehend the material and to assess what you have learned. The features of the Study Guide include a **Chapter Overview** and, for each main section in the text's chapters, **Guided Study** and **Terms for Review** sections.

Make sure to read the "From the Authors" section in the textbook. It provides you with valuable suggestions for reading and studying the text. A plan that includes this Study Guide is offered below.

First, read the Chapter Outlines in the text and the Chapter Overviews in the Study Guide. They describe the contents of the chapters and how the chapters are structured. Having a good idea of what you will be reading will help you organize and comprehend the information.

After surveying the chapter content and organization, you should proceed through the chapter section by section. Use the "You are about to learn..." statements as guides to the content in each section. Pay attention to important terms and their definitions, people, and concepts. You may want to write the terms and their definitions in a notebook or on flashcards to use to test yourself before an exam. In addition, study the illustrations, tables, and figures in the textbook. The tables present summary/comparative information and are excellent reviews. After you finish the section, complete the Quick Quiz in the text to test your knowledge of the information.

Next, complete the Guided Study for the section in the Study Guide. You may want to use another sheet of paper to write your answers so that you may redo the section when preparing for your exams. Reread the material in the text for any questions you have trouble answering. Then, review the terms for the section. Study any terms that you cannot define. Take breaks between studying the main chapter sections because distributed study (i.e., studying small chunks of material more frequently) tends to improve retention compared to massed study (i.e., studying large chunks of material less frequently).

When you've finished studying all the sections in a chapter, review the entire chapter. There are several devices in the textbook and Study Guide to assist you. You should read the Taking Psychology with You section in the textbook. It shows how the chapter content can be applied to your life, which makes the material more meaningful and memorable. Next, review the text's Chapter Summary, and the Guided Study units and the Terms for Review in the Study Guide. Go over any terms that remain unfamiliar. Now you are ready to test your knowledge of the chapter content.

You should test yourself in two ways. First, answer the "You are about to learn..." questions, which precede each major section in the text. Compare your answers to sample answers provided in the Study Guide. Review the content for any questions you had difficulty answering. Then, take both the Key Terms and the Multiple-Choice Progress Tests in the Study Guide. Review any necessary material.

Thank you for reading these suggestions. I hope they are helpful to you. I wish you success in achieving your goals in your psychology course. Please send me your comments and suggestions regarding this study tool. My email address is douglas.johnson@wmich.edu. Thanks to the textbook authors and Pearson Education for the opportunity to work on this Study Guide, and to Fred Whitford for his contributions in previous editions.

Douglas A. Johnson
Psychology Department
Western Michigan University

What is Psychology?

CHAPTER OVERVIEW   Chapter 1 begins by defining psychology and discussing how it is different from other areas that attempt to explain behavior and mental processes, with an emphasis on the distinction between empirical approaches and pseudoscience. A brief history of psychology and the people and events that led to the beginning of research in psychology is provided. Contributions of several early psychologists are noted, including Wilhelm Wundt and William James. Contemporary psychology is discussed in terms of five major theoretical perspectives now dominant in psychology.

The professional activities of psychologists are outlined next. Researchers in psychology study either basic or applied psychology. Regarding psychological practice, the differences among a clinical psychologist, psychotherapist, psychoanalyst, and psychiatrist are explored. The role of psychology in communities is discussed.

The third section presents basic guidelines for critical thinking. The guidelines aid in evaluating whether a psychological claim is valid and in determining whether a theory is scientific. The importance of understanding and applying the principle of falsifiability also is noted.

Descriptive methods are covered next, including advantages and disadvantages of such methods as case studies, observational studies, psychological tests, and surveys. Important issues regarding representative samples, standardization, norms, reliability, and validity are raised. Correlational methods and their uses and limitations are examined. Coefficient of correlation and positive and negative correlations are defined and explained.

The experimental method is detailed using a theoretical study on cell phone use and driving to illustrate such concepts as independent variable, dependent variable, experimental group, control group, and placebo and experimenter effects. Lastly, a brief discussion of statistical methods is presented. Descriptive statistics such as arithmetic mean and standard deviation are discussed. In addition, inferential statistics are introduced along with the concepts of statistical significance and meta-analysis.

GUIDED STUDY

1. The Science of Psychology

Read the section "The Science of Psychology" and then answer the following questions. If you have trouble answering any of the questions, re-study the relevant material before going on to the review of key terms and the progress tests.

1-1. Psychology is defined as the discipline concerned with ___behavior___ and ___mental___ processes and how they are affected by an organism's ___physical___ ___state___, ___mental___ ___state___, and ___external environment___.

1-2. It is important when studying psychology to understand how it differs from other areas that purport to explain human behavior. The authors note that psychology is not psychobabble. One of the differences between psychology and pseudosciences is that psychology is based on research and evidence gathered by careful observation— known as ___empirical___ evidence. Another difference between psychology and its nonscientific competitors is that the predictions made by astrologers, psychics, and the like tend to be so ___vague___ that they become ___meaningless___ when they are tested. Psychology is also not just a fancy name for ___common sense___. Frequently psychological research produces results that ___contradict___ common sense.

1-3. Both great thinkers of history and today's psychologists want to ___describe___, ___predict___, understand, and ___modify___ behavior in order to add to human knowledge and increase human happiness. The forerunners of psychology did not, however, utilize ___empirical___ methods. For example, the attempt to account for specific character and personality traits by studying bumps on the skull was known as _____ and turned out to be complete nonsense. The first psychological laboratory was established in the year ___1879___ by ___Wilhelm Wundt___. The empirical method that involved carefully trained volunteers observing, analyzing, and describing their own sensations, mental images, and emotional reactions was called ___trained introspection___. William James, an American philosopher, was a leader of ___functionalism___ which emphasized the function or purpose of behavior, not its analysis and description. Psychology also has its roots in an approach developed by ___Sigmund Freud___ ~~_____~~, in which he concluded that conflicts and emotional traumas from ___childhood___ were too threatening to be remembered ___consciously___. His broad theory of personality and his method of treating people became known as ___Psychoanalysis___

1-4. There are currently five major perspectives that are dominant in psychology. The __biological__ perspective focuses on how bodily events affect behavior, feelings, and thoughts. A biological specialty, __evolutionary__ psychology, emphasizes how genetically influenced behavior that was functional or adaptive in the past may be reflected in today's behaviors. The __learning__ perspective focuses on the environment and how experience influences our actions. Psychologists from this perspective may refer to themselves as __behaviorists__ when they are especially interested in rewards and punishers. Psychologists who combine behaviorism with research on thoughts, values, and intentions are known as __social~~-~~cognitive__ learning theorists. Those interested in how people reason, remember, explain experiences, and form beliefs follow the __cognitive__ perspective. On the other hand, the approach that focuses on how society and culture affect behavior is known as the __sociocultural__ perspective. The study of unconscious dynamics is undertaken when adopting the __psychodynamic__ perspective.

Terms for Review

The following is a list of the important terms from the section "The Science of Psychology." Make sure you are familiar with each term before taking the progress test on these terms.

psychology
pseudoscience
empirical

psychoanalysis
biological perspective
evolutionary psychology

phrenology
Wilhelm Wundt
trained introspection
functionalism

learning perspective
cognitive perspective
sociocultural perspective
psychodynamic perspective

2. What Psychologists Do

Read the section "What Psychologists Do" and then answer the following questions. If you have trouble answering any of the questions, re-study the relevant material before going on to the review of key terms and the progress tests.

2-1. Psychologists who seek knowledge for its own sake are said to engage in __basic__ psychology. On the other hand, psychologists concerned with the practical uses of knowledge are said to engage in __applied__ psychology.

2-2. __Counseling__ psychologists usually help people deal with more minor day-to-day problems. And, __school__ psychologists work with students, parents, and teachers to aid student performance and resolve emotional difficulties. However, psychologists who are trained in psychotherapy and treat severely disturbed people are typically __clinical__ psychologists. People often confuse the term clinical psychologist with the terms psychotherapist, psychoanalyst, and psychiatrist. A __psychotherapist__ is anyone who does any type of psychotherapy and is not legally regulated. A __psychoanalyst__, on the other hand, is a person who practices psychoanalysis. An M.D. and a three-year residency in psychiatry can earn one the title of __psychiatrist__

2-3. Psychology has expanded quickly since the second half of the _twenith_ century. The American Psychological Association currently has 53 divisions, which represent major fields and specific research or interests, such as the psychology of _women_, the psychology of men, _peace_, _enviromental_ problems, and psychology and the _law_. Psychologists make many contributions to their _communties_. For example, they consult with companies to improve worker _satifaction_ and productivity and they establish programs to reduce _ethnic_ tensions.

Terms for Review

The following is a list of the important terms from the section "What Psychologists Do." Make sure you are familiar with each term before taking the progress test on these terms.

psychological practice
basic psychology
applied psychology
counseling psychologists
school psychologists

clinical psychologists
psychotherapist
psychoanalyst
psychiatrist

3. Critical and Scientific Thinking in Psychology

Read the section "Critical and Scientific Thinking in Psychology" and then answer the following questions. If you have trouble answering any of the questions, re-study the relevant material before going on to the review of key terms and the progress tests.

3-1. The ability to assess claims and make objective judgments on the basis of well-supported reasons and evidence is known as _____ _____. When using the principles of critical thinking one should start by proposing a _____, which is a statement that attempts to predict behavior and is empirically tested. The variables outlined in hypotheses should be elaborated upon in very specific, concrete terms, known as _____ definitions. Critical thinkers are able to analyze their own and others' assumptions and biases. Psychologists put their assumptions to the test by applying the principle of _____, which involves stating a hypothesis in such a way that it can be refuted if contradictory evidence were to be discovered. However, this principle can often be violated because _____ _____, which is the tendency of people to accept evidence that agrees with our position and ignore or reject evidence that disagrees with our position. Critical thinkers also avoid _____ reasoning. They do not make things overly _____ or argue by _____, which can entail arguing from personal experience. When using critical thinking it is also wise to consider other _____ and to tolerate _____. The goal of critical thinking and science is to arrive at a _____, an organized system of assumptions and principles that attempts to explain certain phenomena and how they are related.

Terms for Review

The following is a list of the important terms from the section "Critical and Scientific Thinking in Psychology." Make sure you are familiar with each term before taking the progress test on these terms.

critical thinking	principle of falsifiability
hypothesis	confirmation bias
operational definitions	theory

4. Descriptive Studies: Establishing the Facts

Read the section "Descriptive Studies: Establishing the Facts" and then answer the following questions. If you have trouble answering any of the questions, re-study the relevant material before going on to the review of key terms and the progress tests.

4-1. When conducting research it is important to try to obtain a _____ _____, which is a selected group of individuals who match the population on characteristics that are relevant to the research topic. Research methods that allow a researcher to describe and predict behavior but not to choose one explanation over another are known as _____ methods. One example of this type of method involves a detailed description of a particular individual known as a _____ _____. The main drawback of this method is that it may study individuals who are _____ of the larger population about whom conclusions are to be drawn.

4-2. When researchers are trying not to interfere with people and also are attempting to systematically record their behavior, they are said to be engaging in _____ studies. There are two types of observational studies. One in which the researcher has more control is known as _____ observation. The primary goal of _____ observation is to find out how people or animals act in their usual environments.

4-3. Assessment instruments used to evaluate such things as personality traits and interests are known as _____ _____. A criterion for a good measurement tool is that it is _____, which means there are uniform procedures for giving and scoring the test. Scoring usually involves the use of _____ or established standards of performance. Before using a psychological test, one should be sure that the test is _____, which means that it produces the same results from one time and place to another. In addition, to be _____ the test needs to measure what it was designed to measure.

4-4. In comparison to psychological tests, _____ ask people directly about their experiences, attitudes, or opinions. Frequently, survey results suffer from a sampling bias known as _____ _____. This means that those who participated in the survey did so of their own accord and because of this, probably differ in some way from those who decided not to participate in the survey.

Terms for Review

The following is a list of the important terms from the section "Descriptive Studies: Establishing the Facts." Make sure you are familiar with each term before taking the progress test on these terms.

representative sample	standardize
descriptive methods	norms
case study	reliability
observational studies	validity
naturalistic observation	surveys
laboratory observation	volunteer bias
psychological tests	

5. Correlational Studies: Looking for Relationships

Read the section "Correlational Studies: Looking for Relationships" and then answer the following questions. If you have trouble answering any of the questions, re-study the relevant material before going on to the review of key terms and the progress tests.

5-1. Another type of descriptive research method that enables researchers to examine the _____ between two variables is known as a _____ study. Some correlations are _____, meaning that high values on one variable correspond to high values on the other and that low values on one variable predict low values on the other. Height and weight have this type of relationship. The correlation may also be _____, meaning that there is an inverse relationship, that high values on one variable correspond to low values on

the other and vice versa. An example of this type of correlation is the relationship between self-esteem and depression. The statistic used to express a correlation is called the _____ of _____. It is important to remember that correlation does not mean _____. Sometimes the relationship may be based on a coincidence, causing an _____ correlation. When two variables are correlated, one variable may or may not be _____ the other.

Terms for Review

The following is a list of the important terms from the section "Correlational Studies: Looking for Relationships." Make sure you are familiar with each term before taking the progress test on these terms.

correlational study	negative correlation
correlation	coefficient of correlation
variables	illusory correlations
positive correlation	

6. The Experiment: Hunting for Causes

Read the section "The Experiment: Hunting for Causes" and then answer the following questions. If you have trouble answering any of the questions, re-study the relevant material before going on to the review of key terms and the progress tests.

6-1. To actually track down the causes of behavior, a researcher must use an _____, which allows the researcher to control or manipulate the situation. Prior to conducting an experiment, researchers must obtain

_____ _____ from participants so these individuals know enough about a study to voluntarily make an intelligent decision whether they should participate. In an experiment, the manipulated variable is known as the _____ variable, and the _____ variable measures the reactions of the subjects.

6-2. An experiment minimally requires at least two conditions. The participants in the _____ group are given some level of the independent variable. In the _____ condition, the participants are treated exactly as those in the other group except that they are not exposed to the manipulation of the independent variable. It is necessary to use

_____ _____

when placing participants in the experimental and control groups. Sometimes the control group is given an inactive substance or a fake treatment known as a _____.

6-3. In a _____-_____ study, only the experimenter knows which subjects are in the experimental group and which are in the control group. In a

_____-_____

study, neither the researcher measuring the dependent variable nor the participants know who is in the experimental or control groups. This type of study controls for _____ effects, or expectations

of the experimenter that can influence the study.

6-4. Although experiments have long been the method of choice for psychologists, this method has been criticized because the more _____ exercised over a situation, the more unlike real life it may be. For this reason _____

_____, or the careful study of behavior in natural contexts, is necessary.

Terms for Review

The following is a list of the important terms from the section "The Experiment: Hunting for Causes." Make sure you are familiar with each term before taking the progress test on these terms.

experiment	random assignment
informed consent	placebo
independent variable	single-blind study
dependent variable	experimenter effects
experimental condition	double-blind study
control condition	field research

7. Evaluating the Findings

Read the section "Evaluating the Findings" and then answer the following questions. If you have trouble answering any of the questions, re-study the relevant material before going on to the review of key terms and the progress tests.

7-1. Psychologists use statistics to summarize data in graphs or charts. Such statistics typically are referred to as _____ statistics. One way to organize data is to add all of the scores up and divide by the total number of scores. This is referred to as the _____ _____. Another frequently used descriptive statistic that indicates how spread out a distribution of scores may be is the _____ _____.

_____ statistics differ from descriptive statistics in that they allow researchers to make inferences concerning the importance of the data. When one has determined that it is very unlikely that the results of an experiment occurred due to chance, the results are said to be

_____ _____.

Inferential statistics allow researchers to determine statistical significance.

7-2. A study in which groups of different ages are compared at one time is called a

_____-_____

study. When researchers follow the same group of people over a period of time, this is called a _____ study. The

statistical measure called

_____ _____ can help tell us how powerful the independent variable really is. A _____-

_____ is a statistical technique that combines and analyzes data from many studies instead of evaluating the results of each study separately.

Terms for Review

The following is a list of the important terms from the section "Evaluating the Findings." Make sure you are familiar with each term before taking the progress test on these terms.

descriptive statistics	cross-sectional study
arithmetic mean	longitudinal study
standard deviation	effect size
inferential statistics	meta-analysis
significance tests	

SAMPLE ANSWERS TO *YOU ARE ABOUT TO LEARN* QUESTIONS FROM TEXTBOOK

After you have read through the chapter, go back and review the "You Are About to Learn..." statements that precede each major section. Create your own answer to each question, then compare your answers to the following sample answers. If your answers are not similar to the sample answers, review the relevant sections of the chapter more carefully.

How does "psychobabble" differ from serious psychology?

Unlike psychobabble, serious psychology relies on empirical evidence to make claims.

What's wrong with psychologists' nonscientific competitors, such as astrologers and psychics?

These nonscientific competitors often make claims so broad and vague that they are rendered useless and frequently incorrect.

How and when did psychology become a formal discipline?

During the 19th century, several pioneering researchers began to study psychological issues using scientific methods. And in 1879, Wilhelm Wundt established the first psychological laboratory in Leipzig, Germany.

What are the three early schools of psychology?

The earliest attempt to scientifically study psychology was Wilhelm Wundt's trained introspection, which observed, analyzed, and described various psychological reactions. Later, William James developed functionalism, which focused on the purpose of behavior. A third early school was Sigmund Freud's psychoanalysis, which examined unconscious conflicts and desires.

What are the five major perspectives in psychology?

The five major perspectives in psychology include the biological, learning, cognitive, sociocultural, and psychodynamic perspectives. Each approach offers different explanations of behavior and mental processes.

Why can't you assume that all therapists are psychologists, or that all psychologists are therapists?

You cannot assume that the person is a therapist because not all psychologists are therapists. Many are basic or applied researchers who teach and do research in colleges and universities or conduct research and apply the findings in nonacademic settings.

What are three major areas of psychologists' professional activities?

Most psychologists tend to work in one or more of three categories: (1) teaching and conducting research at academic institutions, (2) providing mental health services to the public, and (3) conducting research or implementing the findings of research in nonacademic settings.

What's the difference between a clinical psychologist and a psychiatrist?

A clinical psychologist typically has a Ph.D., Ed.D., or, Psy.D., whereas a psychiatrist has a medical degree (M.D.) and has done a residency in psychiatry. Except in New Mexico and Louisiana, only psychiatrists can prescribe medication to their clients.

What does it mean to think critically? Most people know that you have to exercise the body to keep it in shape, but they may not realize that clear thinking also requires effort and practice. You must be willing to assess claims and make judgments only in the basis of well-supported reasons and evidence.

Why are not all opinions created equal? Sometimes people justify their mental laziness by proudly telling you they are open-minded. But not all opinions are created equal. Opinions supported by evidence are worth more than other opinions. It's good to be open-minded, many scientists have observed, but not so open that your brains fall out!

What are the eight guidelines for evaluating psychological claims? One should use the eight essential critical thinking guidelines in order to make this distinction. These are (1) ask questions, (2) define your terms, (3) examine the evidence, (4) analyze assumptions and biases, (5) avoid emotional reasoning, (6) do not oversimplify, (7) consider other interpretations, and (8) tolerate uncertainty.

Why is a psychological theory unscientific if it explains anything that could conceivably happen? This theory would be unscientific because it does not meet the principle of falsifiability. All scientific theories must not only be able to predict what will happen but also what will not happen. A theory that can explain anything never opens itself up to the possibility of falsification.

What's wrong with drawing conclusions about behavior from a collection of anecdotes? Anecdotes represent only one or two examples of a category. Critical thinkers require more evidence than this before drawing conclusions.

How are participants selected for psychological studies and why does it matter? A group of individuals are selected from a population for study, which matches that population on important characteristics such as age and sex.

What are the methods psychologists use to describe behavior? Psychologists will employ case studies, observational studies (including naturalistic and laboratory), psychological tests, and surveys.

What are the advantages and disadvantages of each descriptive method? Case studies can generate very detailed information using a small sample, but suffer from a higher risk of data being unrepresentative of the general population. Observational studies can allow us to better witness of wide range of people in various settings, but run the risk of people reacting abnormally due to being observed. Tests can be easy to administer but the development of reliable and valid tests are difficult. Surveys can produce very large quantities of data quickly, but these self-reports often provide distorted and inaccurate views. Finally, none of these methods help us establish cause and effect relationships.

What does it mean to say that two things, such as grades and TV watching, are "negatively" correlated? A negative correlation means that high values of one variable are associated with low values of the other. In the example of grades and TV watching, students who spend many hours in front of the TV tend to have lower GPAs and those who spend fewer hours in front of the TV tend to have higher GPAs.

Does a positive correlation between TV watching and hyperactivity mean that too much TV makes kids hyperactive?

No, it simply means that there is a relationship between these variables. As children watch more TV, it can be predicted that their hyperactivity will increase. Remember that a correlation does not show causation. When two variables are correlated, changes in one variable may or may not be causing changes in the other.

Why do psychologists rely so heavily on experiments?

Because the experimental method allows researchers to track down the causes of behavior and give explanations. None of the other methods allow this.

What is a control group used for?

Control groups allow the researcher to evaluate whether the independent variable had an effect by comparing the experimental group, which receives some level of the independent variable, with the control group, which is treated the same as the experimental group except that they do not receive the independent variable. Without a control group, one cannot be sure that the behavior one is interested in would not have occurred anyway, even without the manipulation.

Who is "blind" in single- and double-blind experiments and what are they supposed to not "see?"

In a single-blind experiment, only the participants are unaware of what condition they are assigned to. In a double-blind experiment, the experimenter is "blind" as to which condition the participants were assigned and the participants are also "blind" as to the condition in which they were placed.

Why can averages be misleading?

Averages may be misleading because they do not indicate anything about the variability in the participants' responses.

How can psychologists tell whether a finding is impressive or trivial?

Psychologists use inferential statistics to determine whether a finding is impressive or trivial. Inferential statistics tell researchers how likely it is that a result occurred by chance. If a result is impressive, it is said to be statistically significant. This means that the likelihood it occurred by chance is low (5 or fewer times in 100 repetitions of the study).

Why are some findings statistically significant but unimportant in practical terms?

A result may be statistically significant but of minor consequence in everyday life. This means that the result was significant according to inferential statistics but that it has very little application or meaning in people's lives.

How can psychologists combine results from many studies of a problem to get a better overall understanding of it?

Meta-analyses take into account the variation shown across a series of studies, which can sometimes provide a clearer summary of a phenomenon.

KEY TERMS FILL-IN-THE-BLANKS PROGRESS TEST

Fill in the blanks with the key terms from the chapter that match the definitions provided. When you have finished this progress test, check your answers with those at the end of this chapter. You should review any key terms that you do not define correctly.

1. _____ A perspective focusing on how bodily events affect behavior, feelings, and thoughts.

2. _____ An early psychological approach that emphasized the function or purpose of behavior and consciousness.

3. _____ The discipline concerned with behavior and mental processes and how they are affected by an organism's physical state, mental state, and external environment.

4. _____ Relying on or derived from observation, experimentation, or measurement.

5. _____ The father of psychology who used the method of trained introspection.

6. _____ A perspective focusing on the environment and how experience influences us.

7. _____ A tendency to look for or pay attention only to information that confirms one's own belief, and ignore, trivialize, or forget information that disconfirms that belief.

8. _____ The study of psychological issues that have direct practical significance and the application of psychological findings.

9. _____ A psychologist who helps people deal with minor day-to-day problems.

10. _____ A professional in psychological practice who also holds a medical degree (M.D.).

11. _____ The study of psychological issues in order to seek knowledge for its own sake rather than for its practical application.

12. _____ The proposition that a scientific theory must make predictions that expose the theory to the possibility of disconfirmation.

13. _____ A statement that attempts to predict or to account for a set of phenomena.

14. _____ The ability and willingness to assess claims and to make objective judgments on the basis of well-supported reasons.

15. _____ A precise definition of a term that specifies the operations for observing or measuring the process or phenomenon being defined.

16. _____ Procedures used to measure and evaluate personality traits, emotional states, aptitudes, interests, abilities, and values.

17. _____ A group of participants selected from a population for study that matches the population on important characteristics such as age, ethnicity, and gender.

18. _____ A detailed description of a particular individual being studied or treated.

19. _____ A shortcoming of findings derived from a sample of volunteers instead of a

representative sample.

20. _____ In test construction, to develop uniform procedures for giving and scoring a test.

21. _____ The ability of a test to measure what it was designed to measure.

22. _____ Measures that yield descriptions of behavior but not necessarily causal explanations.

23. _____ A relationship characterized by increases in one variable and decreases in another.

24. _____ A measure of correlation that ranges in value from -1.00 to +1.00.

25. _____ Characteristics of behavior or experience that can be measured or described by a numeric scale.

26. _____ A descriptive study that looks for a consistent relationship between two phenomena.

27. _____ An inactive substance or fake treatment used as a control in an experiment or given by a medical practitioner to a patient.

28. _____ An experiment in which neither the participants nor the individuals that have contact with them know which participants are in the control group and which are in the experimental group until after the results are tallied.

29. _____ A variable that an experimenter manipulates in an experiment.

30. _____ Unintended changes in participants' behavior due to cues inadvertently given by the experimenter.

31. _____ A controlled test of a hypothesis in which the researcher manipulates one variable to discover its effect on another.

32. _____ In an experiment, a comparison condition in which participants are not exposed to the independent variable.

33. _____ A measure of variability that indicates the average difference between scores in a distribution and their mean.

34. _____ A procedure for combining and analyzing data from many studies; it determines how much of the variance in scores across all studies can be explained by a particular variable.

35. _____ Assess how likely it is that a study's results occurred merely by chance.

36. _____ Statistics that organize and summarize research data.

37. _____ A study in which the same subjects are followed and periodically reassessed over a period of time.

MULTIPLE-CHOICE PROGRESS TEST

Choose the single best answer for each of the following questions. When you have finished this progress test, check your answers with those at the end of this chapter. You should review the relevant pages in the text for the questions you do not answer correctly.

1. According to the text's definition of psychology, behavior and mental processes are affected by an organism's:
    a. physical state.
    b. mental state.
    c. external environment.
    d. all of the above

2. Which of the following relies heavily on empirical evidence?
    a. Astrology
    b. Numerology
    c. Graphology
    d. None of the above

3. An early research method in which specially trained volunteers carefully observed, analyzed, and described their own sensations, mental images, and emotional reactions was called:
    a. introspection.
    b. functionalism.
    c. psychoanalysis.
    d. phrenology.

4. Phrenology is to _____ as functionalism is to _____.
    a. William James; Joseph Gall
    b. Joseph Gall; William James
    c. Wilhelm Wundt; Sigmund Freud
    d. Sigmund Freud; Wilhelm Wundt

5. The learning perspective is to the psychodynamic perspective as _____ are to _____.
    a. bodily events; social and cultural forces
    b. social and cultural forces; bodily events
    c. environmental conditions; unconscious dynamics
    d. unconscious dynamics; environmental conditions

6. Which of the following therapists is most likely to look for biochemical causes of mental disorders?
    a. A counseling psychologist
    b. A psychiatrist
    c. A clinical psychologist
    d. A social worker

7. If you test a hypothesis by stating it in such a way that it can be refuted by counterevidence, you are:
    a. conducting a single-blind study.
    b. conducting a double-blind study.
    c. using operational definitions.
    d. employing the principle of falsifiability.

8. On a radio talk show, the host argues that smoking is not dangerous to your health because his grandfather smoked two packs a day for most of his adult life and lived to be 93 years old. The host is guilty of:
    a. reasoning emotionally.
    b. arguing by anecdote.
    c. examining the evidence.
    d. considering alternative interpretations.

9. Which descriptive research method provides in-depth information about an individual being studied or treated?
   a. Case study
   b. Naturalistic observation
   c. Test
   d. Survey

10. A test producing the same results from one time to another is to a test measuring what it is supposed to as _____ is to _____.
   a. validity; reliability
   b. reliability; validity
   c. reliability; standardization
   d. standardization; reliability

11. Volunteer bias is a problem that is most likely to occur with which one of the following descriptive research methods?
   a. Case study
   b. Survey
   c. Test
   d. Naturalistic observation

12. Which of the following coefficients of correlation indicates the strongest relationship?
   a. +.50
   b. +.10
   c. -.25
   d. -.75

13. If a researcher observes a strong negative correlation between income and mental illness, you can conclude that:
   a. being poor causes mental illness.
   b. having wealth makes you resistant to mental illness.
   c. those with lower incomes tend to suffer from higher rates of mental illness and those with higher incomes tend to suffer from lower rates of mental illness.
   d. lower income levels lead to lower levels of mental illness.

14. Which of the following relationships is a negative correlation?
   a. Height and weight
   b. IQ scores and school grades
   c. Educational level and annual income
   d. None of the above

15. Only _____ permits a researcher to identify cause and effect.
   a. a correlational study
   b. an experiment
   c. a survey
   d. naturalistic observation

16. In an experiment, the _____ variable is manipulated and the _____ variable is measured.
   a. control; independent
   b. independent; control
   c. independent; dependent
   d. dependent; independent

17. To control for experimenter effects, a researcher conducts a _____ study.
   a. single-blind study
   b. double-blind study
   c. case
   d. correlational

18. The mean and standard deviation are _____ statistics.
   a. inferential
   b. descriptive
   c. correlational
   d. case study

19. Significance tests tell the researcher how likely it is that the results of the study are due to _____, and the results are said to be significant if this likelihood is very _____.
   a. chance; low
   b. the independent variable; low
   c. chance; high
   d. the independent variable; high

20. Cross-sectional studies of mental abilities across the life span usually find that mental ability _____ with age, and longitudinal studies usually find that mental ability _____ with age.
   a. declines; declines
   b. declines; does not decline
   c. does not decline; declines
   d. does not decline; does not decline

Guided Study

1. The Science of Psychology

1-1. behavior
mental
physical state
mental state
external environment

1-2. empirical
vague
meaningless
common sense
contradict

1-3. describe
predict
modify
empirical
1879
Wilhelm Wundt
trained introspection
functionalism
Sigmund Freud
childhood
consciously
psychoanalysis

1-4. biological
evolutionary
learning
behaviorists
social-cognitive
cognitive
sociocultural
psychodynamic

2. What Psychologists Do

2-1. basic
applied

2-2. counseling
school
clinical
psychotherapist
psychoanalyst
psychiatrist

2-3. twentieth
women
peace
environmental
law
communities
satisfaction
ethnic

3. Critical and Scientific Thinking in Psychology

3-1. critical thinking
hypothesis
operational
falsifiability
confirmation bias
emotional
simplified
anecdote
interpretations
uncertainty
theory

4. Descriptive Studies: Establishing the Facts
4-1. representative sample   descriptive   case study   unrepresentative
4-2. observational   laboratory   naturalistic
4-3. psychological tests   standardized   norms   reliable   valid
4-4. surveys   volunteer bias

5. Correlational Studies: Looking for Relationships
5-1. relationship   correlational   positive   negative   coefficient   correlation   causation   illusory   causing

6. The Experiment: Hunting for Causes
6-1. experiment   informed consent   independent   dependent
6-2. experimental   control   random assignment   placebo
6-3. single-blind   double-blind   experimenter
6-4. control   field research

7. Evaluating the Findings
7-1. descriptive   arithmetic mean   standard deviation   inferential   statistically significant
7-2. cross-sectional   longitudinal   effect size   meta-analysis

Answers to Key Terms Progress Test

1. biological perspective
2. functionalism
3. psychology
4. empirical
5. Wilhelm Wundt
6. learning perspective
7. confirmation bias
8. applied psychology
9. counseling psychologist
10. psychiatrist
11. basic psychology
12. principle of falsifiability
13. hypothesis
14. critical thinking
15. operational definition
16. psychological tests
17. representative sample
18. case study
19. volunteer bias
20. standardization
21. validity
22. descriptive methods
23. negative correlation
24. coefficient of correlation
25. variable
26. correlational study
27. placebo
28. double-blind study
29. independent variable
30. experimenter effects
31. experiment
32. control condition
33. standard deviation
34. meta-analysis
35. significance tests
36. descriptive statistics
37. longitudinal study

Item Number	Answers
1.	d. all of the above
2.	d. none of the above
3.	a. introspection
4.	b. Joseph Gall; William James
5.	c. environmental conditions; unconscious dynamics
6.	b. a psychiatrist
7.	d. employing the principle of falsifiability
8.	b. arguing by anecdote
9.	a. case study
10.	b. reliability; validity
11.	b. survey
12.	d. -0.75
13.	c. those with lower incomes tend to suffer from higher rates of mental illness and those with higher incomes tend to suffer from lower rates of mental illness.
14.	d. none of the above
15.	b. experiment
16.	c. independent; dependent
17.	b. double-blind study
18.	b. descriptive
19.	a. chance; low
20.	b. declines; does not decline

CHAPTER 2

Theories of Personality

CHAPTER OVERVIEW

Chapter 2 begins with a definition of personality, which is the distinctive pattern of behavior, thoughts, motives, and emotions that characterize people over time. Personality consists of characteristics known as traits that describe the individual across situations. The various perspectives on personality presented in this chapter offer different views of the formation of personality and the stability of personality traits.

Freud's theory and other psychodynamic approaches to the study of personality are examined first. Topics such as psychoanalysis, defense mechanisms, psychosexual stages of personality development, Jungian theory, and the object-relations school are covered. An evaluation of the psychodynamic approach also is offered.

Next, modern theories of personality are explored, which includes a description of the trait perspective on personality. The theories of Allport and Cattell are discussed along with a description of the five fundamental personality traits, known as the "Big Five." The genetic influences on personality are described next, with coverage of issues such as temperament, genes, and the heritability of personality traits. Strategies to determine heritability are examined, including studies comparing identical twins to fraternal twins.

Then, the environmental influences on personality are explored, which includes a discussion of the contributions of social-cognitive learning theory. Coverage of such concepts as reciprocal determinism and nonshared environments is presented. Also, the relative power of parents and peers to determine the personality traits of children is examined. Following this discussion, cultural influences on personality are considered. Differences in personality across cultures are described, including those in individualist versus collectivist cultures and regional differences within a culture, such as the culture of honor that affects the aggressiveness of males.

Finally, looking at the inner experience requires examining the humanist perspective. The humanist ideas of Maslow, Rogers, and May are presented, including such terms as self-actualization, unconditional positive regard, and the existential approach.

GUIDED STUDY

1. Psychodynamic Theories of Personality

Read the section "Psychodynamic Theories of Personality" and then answer the following questions. If you have trouble answering any of the questions, re-study the relevant material before going on to the review of key terms and the progress tests.

1-1. Psychodynamic theory, which emphasizes the movement of psychological energy within the person, was originated by _____ _____. His theory of personality called _____ emphasized unconscious motives and conflicts. Freud identified three structures of personality. The _____ is present at birth and is responsible for psychological energies and instincts. The _____ is a referee between the needs of instincts and the demands of society. Lastly, the _____ represents one's morality. The weapons used by the ego to aid in reducing anxiety are known as _____ _____. For example, _____ is a defense mechanism in which threatening ideas, memories, or emotions are blocked off from consciousness. Another defense mechanism, _____ occurs when people direct their emotions, such as anger, toward things, animals, or other people that are not the source of these emotions. When someone refuses to admit that something unpleasant is happening, they are experiencing the defense mechanism of _____. Freud also developed a five-stage psychosexual theory of personality development. The first is the _____ stage. The second is the _____ stage. Thirdly, during the _____ stage, the child wishes to possess the parent of the opposite sex and to get rid of the parent of the same sex. Freud called this phenomenon the _____ _____. The fourth stage, in which the child's sexual urges are repressed, is called the _____ stage. Lastly, the fifth stage, which begins at puberty, is called the _____ stage. Freud's ideas were received positively by many, while others think that psychoanalytic theory is worthless because it has little _____ support.

1-2. Other psychologists from the psychodynamic perspective broke away from Freud. In _____ _____'s theory, a _____ unconscious that contains universal memories, symbols, and images, which are the legacy of human history, was proposed. Jung studied myths and folklore from which he identified common themes that he referred to as _____. Another approach, the _____-_____ school, holds that the central problem in life is to find a balance between the need for _____ and the need for others. According to this view, the way people react to _____ is influenced by experiences in the first two years of life.

1-3. Empirical psychologists criticize psychodynamic approaches to personality for failing scientifically on three dimensions. Firstly, they feel that they violate the principle of _____. Secondly, the principles were outlined based on observations of a few _____ patients. Lastly, psychodynamic theories of development were based on _____ accounts. This creates an _____ of causality between events.

Terms for Review

The following is a list of the important terms from the section "Psychodynamic Theories of Personality." Make sure you are familiar with each term before taking the progress test on these terms.

Sigmund Freud
psychoanalysis
psychodynamic theories
id
libido
ego
superego
defense mechanisms
repression
projection
displacement
regression
denial

psychosexual stages
oral stage
anal stage
phallic stage
Oedipus complex
latency stage
genital stage
Carl Jung
collective unconscious
archetypes
object-relations school
illusion of causality

2. The Modern Study of Personality

Read the section "The Modern Study of Personality" and then answer the following questions. If you have trouble answering any of the questions, re-study the relevant material before going on to the review of key terms and the progress tests.

2-1. Measures of personality traits that are useful in research are called _____ tests (inventories). One of the first trait theorists was _____ _____, who proposed five to ten different types of traits. Most individuals have what are known as _____ traits, which encompass the individual's general personality. These traits are fairly fixed. _____ traits, on the other hand, are more apt to change over time. A second trait theorist, _____ _____, used a statistical method known as _____ _____ to identify personality traits. Today, researchers discuss what are called the "Big Five" personality traits. These consist of _____ versus introversion, _____ versus emotional stability, _____ versus antagonism, _____ versus impulsiveness, and _____ to experience versus resistance to new experience.

Terms for Review

The following is a list of the important terms from the section "The Modern Study of Personality." Make sure you are familiar with each term before taking the progress test on these terms.

objective tests (inventories)
Gordon Allport
central traits
secondary traits

Raymond Cattell
factor analysis
Big Five

3. Genetic Influences on Personality

Read the section "Genetic Influences on Personality" and then answer the following questions. If you have trouble answering any of the questions, re-study the relevant material before going on to the review of key terms and the progress tests.

3-1. Some aspects of your personality may be influenced by your _____, which are the basic units of heredity. One way to examine genetic influences on personality is to study _____, which, according to biological psychologists, are the individual's physiological dispositions to respond to the environment in a certain way. For example, reactive children show increased _____ _____ and high levels of _____ hormones during mildly stressful tasks.

3-2. Another method to study genetic contributions to personality is used by behavioral _____. These researchers estimate the _____ of traits. This involves estimating the proportion of the total variation in a trait that is attributable to genetic variation among individuals within a group. This is an estimate of how much of the _____ for a trait within a population is based on genes. It does not give us the impact of genetics on any particular individual's traits. Heritability is typically studied using either adopted children or by comparing _____ twins with fraternal twins. Researchers also study such twins that were separated at birth. This allows them to make a better estimate of

heritability as these twins are genetically _____, yet reared in different _____. Regarding personality traits, the heritability estimate based on twin research is typically ranges from _____ to _____. In other words, within a group of people, up to 50 percent of the variability in a trait is attributable to genetic differences among the individuals in the group.

3-3. When evaluating genetic theories of personality, it is important not to _____ and assume that personality is purely genetic, overlooking the role of the environment and experience. A genetic predisposition does not mean a genetic _____. The data from heritability research also support the role of _____ influences on personality.

Terms for Review

The following is a list of the important terms from the section "Genetic Influences on Personality." Make sure you are familiar with each term before taking the progress test on these terms.

genes	behavioral genetics
temperaments	identical twins
heritability	fraternal twins

4. Environmental Influences on Personality

Read the section "Environmental Influences on Personality" and then answer the following questions. If you have trouble answering any of the questions, re-study the relevant material before going on to the review of key terms and the progress tests.

4-1. In behavioral learning terms, people act inconsistently from one situation to another because different behaviors are _____, _____, or _____ in different contexts. For behavioral psychologists, personality is a collection of acquired behavioral patterns. Another learning view, _____ _____ learning theory proposes that personality traits result from one's learning history and the resulting _____ and beliefs. This theory also stresses the continual _____ between one's personal qualities and the person's situation. This two-way relationship between aspects of the environment and aspects of the individual is referred to as _____ _____. The study of this interaction requires the consideration of the _____ environment, which helps explain why two siblings raised in the same family can appear so different.

4-2. The notion that parents are the only influence on the development of their children's _____ has been questioned. This belief lacks evidence because the _____ environment of the home has little effect, parents rarely use one _____ style that is consistently used over time and with all their children, and even when parents try to be _____, there may be little similarity between what they do and the personality of their children. The relationship between parents and children is not a _____ relationship. The influence is bi-directional.

4-3. It has been difficult to separate the relative effects of parents and _____ on the development of children's personality traits. To see which has a stronger influence, researchers look at situations where the influences of parents and peers _____. Peer pressures do play a role in shaping personality traits, leading to the emphasis of some traits and the _____ of others.

Terms for Review

The following is a list of the important terms from the section "Environmental Influences on Personality." Make sure you are familiar with each term before taking the progress test on these terms.

social-cognitive learning theory
reciprocal determinism
nonshared environment

5. Cultural Influences on Personality

Read the section "Cultural Influences on Personality" and then answer the following questions. If you have trouble answering any of the questions, re-study the relevant material before going on to the review of key terms and the progress tests.

5-1. A _____ is a program of shared rules that govern the behavior of members of a community or society and a set of

24

_____, _____, and _____ shared by most members of that community. Cultures that emphasize the independence of the individual over the needs of the group are considered _____ cultures. On the other hand, cultures that emphasize group harmony over the wishes of the individual are known as _____ cultures. People often attribute another's actions to personality traits when in fact they may be due to cultural _____. An example involves people's perception of _____, which can be either linear or parallel depending on cultural norms. Studies of male _____ also point to the influence of culture. People who herded animals in the American South and in some western regions of the U.S. developed a culture of _____ to protect their livelihood. This culture requires men to respond with _____ to restore their status even in response to minor disputes and trivial insults. Cultures of honor have higher rates of _____ violence and higher rates of honor-related _____ compared to other cultures. In cultures in which competition for _____ is intense, men are pushed to take risks and act tough.

5-2. One problem for cultural psychologists is how to describe cultural influences on personality without oversimplifying or

_____. The study of culture does not rely on the assumption that all members of a culture have the same personality _____. Variation occurs within every _____. And, similarities between cultures do exist. However, some key aspects of _____ are influenced by the culture in which one is raised.

Terms for Review

The following is a list of the important terms from the section "Cultural Influences on Personality." Make sure you are familiar with each term before taking the progress test on these terms.

culture
individualist cultures
collectivist cultures
culture of honor

6. The Inner Experience

Read the section "The Inner Experience" and then answer the following questions. If you have trouble answering any of the questions, re-study the relevant material before going on to the review of key terms and the progress tests.

6-1. The humanist approach began in the early 1960s due to dissatisfaction with _____ and behaviorism. The main figureheads in the humanist movement were Abraham _____, Rollo _____, and Carl _____. Maslow emphasized the positive aspects of human nature, such as _____ _____. The traits that he thought were important to personality were not the Big Five, but those qualities he saw as pertaining to a

_____-_____ person.
This is a person who strives for a life that is
meaningful, challenging, and satisfying.
Carl Rogers studied individuals whom he
felt had attained congruence or harmony.
He called these individuals

_____ _____ people.
To become fully functioning, Rogers
claimed that we need _____

_____ _____, or love
and support without conditions or strings
attached. Rollo May differed from other
humanists in that he ascribed to the
European philosophy of _____,
meaning that May believed in freedom of
choice for humans, but he also felt that
freedom brings with it a burden of
responsibility.

6-2. The major criticism of the humanist
perspective is that many of its proposals are
_____. Many humanist concepts
can be hard to _____
operationally. However, humanist
psychologists have added _____
to the study of personality.

Terms for Review

*The following is a list of the important terms
from the section "The Inner Experience." Make
sure you are familiar with each term before
taking the progress test on these terms.*

humanist psychology   congruence
Abraham Maslow   unconditional positive regard
peak experiences   Rollo May
self-actualized person   existentialism
Carl Rogers

SAMPLE ANSWERS TO *YOU ARE ABOUT TO LEARN* QUESTIONS FROM TEXTBOOK

After you have read through the chapter, go back and review the "You Are About to Learn..." statements that precede each major section. Create your own answer to each question, then compare your answers to the following sample answers. If your answers are not similar to the sample answers, review the relevant sections of the chapter more carefully.

What was Freud's theory of the structure and development of personality?

In Freud's theory, your personality consists of three major systems: the id, ego, and superego. The id develops at birth, the ego develops next, and the superego is the last system to develop.

What would Carl Jung have to say about Harry Potter's archenemy, Lord Voldemort?

Carl Jung would most likely say that Lord Voldemort represents the shadow archetype. This archetype represents the sinister, evil side of human nature.

What are the "objects" in the object-relations approach to personality?

The objects are the numerous representations of the self and others that a child eventually constructs. The psychodynamic interplay among them comprises the relations.

Why do many psychologists reject most psychodynamic ideas?

Freud's ideas have very little empirical support and as such, are not a scientific view of human behavior. Furthermore, they violate the principle of falsifiability, draw universal principles from a few atypical patients, and base their theories on the retrospective accounts of adults.

Can you trust tests that tell you what "personality type" you are?

Some personality tests are not very reliable. Other measures of personality are scientifically valid and useful. Well-constructed, standardized questionnaires, called objective tests or inventories, can reliably and validly assess personality traits.

How can psychologists tell which personality traits are more central or important than others?

Allport distinguished between central traits and secondary traits, which are more changeable. Typically, psychological tests are used to identify basic personality traits. Also used is factor analysis, a statistical procedure that identifies clusters of correlated test items that seem to be measuring some common underlying trait. For example, Raymond Cattell identified 16 personality factors that he thought identified basic personality traits.

Which five dimensions of personality seem to describe people the world over?

The five dimensions identified by psychologists are (1) extroversion versus introversion; (2) neuroticism; (3) agreeableness; (4) conscientiousness; and (5) openness to experience.

Can animals have "personalities" just like people do?

When we think of an individual who has a personality, we usually think of a human being. But bears, dogs, pigs, hyenas, goats, cats, and, of course, our fellow primates also have distinctive, characteristic ways of behaving that make them different from their fellows (Gosling, 2001). So, surprisingly, does the humble, squishy octopus! When researchers dropped a crab into a tank of octopuses, some of them would aggressively grab that dinner right away; others seemed more passive and waited for the crab to swim near them; and some waited and attacked the crab when no one was watching (Mather & Anderson, 1993).

To what extent are temperamental and personality differences among people influenced by their genetic differences?

Heritability has been estimated at 50 percent for many personality traits. Thus, in a group of people, 50 percent of the variance in personality traits can be attributed to genetic differences.

Are people who have highly heritable personality traits stuck with them forever?

No, a genetic predisposition does not equal a genetic inevitability. Environmental influences also play a role in the development of personality traits.

How does the social-cognitive theory account for apparent changes in personality across situations?

The expression of people's personality can be inconsistent across situations. Personality can be variable due to different behaviors being rewarded, punished, or ignored, depending on the environmental context.

How much can parents influence their children's personalities?

The notion that parents have supreme influence over their children's personalities now faces disconfirming evidence. Parents and children continually affect each other, as predicted by reciprocal determinism.

How do peers shape and suppress the aspects of personality?

Peers can affect personality by shaping the expression of personality traits leading to the promotion of some attributes or abilities and the devaluing of others.

How does your culture influence your personality—and even whether you think you have a stable "self"?

Your response to "Who are you?" will be influenced by your cultural background, particularly whether your culture emphasizes individualism or community. In individualist cultures, the independence of the individual often takes precedence over the needs of the group, and the self is often defined as a collection of personality traits "I am outgoing, agreeable, and ambitious" or in occupational terms "I am a psychologist." In collectivist cultures, group harmony often takes precedence over the wishes of the individual, and the self is defined in the context of relationships and the community "I am the son of a farmer, descended from three generations of storytellers on my mother's side and five generations of farmers on my father's side."

How does culture influence your personality, even if you think you have a stable one?

Culture has a profound effect on people's behavior, attitudes, and the traits they value or reject. Behavior is a function of both the individual and the individual's culture. For example, individualist and collectivist cultures define the self in different ways, which influences personality traits we value, how we express emotions, how much we value having relationships or maintaining freedom, and even whether we think personality is stable across situations.

Why are men in the South and the West more likely to get angry at personal insults than other American men are?

Men from the South and the West come from a culture of honor that requires men to respond with anger and aggression when they feel that their status has been demeaned. Compared to men raised in the North, men raised in the South experience heightened levels of stress hormones and testosterone when they are offended and are more likely to retaliate aggressively.

How can one appreciate cultural influences on personality without stereotyping?

It is important to recognize that while all members of a culture are influenced by that culture, they are still individuals who can show a great deal of variability in their own behaviors.

How does the humanist approach to human nature differ from psychodynamic and genetic ones?

Humanists believe in complete freedom of choice and free will. Psychologists representing the psychodynamic and genetic view do not always share this view.

What were the contributions of Abraham Maslow, Carl Rogers, and Rollo May to understanding our inner lives?

Maslow stressed the importance of building towards a meaningful and challenging life, Rogers emphasized the need for acceptance without qualifications, and May popularized the notion of choosing the best aspects of ourselves.

How do psychological scientists evaluate humanist views?

Humanist views are not scientific because they are primarily untestable and lack operational definitions.

KEY TERMS FILL-IN-THE-BLANKS PROGRESS TEST

Fill in the blanks with the key terms from the chapter that match the definitions provided. When you have finished this progress test, check your answers with those at the end of this chapter. You should review any key terms that you do not define correctly.

1. _____ In psychoanalysis, the part of personality that represents reason, good sense, and rational self-control.

2. _____ In psychoanalysis, a conflict in which a child desires the parent of the opposite sex and views the same-sex parent as a rival.

3. _____ Methods used by the ego to prevent unconscious anxiety or threatening thought from entering consciousness.

4. _____ In psychoanalysis, the part of the personality containing inherited psychological energy, particularly sexual and aggressive instincts.

5. _____ A psychodynamic approach that emphasizes the importance of the infant's first two years of life and the baby's formative relationships.

6. _____ To Carl Jung, the universal memories and experiences of humankind, represented in the unconscious images and symbols of all people.

7. _____ They typically include scales on which people are asked to rate themselves.

8. _____ A statistical method used by Cattell for analyzing the intercorrelations among various measures or test scores.

9. _____ According to Allport, each of us has five to ten of these fairly fixed traits that encompass an individual's personality.

10. _____ These are changeable aspects of personality, such as habits and music preferences.

11. _____ Twins that develop when a fertilized egg divides into two parts that become separate embryos.

12. _____ Characteristic styles of responding to the environment that are present in infancy and are assumed to be innate.

13. _____ A statistical estimate of the proportion of the total variance in some trait within a group that is attributable to genetic differences among individuals within the group.

14. _____ The functional units of heredity, which are composed of DNA.

15. _____ The two-way interaction between aspects of the environment and aspects of the individual in the shaping of personality traits.

16. _____ Unique aspects of the situation that are not shared with family members.

17. _____ Cultures in which the self is regarded as embedded in relationships and harmony with one's group is prized above individual goals and wishes.

18. _____ A program of shared rules that govern the behavior of members of a community or society and a set of values, beliefs, and attitudes shared by most members of the community.

19. _____ Cultures in which the self is regarded as autonomous, and individual goals and wishes are prized above duty and relations with others.

20. _____ To Carl Rogers, love or support given to another person with no conditions attached.

21. _____ A philosophic approach that emphasizes the inevitable dilemmas and challenges of human existence.

22. _____ Harmony between the image people project to others and their true feelings and wishes.

23. _____ A psychological approach that emphasizes personal growth, resilience, and the achievement of human potential.

24. _____ Rare moments of rapture caused by the attainment of excellence or the experience of beauty.

MULTIPLE-CHOICE PROGRESS TEST

Choose the single best answer for each of the following questions. When you have finished this progress test, check your answers with those at the end of this chapter. You should review the relevant pages in the text for the questions you do not answer correctly.

1. In Freud's theory of personality, the _____ represents reason, good sense, and rational self-control.
   a. ego
   b. superego
   c. libido
   d. id

2. When displacement serves a higher cultural or useful purpose, as in the creation of art or inventions, it is called _____.
   a. projection
   b. reaction formation
   c. sublimation
   d. repression

3. Which of the following is the correct sequence of stages in Freud's theory of personality development?
   a. Oral; genital; latency; anal; phallic
   b. Anal; latency; genital; oral; phallic
   c. Oral; phallic; anal; latency; genital
   d. Oral; anal; phallic; latency; genital

4. According to Freud's theory of personality development, the Oedipus complex occurs in the _____ stage.
   a. oral
   b. anal
   c. phallic
   d. genital

5. Which of the following concepts is NOT part of Jungian theory?
   a. Collective unconscious
   b. Archetypes
   c. Collectivist cultures
   d. All of the above

6. Psychodynamic theories have been criticized for:
   a. violating the principle of falsifiability.
   b. overgeneralizing from atypical patients to everyone.
   c. being based on the unreliable and retrospective accounts of patients.
   d. all of the above

7. Which of the following statements about object-relations theory is FALSE?
   a. The first two years of life are the most critical for development of personality.
   b. The basic human drive is the need to be in relationships.
   c. Children of both sexes identify first with the mother.
   d. Women develop more rigid ego boundaries between themselves and other people.

8. Central and secondary personality traits were proposed by:
   a. Cattell.
   b. Freud.
   c. Allport.
   d. Jung.

9. Bill is a very anxious person who is unable to control his impulses and who has a tendency to worry and complain even though he has no major problems. Which of the Big Five personality traits is most relevant to Bill's behavior?
   a. Conscientiousness
   b. Neuroticism
   c. Agreeableness
   d. Openness to experience

10. Physiological dispositions to respond to the environment in certain ways are called:
    a. central traits.
    b. temperaments.
    c. generalized expectancies.
    d. archetypes.

11. Which of the following groups should have the highest heritability for a given trait?
  a. A group of genetically very similar people raised in very dissimilar environments
  b. A group of genetically very similar people raised in very similar environments
  c. A group of genetically very dissimilar people raised in very dissimilar environments
  d. A group of genetically very dissimilar people raised in very similar environments

12. Which would be the most useful comparison to make if one was looking at the relationship between genes and a certain personality trait?
  a. Comparing identical twins raised in the same environment
  b. Comparing fraternal twins raised in different environments
  c. Comparing identical twins raised in different environments
  d. Comparing adopted children and their adoptive parents

13. Based on adoption and twin studies, heritability of personality traits is typically around:
  a. .10 - .15.
  b. .33 - .66.
  c. .20 - .50.
  d. .70 - .95.

14. Mary sees personality as a result of the two-way interaction between aspects of the environment and aspects of the individual. She is most likely a _____.
  a. social-cognitive learning theorist
  b. evolutionary theorist
  c. behavioral geneticist
  d. psychodynamic theorist

15. Which statement best describes the relative power of parents and peers to influence the development of children's personality traits?
  a. Parents do not have much influence over their children's personality traits.
  b. Parents have much influence over their children's personality traits.

  c. Peers are more influential than parents are in the development of children's personality.
  d. Both peers and parents shape the expression of personality traits and the relationships between individuals and their parents and peers are reciprocal.

16. Cultures whose members regard the "self" as embedded in the context of relationships and the larger community are _____ cultures.
  a. individualist
  b. collectivist
  c. monochronic
  d. polychronic

17. The idea that fully functioning people experience congruence between their self image and their true feelings, perceptions, and wishes was proposed by:
  a. Carl Rogers.
  b. Gordon Allport.
  c. B.F. Skinner.
  d. Carl Jung.

18. Rollo May added the element of _____ to American psychology.
  a. peak experiences
  b. existentialism
  c. archetypes
  d. illusion of causality

19. Free will falls under which category of major influences on personality?
  a. Humanistic
  b. Genetic
  c. Cultural
  d. Environmental

20. Which of the following pairs of personality theorists and perspectives is INCORRECT?
  a. Abraham Maslow; humanist
  b. Carl Rogers; humanist
  c. Carl Jung; genetic
  d. Sigmund Freud; psychodynamic

Guided Study

1. Psychodynamic Theories of Personality

1-1. Sigmund Freud
psychoanalysis
id
ego
superego
defense mechanisms
regression
displacement
denial
oral
anal
phallic
Oedipus complex
latency
genital
empirical

1-2. Carl Jung
collective
archetypes
object-relations
independence
separation

1-3. falsifiability
atypical
retrospective
illusion

2. The Modern Study of Personality

2-1. objective
Gordon Allport
central
secondary
Raymond Cattell
factor analysis
extroversion
neuroticism
agreeableness
conscientiousness
openness

3. Genetic Influences on Personality

3-1. genes
temperaments
heart rates
stress

3-2. genetics
heritability
variability
identical
identical
environments
.20
.50

3-3. oversimplify
inevitability
environmental

4. Environmental Influences on Personality

4-1. rewarded
    punished
    ignored
    social-cognitive
    expectations
    interaction
    reciprocal determinism
    nonshared

4-2. personality
    shared
    child-rearing
    consistent
    one-way

4-3. peers
    clash
    downplaying

5. Cultural Influences on Personality

5-1. culture
    values
    beliefs
    attitudes
    individualist
    collectivist
    norms
    time
    aggressiveness
    honor
    violence
    domestic
    homicides
    resources

5-2. stereotyping
    traits
    culture
    personality

6. The Inner Experience

6-1. psychoanalysis
    Maslow
    May
    Rogers
    peak experiences
    self-actualized
    fully functioning
    unconditional positive regard
    existentialism

6-2. untestable
    define
    balance

Answers to Key Terms Progress Test

1. ego
2. Oedipus complex
3. defense mechanisms
4. id
5. object-relations school
6. collective unconscious
7. objective tests (inventories)
8. factor analysis
9. central traits
10. secondary traits
11. identical twins
12. temperaments
13. heritability
14. genes
15. reciprocal determinism
16. nonshared environment
17. collectivist cultures
18. cultures
19. individualist cultures
20. unconditional positive regard
21. existentialism
22. congruence
23. humanist psychology
24. peak experiences

Answers to Multiple-Choice Progress Test

Item Number	Answers
1.	a. ego
2.	c. sublimation
3.	d. oral; anal; phallic; latency; genital
4.	c. phallic
5.	c. collectivist cultures
6.	d. all of the above
7.	d. Women develop more rigid ego boundaries between themselves and other people.
8.	c. Allport
9.	b. neuroticism
10.	b. temperaments
11.	a. a group of genetically very similar people raised in very dissimilar environments
12.	c. comparing identical twins raised in different environments
13.	c. .20 - .50
14.	a. social-cognitive learning theorist
15.	d. Both peers and parents shape the expression of personality traits and the relationships between individuals and their parents and peers are reciprocal.
16.	b. collectivist
17.	a. Carl Rogers
18.	b. existentialism
19.	a. humanistic
20.	c. Carl Jung; genetic

CHAPTER 3

Development Over the Life Span

CHAPTER OVERVIEW

Developmental psychologists study universal and specific aspects of people across the life span. They focus on physiological and cognitive changes and on socialization, which is the process by which children learn the behaviors, attitudes, and expectations required of them by their society or culture.

The chapter begins with a discussion of prenatal development including a description of the three stages of prenatal development. In addition, possible harmful influences to the embryo and fetus are outlined. These influences include German measles, radiation, sexually transmitted diseases, cigarette smoking, alcohol, and other drugs. Following coverage of infants' sensory and motor abilities, attachment in infancy is explored. This includes a description of separation anxiety and research in this area.

The basic progression of language development is provided next, along with Chomsky's theory of language acquisition. Following this section, Piaget's stages of cognitive development are detailed. Terms central to Piaget's theory including assimilation, accommodation, object permanence, conservation, and egocentric thinking are defined. Several corrections to Piaget's theory of cognitive development also are presented. Next, Kohlberg's levels of moral reasoning are discussed and critiqued. A discussion on how to develop a moral conscience in children follows.

The biological, cognitive, and learning influences on gender development are considered next. This includes a description of such phenomena as gender identity, gender typing, and gender schemas. The influence of parents is explored including consideration of other factors that affect children's gender development. And, what happens to gender over the life span is discussed.

The time period known as adolescence is covered next. Important terms such as puberty, menarche, and secondary sex characteristics are defined along with a discussion of the effects of early maturation and late maturation on adolescent males and females. The psychology of adolescence also is examined.

The next developmental stage is adulthood. Erik Erikson's eight-stage theory of development is described along with the concept of emerging adulthood. The physical and emotional effects of menopause in women are reported. Finally, the work of gerontologists is presented, which includes a discussion of crystallized versus fluid intelligence. The chapter concludes by addressing whether adults are prisoners of their childhood experiences.

GUIDED STUDY

1. From Conception Through the First Year

Read the section "From Conception Through the First Year" and then answer the following questions. If you have trouble answering any of the questions, re-study the relevant material before going on to the review of key terms and the progress tests.

1-1. The first stage of prenatal development, in which the male sperm unites with the female egg, is called the _____ stage. The fertilized egg is called a _____. When the zygote becomes implanted in the wall of the uterus, the second stage of prenatal development, called the _____ stage, begins. The last stage, the _____ stage, begins at eight weeks. Several things can pass the placental barrier and damage the embryo and fetus. One substance that is damaging to the fetus is alcohol, which can lead to _____ _____ syndrome. This syndrome causes facial deformities, smaller brains, lack of coordination, and mental retardation. Other potentially harmful influences are rubella or German _____, radiation, _____ transmitted diseases, _____ smoking, and the use of other _____.

1-2. A newborn is equipped with automatic behaviors that are necessary for survival and are known as _____ _____. For example, when touched on the side of the face or near the mouth the infant will turn his or her head in search of something on which to suck. This is known as the _____ reflex.

1-3. Infants form attachments very early in life. The Harlows' first demonstrated the importance of touching, or _____ _____ in an experiment with rhesus monkeys. The monkeys spent _____ time with the cloth "mother" than with the mother that provided _____. Between _____ months, after babies are emotionally attached to their primary caregivers, they will frequently be frightened of strangers. They will also be upset if their primary caregiver leaves them, showing what is called _____ _____.

Ainsworth developed an experimental situation, known as the _____ _____, to identify styles of attachment between mothers and infants. Based on children's reactions, Ainsworth classified children as having different styles of _____. The children that were most attached to their mothers were said to be _____ attached. Other children were described as displaying a(n) _____ attachment which has two forms. Some of these infants were said to be _____; they did not seem to care where the mother was. Others were described as being _____ or _____; resisting contact with the mother and acting angry with her when she returned, but protesting loudly when she left them. Most children form secure attachments with their mothers in spite of large variations in _____ customs.

Terms for Review

The following is a list of the important terms from the section "From Conception Through the First Year." Make sure you are familiar with each term before taking the progress test on these terms.

maturation	contact comfort
germinal stage	separation anxiety
zygote	Strange Situation
embryonic stage	securely attached
fetal stage	insecurely attached
fetus	avoidant attachment
fetal alcohol syndrome	anxious/ ambivalent attachment
motor reflexes	

2. Language Development

Read the section "Language Development" and then answer the following questions. If you have trouble answering any of the questions, re-study the relevant material before going on to the review of key terms and the progress tests.

2-1. _____ is the set of rules for combining meaningless elements into a manner that conveys meaning. Adults' use of _____, which is characterized by higher and more varied pitch and exaggerated intonation when speaking to babies, appears to be universal. This speech helps babies learn the melody and _____ of their native language. According to linguists who study language acquisition, by _____ babies have learned many key consonant and vowel sounds of their native language. They start to _____ between the ages of 6 months and 1 year, which

involves the repetition of sounds and syllables. At about _____ they typically will begin to name things. The two or three word brief communications used by the 18-month to 2-year-old child is referred to as _____ speech. Psychologists first thought that children learn to speak by imitating adults. However, some theorists have suggested that we are born with a _____ _____. This innate mental module that allows children to develop language when they are exposed to it was proposed by _____. Evidence supporting this notion comes from children's understanding of not only the _____ structure of a sentence, but also their understanding of the underlying meaning of the sentence, known as the _____ structure of the sentence. Supporters of this view have noted that many children go through similar stages of linguistic _____; that children combine words in ways that adults never would, thereby committing errors called _____; and that children learn to speak in a _____ correct manner even though adults are not consistently correcting them. Also, children may _____ their own language if they are not exposed to adult language. It does appear, however, that _____ plays at least as great a role in language development. Despite not having pre-existing mental modules, _____ programs are able to

39

learn the rules of language. The idea that language has to be learned at a certain time period in life is known as a

_____ _____.

Terms for Review

The following is a list of the important terms from the section "Language Development." Make sure you are familiar with each term before taking the progress test on these terms.

language   deep structure
parentese   universal grammar
telegraphic speech   overregularizations
surface structure

3. Cognitive Development

Read the section "Cognitive Development" and then answer the following questions. If you have trouble answering any of the questions, re-study the relevant material before going on to the review of key terms and the progress tests.

3-1. The psychologist who created a theory of cognitive development in the 1920s was _____ _____. He proposed children may _____ new information, allowing it to fit into existing mental categories. They may also_____ new experiences, especially when faced with new information that doesn't fit and requires a change or modification of existing categories. Piaget further stated that all children go through four stages of cognitive development. The first, from birth to 2 years of age, is called the _____ stage, in which children learn through coordinating sensory information with motor movements. A major accomplishment during this stage is the

development of _____ _____, knowing that something continues to exist when you cannot sense it. During the_____ stage, from ages 2 to 7 years, the use of symbols and language increases. However, Piaget felt that children in this stage were lacking in other mental abilities such as reasoning. For example, according to Piaget, children in this stage cannot take another person's perspective or point of view. In other words, such children are described as being _____. Another limitation of the preoperational child is that they believe that physical properties change when their appearances change. In other words, they do not understand _____. In the third stage, known as the _____ _____ stage, children between 7 to 11 years old master many of the skills they were lacking in the preoperational stage. Their thinking abilities, however, are still limited to actual experiences and tangible concepts. Lastly, the fourth stage or _____ _____ stage, from ages 12 to adulthood, signals the beginning of _____ reasoning abilities. Although Piaget's research contributed greatly to the field of developmental psychology, there are some corrections to his theories. Cognitive abilities tend to develop _____ and not in discrete steps or stages. Further, preschoolers are not as _____ as Piaget claimed. As early as ages 3 to 4, they begin developing a _____ of _____, which is a system of beliefs about how their mind and the minds of other people work. Children also reveal cognitive abilities much _____ than Piaget thought possible. Finally, cognitive development is influenced by the _____ in which the child lives.

Terms for Review

The following is a list of the important terms from the section "Cognitive Development." Make sure you are familiar with each term before taking the progress test on these terms.

Jean Piaget	egocentric
assimilate	conservation
accommodate	concrete operations stage
sensorimotor stage	formal operations stage
object permanence	theory of mind
preoperational stage	

4. Moral Development

Read the section "Moral Development" and then answer the following questions. If you have trouble answering any of the questions, re-study the relevant material before going on to the review of key terms and the progress tests.

4-1. _____ _____ used Piaget's ideas to develop a stage theory of moral reasoning. Very young children obey rules because they fear being _____ and believe it is in their best interest to obey. Around age 10 their moral judgments shift such that they are based on _____ and a _____ to others. Next, they come to understand the _____ of _____. Some eventually reach the highest level of moral reasoning, which is based on _____ _____ _____.

4-2. One method frequently used by parents in an attempt to enforce proper behavior and instill moral standards in their children is _____ _____, which involves threatening some sort of punishment in order to encourage the child to act morally. Power assertion, however, is associated with greater _____ and reduced _____. A better approach to teaching moral behavior is _____. When using this method, parents appeal to the child's own abilities, empathy, helpful nature, and sense of _____ for others. One of the most important skills to acquire is _____-_____, the ability to suppress initial wish in favor of something else that is less appealing.

Terms for Review

The following is a list of the important terms from the section "Moral Development." Make sure you are familiar with each term before taking the progress test on these terms.

Lawrence Kohlberg	induction
power assertion	self-regulation

5. Gender Development

Read the section "Gender Development" and then answer the following questions. If you have trouble answering any of the questions, re-study the relevant material before going on to the review of key terms and the progress tests.

5-1. _____ _____ is used to refer to one's sense of being male or female. Gender _____, however, is society's beliefs about which skills and behaviors are appropriate for males or females. Therefore, it is possible to have a strong gender identity and not be gender _____. Identity can be complicated by _____ _____, which is when a child is born with ambiguous genitals. Further, some adults choose to call themselves _____, reflecting the fact they do not fit comfortably into the usual gender categories.

5-2. Biological psychologists assert that differences between males and females may be due to prenatal _____. Another approach to gender development investigates _____ abilities and their influence on gender development. According to this approach, children develop a _____ _____, a mental network of beliefs, metaphors, and expectations about what it means to be male or female, which can influence behavior. According to learning theorists, differences between boys and girls are a result of the subtle and not-so-subtle messages found in the _____. Parents, teachers, and other adults will convey their _____ and _____ about gender even when they are unaware of their actions.

Terms for Review

The following is a list of the important terms from the section "Gender Development." Make sure you are familiar with each term before taking the progress test on these terms.

gender identity	transgender
gender typing	transsexual
intersex conditions	gender schema

6. Adolescence

Read the section "Adolescence" and then answer the following questions. If you have trouble answering any of the questions, re-study the relevant material before going on to the review of key terms and the progress tests.

6-1. The point at which a person becomes capable of sexual reproduction is known as _____. The interval of time between becoming sexually mature and adulthood is referred to as _____. From puberty on, boys have a higher level of the hormones called _____ and girls have higher levels of _____. Signs of sexual maturity in girls include the onset of menstruation, called _____. For boys, the growth of the _____, scrotum, and testes signal puberty. In addition, boys develop a deepened voice and facial and chest hair, and both boys and girls develop _____ hair. These changes reflect _____ _____ characteristics and are a result of _____. The length and onset of puberty varies tremendously across individuals due to _____ and environmental influences. The _____ changes significantly during adolescence, as well. Changes occur in the _____ cortex and the _____ system. Further,

_____ occurs when fatty sheaths of insulation develop for cells.

6-2. The rates of violent crimes committed by adolescents in the U.S. has been _____ steadily since 1993. Problems that are more common are _____ with parents, _____ swings and depression. _____ _____ often occurs because teenagers are developing their own standards and values, which may clash with those of their parents. Boys tend to _____ emotional problems by acting aggressively. Girls, on the other hand, tend to _____ their feelings and problems.

Terms for Review

The following is a list of the important terms from the section "Adolescence." Make sure you are familiar with each term before taking the progress test on these terms.

adolescence   secondary sex characteristics
puberty   myelinization
menarche

7. Adulthood

Read the section "Adulthood" and then answer the following questions. If you have trouble answering any of the questions, re-study the relevant material before going on to the review of key terms and the progress tests.

7-1. A comprehensive stage theory of development was put forth by _____ _____, who proposed that people go through eight stages in their lives, and face a _____ at each stage. For

example, _____ versus _____ is the crisis during infancy. Autonomy versus shame and doubt is the challenge facing a _____. The crisis in the preschool years is _____ versus guilt. School-age children face the challenge of _____ versus _____. Identity versus role confusion is the challenge of _____, during which they typically experience an _____ crisis. Adults face the challenge of _____ versus isolation. The crisis of middle adulthood is one of _____ versus _____, and the crisis of old age is one of ego _____ versus _____. Erikson acknowledged that cultural and _____ factors affect the passage through these stages and that development is an ongoing process. Current researchers have found that people's psychological challenges can occur at different ages depending on internal factors and their experiences in life.

7-2. Researchers today do not focus as much on stages as they do on the _____ of life. Changing demographics have created a new stage of development known as _____ _____. During this stage, people have moved beyond adolescence into maturity but do not feel fully secure as adults. The middle years are not a time of crisis for most

43

people. Women during this time experience _____, which is when the ovaries stop producing estrogen and progesterone and menstruation ends. Although menopause does produce negative side effects in some women, only about _____ percent of women have severe physical symptoms. Only 3 percent even report _____ at having reached menopause. Men experience biological changes, as well since their _____ levels diminish as they get older.

7-3. Researchers who study aging and the elderly are called _____. Negative consequences of aging include the decline in aspects of intelligence, _____, and other forms of mental functioning. However, gerontologists distinguish between _____ intelligence, which is the capacity for deductive reasoning and the ability to solve problems that does decline with age and _____ intelligence, which is the knowledge and skills that accumulate over one's lifetime and that remains stable or can increase as one gets older.

Terms for Review

The following is a list of the important terms from the section "Adulthood." Make sure you are familiar with each term before taking the progress test on these terms.

Erik Erikson	gerontologists
identity crisis	fluid intelligence
emerging adulthood	crystallized intelligence
menopause	

8. The Wellsprings of Resilience

Read the section "The Wellspring of Resilience" and then answer the following questions. If you have trouble answering any of the questions, re-study the relevant material before going on to the progress tests.

8-1. Many studies that have followed people from childhood to adulthood contradict the widespread assumption that early traumas always have long-lasting, negative effects. Most children are _____ and have recovered from _____, childhood illness, abusive or _____ parents, and from _____ abuse.

SAMPLE ANSWERS TO *YOU ARE ABOUT TO LEARN* QUESTIONS FROM TEXTBOOK

After you have read through the chapter, go back and review the "You Are About to Learn..." statements that precede each major section. Create your own answer to each question, then compare your answers to the following sample answers. If your answers are not similar to the sample answers, review the relevant sections of the chapter more carefully.

What are the stages of prenatal development?

The germinal stage begins at fertilization. It is followed by the embryonic stage and then the fetal stage.

What are factors that can harm an embryo or fetus during pregnancy?

A pregnant woman should abstain from smoking, avoid alcohol and x-rays, and take no drugs unless they are necessary.

How does culture affect how a baby physically matures?

Babies' physical maturation is affected by cultural customs that govern how their parents hold, touch, feed, and talk to them. Whereas these various customs impact the rate of maturation eventually healthy children everywhere are able to crawl, sit, and walk.

Why is contact comfort and attachment so important for infants (not to mention adults)?

According to research by the Harlows, infant monkeys formed attachments to artificial mothers that provided contact comfort, or cuddling. Depriving infants of affection and cuddling may lead to behavioral and cognitive problems, low self-esteem, and increased risk of depression later in life.

What are some of the varieties of infant attachment?

Babies can be securely attached so that they will cry or protest if the caregiver leaves or they can be insecurely attached, resulting in either disinterest or resistance to the caregiver.

What is language and what does it allow humans to accomplish?

Language involves combining meaningless elements together so that they acquire meaning, which allows us to refer to the past and future and convey precise information that aids in survival.

Why is "baby talk" important for language development?

When parents speak to babies, their pitch is higher and more varied than usual, and their intonation is more exaggerated. This "baby talk" or parentese helps babies learn the "melody" and rhythm of their native language.

What are some milestones in the development of language?

Initially, infants engage in babbling, the repetition of the basic units of sound. Eventually, certain sounds are selected out of language and common patterns emerge. Symbolic gestures begin occurring and telegraphic speech happens.

Is language an innate ability or an acquired one?

Language depends upon both biological readiness and social experience. Although normal children may have an inborn capacity to acquire language from mere exposure to it, parents help things along by correcting children's mistakes. There is a critical period in language development during the first few years of life. Children who are not exposed to language during this period rarely speak normally. Thus, as usual, nature and nurture interact in the development of language.

What are Piaget's stages of cognitive development and their hallmarks?

Babies are born into the sensorimotor stage. At some point during this stage, infants begin to reveal an understanding of object permanence. Preoperational stage occurs next, during which children do not understand conservation. They believe that when something changes form or appearance, it also changes in quantity or amount. The third stage is concrete operations in which conservation is understood but knowledge is grounded in direct experiences and tangible objects. Finally, during the formal operations stage, the capacity for abstract thought emerges.

What are modern approaches to the mental development of children?

Current views of mental development suggest that development occurs in continuous waves, that the very young are not necessarily egocentric, children can understand more than Piaget gave them credit for, and that culture is a critical element in cognitive development.

How do moral feelings and behavior develop?

How do children learn to tell right from wrong, resist the temptation to behave selfishly, and obey the rules of social conduct? In the 1960s, Lawrence Kohlberg (1964), inspired by Piaget's work, argued that children's ability to understand right from wrong evolved along with the rest of their cognitive abilities and argued that moral understanding develops through stages. Initially, moral behavior is simply motivated by avoidance of punishment that is in the best interest of the individual. Later, motivating factors such as conformity and loyalty become relevant. For some individuals, following a universal code of ethics becomes more important than other considerations.

Why is it likely that shouting "Because I say so!" will not succeed in getting children to behave well?

This method, called power assertion, is based on a child's fear of punishment and is associated with aggressive behavior and poor moral reasoning in children. In addition, longitudinal studies show that when paired with intermittent discipline, power assertion can lead to children whose aggressiveness is difficult to manage.

Why is a child's ability to delay gratification so important? Why do some people fail to identify themselves as either male or female?

To ability to engage in such self-regulation predicts the control of negative emotions and ability to perform well. The complexity of sex and gender development is especially apparent in the cases of people who do not fit the familiar categories of male and female. Every year, thousands of babies are born with intersex conditions, formerly known as hermaphroditism. In these conditions, which occur in about one of every 2,000 births, chromosomal or hormonal anomalies cause the child to be born with ambiguous genitals, or genitals that conflict with the infant's chromosomes. A child who is genetically female, for example, might be born with an enlarged clitoris that looks like a penis. A child who is genetically male might be born with androgen insensitivity, a condition that causes the external genitals to appear to be female.

How would a biologically oriented psychologist explain why most little boys and girls are "sexist" in their choice of toys?

Biological psychologists believe that differences between the sexes are largely a matter of prenatal hormones, genes, and possibly brain organization. They feel that gender differences will surface no matter what parents or teachers do. Even when parents and teachers attempt to treat girls and boys in the same manner, many find that boys still prefer mechanical toys and girls still prefer more "feminine" toys.

When and how do children learn that they are male or female?

As soon as children have a gender schema, they change their behavior to conform to it. They begin to prefer same-sex playmates and sex-traditional toys, without being explicitly taught to do so. They become more gender typed in their toy preferences, play, games, aggressiveness, and verbal skills. Girls stop being physically aggressive. In addition, boys' gender schemas are more rigid than girls' are.

What is a learning explanation of typical sex differences in childhood behavior?

Significant individuals in the child's environment may reward and punish certain behaviors thought to be gender appropriate. For example, in one observational study, teachers responded far more to boys when they acted aggressively. On the other hand, they responded far more to girls when they acted dependently. Thus, boys receive more attention from teachers, parents, and peers when they act aggressively than do girls. When girls call for help from a teacher, they receive more attention than do boys who engage in the same behavior.

What are the physiological changes of adolescence?

During puberty, sex organs mature and individuals become capable of reproduction. Breast development and menarche occurs in females. Nocturnal emissions and the growth of testes, scrotum, and penis occur in males. Hormones result in the emergence of secondary sex characteristics.

What are the psychological issues of adolescence?

Both sexes usually encounter problems when there is early maturation. Boys who mature early are more likely to use drugs, break the law, and have less self-control. Girls who mature early are more likely to have emotional problems, drop out of school, have conflicts with their parents, and have a negative body image. However, results from most studies have indicated that only a minority of teenagers conforms to the stereotype of the troubled, angry, unhappy adolescent. The majority of teenagers have supportive families, a sense of purpose and self-confidence, good friends, and adequate coping skills.

What are some findings on brain development in adolescence?

Research has shown that adolescents often get into trouble because of the neurological immaturity of their brains.

What is Erik Erikson's theory of the stages of development?

Erikson saw the entire lifespan as consisting of a series of eight conflicts or crises that must be resolved before an individual can progress normally in their development.

What the typical attitudes during "emerging adulthood," the years from 18 to 25?

During this time, people may not feel like they are adolescents or adults. Although in some respects they are more emotionally mature, they also are more likely to take risks, such as drunk driving, than are people of any other age group. It is considered by some to be a period of prolonged exploration and freedom.

What are some common midlife changes for women and men?

Women will enter menopause, which appears to have no effect on most women's mental health. In men, testosterone levels drop as they age.

Which mental abilities decline in old age, and which do not?

Fluid intelligence declines in old age. This includes the capacity for deductive reasoning and the ability to use new information to solve problems. Crystallized intelligence, on the other hand, does not decline with age. This includes the knowledge and skills that are built up over a lifetime and allows people to engage in such behaviors as solving math problems and defining words.

Do traumatic childhood experiences affect a person forever?

No, they do not. Studies that follow people from childhood to adulthood find that most children recover from war, abusive or alcoholic parents, and sexual abuse.

What makes most children resilient in the face of adversity?

Children who experience violence or neglect are at risk of having emotional and physical problems later in life. But the majority of children are resilient and are able to overcome early traumatic experiences. Psychologists now study not only the sad consequences of neglect, poverty, and violence but also the origins of resilience under adversity, which they find more common than was once believed.

KEY TERMS FILL-IN-THE-BLANKS PROGRESS TEST

Fill in the blanks with the key terms from the chapter that match the definitions provided. When you have finished this progress test, check your answers with those at the end of this chapter. You should review any key terms that you do not define correctly.

1. _____ Automatic behaviors that are necessary for survival and with which newborns begin life.

2. _____ The stage in prenatal development that begins with the implantation of the zygote.

3. _____ The sequential unfolding of genetically influenced behavior and physical characteristics.

4. _____ Negative emotions displayed when the primary caregiver temporarily leaves the infant.

5. _____ The basis of an infant's first attachment.

6. _____ The understanding, which develops throughout the first year, that an object continues to exist even when you cannot see it or touch it.

7. _____ A child's first combination of words, which omits (as a telegram does) unnecessary words.

8. _____ In Piaget's theory, the process of absorbing new information into existing cognitive structures.

9. _____ The inability to take another person's perspective.

10. _____ In Piaget's theory, the process of modifying existing cognitive structures in response to experience and new information.

11. _____ The understanding that the physical properties of objects can remain the same even when their form or appearance changes.

12. _____ An innate mental module proposed to explain language acquisition and involves the sensitivity of the brain of the core features common to all languages.

13. _____ A method of child rearing in which the parent uses punishment and authority to correct the child's misbehavior.

14. _____ A method of child rearing in which the parents appeal to the child's own resources, abilities, sense of responsibility, and feelings for others in correcting the child's misbehavior.

15. _____ The process by which children learn the abilities, interests, personality traits, and behaviors, associated with being masculine or feminine in their culture.

16. _____ A mental network of knowledge, beliefs, metaphors, and expectations about what it means to be male or female.

17. _____ The onset of menstruation.

18. _____ The age at which a person becomes capable of sexual reproduction.

19. _____ Examples are chest hair, the deepening of the voice, and breast development.

20. _____ Having developed past adolescence, but not yet fully developed as an adult.

21. _____ Cognitive skills and specific knowledge of information acquired over a lifetime.

22. _____ The cessation of menstruation and of the production of ova.

23. _____ It is relatively independent of education and tends to decline in old age.

Choose the single best answer for each of the following questions. When you have finished this progress test, check your answers with those at the end of this chapter. You should review the relevant pages in the text for the questions you do not answer correctly.

1. Which of the following is the correct order of the three stages of prenatal development?
    a. Germinal; embryonic; fetal
    b. Germinal; fetal; embryonic
    c. Embryonic; germinal; fetal
    d. Fetal; embryonic; germinal

2. Which of the following is (are) potentially harmful to fetal development?
    a. Cigarette smoking
    b. Father's cocaine use
    c. Lead
    d. all of the above

3. In response to stimulation to their cheek, an infant will orient their head towards the source of stimulation. This is the _____ reflex.
    a. Moro
    b. Babinski
    c. rooting
    d. stepping

4. Which of the following statements about an infant's physical abilities is FALSE?
    a. Newborns begin life with several motor reflexes, such as the "rooting reflex."
    b. Newborns cannot discriminate their mother or other primary caregiver until they are two or three months old.
    c. Newborns have a preference for faces.
    d. none of the above

5. In Ainsworth's Strange Situation, a child who does not care whether the mother leaves the room, makes little effort to seek contact with her on return, and treats the stranger about the same as the mother is categorized as:
    a. securely attached.

    b. avoidant.
    c. anxious.
    d. ambivalent.

6. With respect to language development, which of the following statements is FALSE?
    a. Infants are responsive to the pitch, intensity, and sound of language.
    b. By 4 to 6 months, babies can distinguish the key sounds of their native language from those of a foreign language.
    c. From age 6 months to 1 year, babies begin to speak in two- or three-word telegraphic sentences.
    d. none of the above

7. Which of the following kinds of evidence supports Chomsky's argument for a language acquisition device?
    a. Children everywhere go through similar stages of linguistic development.
    b. Children simply imitate adults in their use of language.
    c. Adults consistently correct their children's syntax.
    d. all of the above

8. In Piaget's theory, the process of modifying existing cognitive structures in response to experience and new information is called _____.
    a. assimilation
    b. accommodation
    c. egocentric thinking
    d. conservation

9. According to Piaget, object permanence is a major accomplishment of the _____ stage.
    a. formal operations
    b. concrete operations
    c. preoperational
    d. sensorimotor

10. An understanding of conservation occurs in the _____ stage and an understanding of abstract reasoning occurs in the _____ stage.

a. sensorimotor; preoperational
b. preoperational; sensorimotor
c. concrete operations; formal operations
d. formal operations; concrete operations

11. With respect to the text's evaluation of Piaget's theory, which of the following statements is FALSE?
a. The changes from one stage to another are not as discrete as he implied.
b. Preschoolers are more egocentric than Piaget thought.
c. Piaget overestimated the cognitive abilities of many adults.
d. none of the above

12. According to Kohlberg, if someone obeys a rule because she fears being punished if she disobeys, then her moral reasoning is at an _____ stage of development.
a. early
b. average
c. advanced
d. none of the above

13. Being rewarded for gender specific behaviors is to gender schemas as _____ psychologists are to _____ psychologists.
a. biological; learning
b. learning; biological
c. learning; cognitive
d. cognitive; learning

14. _____ intelligence reflects an inherited predisposition and tends to _____ over the life span.
a. Fluid; not decline.
b. Fluid; decline
c. Crystallized; not decline
d. Crystallized; decline

15. According to Erik Erikson, _____ is the crisis of adolescence, when teenagers must decide what they are going to be and what they hope to make of their lives.
a. autonomy versus shame and doubt
b. trust versus mistrust
c. identity versus role confusion
d. intimacy versus isolation

16. Menarche refers to a girl's first:
a. sexual activity.
b. menstruation.
c. baby.
d. breast growth.

17. Which of the following statements about victims of child trauma is TRUE?
a. By adulthood, most victims of childhood abuse are as well adjusted as people in the general population.
b. The majority of children of abusive or alcoholic parents become abusive or alcoholic.
c. Meta-analyses of studies on the effects of abuse have found several links between childhood sexual abuse and later emotional disorders.
d. none of the above

Guided Study

1. From Conception Through the First Year

1-1. germinal
   zygote
   embryonic
   fetal
   fetal alcohol
   retardation
   measles
   sexually
   cigarette
   drugs

1-2. motor reflexes
   rooting

1-3. contact comfort
   more
   food
   6 and 8
   separation anxiety
   Strange Situation
   attachment
   securely
   insecure
   avoidant
   anxious
   ambivalent
   child-rearing

2. Language Development

2-1. language
   parentese
   rhythm
   4 to 6 months
   babble
   1 year
   telegraphic
   universal grammar
   Chomsky
   surface
   deep
   development
   overregularizations
   grammatically
   invent
   experience
   computer
   critical period

3. Cognitive Development

3-1. Jean Piaget
   assimilate
   accommodate
   sensorimotor
   object permanence
   preoperational
   egocentric
   conservation
   concrete operations
   formal operations
   abstract
   continuous
   egocentric
   theory
   mind
   earlier
   culture

4. Moral Development

4-1. Lawrence Kohlberg
punished
conformity
loyalty
rule
law
universal human rights

4-2. power assertion
aggressiveness
empathy
induction
responsibility
self-regulation

5. Gender Development

5-1. Gender identity
typing
typed
intersex conditions
transgender

5-2. hormones
cognitive
gender schema
environment

6. Adolescence

6-1. puberty
adolescence
androgens
estrogens
menarche
penis
pubic
secondary sex
hormones
brain
prefrontal
limbic
myelinization

6-2. declining
conflict
mood
rule breaking
externalize
internalize

7. Adulthood

7-1. Erik Erikson
crisis
trust
mistrust
toddler
initiative
competence
inferiority
adolescence
identity
intimacy
generativity
stagnation
integrity
despair
economic
development

7-2. transitions
emerging adulthood
menopause
10
regret
testosterone

7-3. gerontologists
memory
fluid
crystallized

8. The Wellsprings of Resilience

8-1. resilient
war
alcoholic
sexual

Answers to Key Terms Progress Test

1. motor reflexes
2. embryonic
3. maturation
4. separation anxiety
5. contact comfort
6. object permanence
7. telegraphic speech
8. assimilation
9. egocentric thinking
10. accommodation
11. conservation
12. universal grammar
13. power assertion
14. induction
15. gender typing
16. gender schema
17. menarche
18. puberty
19. secondary sex characteristics
20. emerging adulthood
21. crystallized intelligence
22. menopause
23. fluid intelligence

Item Number	Answers
1.	a. germinal; embryonic; fetal
2.	d. all of the above
3.	c. rooting
4.	b. Newborns cannot discriminate their mother or other primary caregiver until they are two or three months old.
5.	b. avoidant
6.	c. From age 6 months to 1 year, babies begin to speak in two- or three-word telegraphic sentences.
7.	a. Children everywhere go through similar stages of linguistic development.
8.	b. accommodation
9.	d. sensorimotor
10.	c. concrete operations; formal operations
11.	b. Preschoolers are more egocentric than Piaget thought.
12.	a. early
13.	c. learning; cognitive
14.	b. Fluid; decline
15.	c. identity versus role confusion
16.	b. menstruation
17.	a. By adulthood, most victims of childhood abuse are as well adjusted as people in the general population.

CHAPTER 4

Neurons, Hormones, and the Brain

CHAPTER OVERVIEW

The chapter begins with an overview of the nervous system. This includes coverage of the central versus peripheral nervous systems. In addition, the various subsystems within the peripheral nervous system are outlined including the somatic versus autonomic nervous systems and the sympathetic versus parasympathetic nervous systems.

Communication within the nervous system is covered next. This includes discussion of the types of cells found in the nervous system, the basic structure of a neuron, new findings in neuroscience, how an action potential is generated, and how neurons communicate with each other at the synapse via neurotransmitters. Several different neurotransmitters and their functions are described. The role of hormones in the endocrine system and the differences between hormones and neurotransmitters also are discussed.

Various methods of viewing or studying the brain are detailed. These include an EEG (electroencephalogram), TMS (transcranial magnetic stimulation), a PET (positron emission tomography) scan, and an MRI (magnetic resonance imaging). Next, various brain structures are identified and their locations and functions are described. The structures discussed include those in the brain stem (medulla, pons, and reticular activating system), the cerebellum, the thalamus, the hypothalamus and the pituitary gland, the amygdala, the hippocampus, and the two cerebral hemispheres. The structure and functions of the cerebral hemispheres are examined in some detail, including coverage of the four lobes within each hemisphere, the visual, auditory, motor, and somatosensory cortices, and Broca's and Wernicke's areas.

The differences in specialization between the two hemispheres are presented next. These differences are explained by exploring research on split-brain patients, who have had their corpus callosums severed. Lastly, the issues of the self and consciousness and whether there are sex differences in the brain are discussed.

1. The Nervous System: A Basic Blueprint

Read the section "The Nervous System: A Basic Blueprint" and then answer the following questions. If you have trouble answering any of the questions, re-study the relevant material before going on to the review of key terms and the progress tests.

1-1. The human nervous system is divided into two parts. The _____ nervous system contains the brain and the _____ _____. The _____ nervous system contains all portions of the nervous system outside of the brain and spinal cord. The spinal cord is an extension of the brain and can produce some behaviors on its own without the brain, called _____ _____.

1-2. The peripheral nervous system is responsible for handling input into the central nervous system (CNS) and output from the CNS. The neurons that carry information to the CNS are known as _____ nerves. _____ nerves carry information away from the CNS to muscles, glands, and internal organs. The peripheral nervous system is further divided into the skeletal nervous system also called the _____ nervous system and the self-governing or _____ nervous system. The somatic nervous system permits _____ actions whereas the autonomic nervous system works in an _____ fashion. The autonomic nervous system is subdivided into two parts. One subsystem, the _____ nervous system, mobilizes the body for action in dangerous situations. The other subsystem, the _____ nervous system, calms down the body's systems and conserves energy.

Terms for Review

The following is a list of the important terms from the section "The Nervous System: A Basic Blueprint." Make sure you are familiar with each term before taking the progress test on these terms.

central nervous system	motor nerves
spinal cord	somatic nervous system
spinal reflexes	autonomic nervous system
peripheral nervous system	sympathetic nervous system
sensory nerves	parasympathetic nervous system

2. Communication in the Nervous System

Read the section "Communication in the Nervous System" and then answer the following questions. If you have trouble answering any of the questions, re-study the relevant material before going on to the review of key terms and the progress tests.

2-1. The nervous system contains communication specialist cells called _____. The _____ cells, which greatly outnumber neurons, act as a type of glue and provide nutrients and insulation to the neurons. A neuron has multiple parts to it. The _____ receive incoming information. The _____ _____ is responsible for keeping the neuron alive, and it also processes the information it receives from the dendrites. Lastly, the _____ carries information away from the cell body and toward other neurons. Most axons divide at their ends into _____ _____. In addition, some axons are insulated with a fatty substance called a _____ _____, which improves neural communication. In the peripheral nervous system, axons (and sometimes dendrites) that are bundled together comprise _____.

2-2. Recently, scientists changed their thoughts regarding the ability of neurons in the _____ nervous system to regenerate. Research in this area involves studying _____ _____, which are immature cells that renew themselves and have the potential to develop into mature cells. The growth of new neurons from these immature stem cells is known as _____.

2-3. The billions of neurons in the nervous system are not physically _____ to each other. The space between the axon terminal of one neuron and the dendrites of another neuron is referred to as the _____ _____. This

entire area, the axon terminal, the synaptic cleft, and the receiving dendrite, is called the _____. The communication system for neurons is both electrical and _____ in nature. When a neuron is stimulated, a brief change in electrical voltage called an _____ _____ occurs, which produces an electrical impulse. In an unmyelinated axon, the action potential travels at a _____ speed than it does in a myelinated axon. The sacs located in the axon terminal, which contain the chemicals used by the nervous system, are called _____ _____. The chemicals used by the nervous system to carry information from one neuron to another are called _____. These neurotransmitters bind to _____ _____ on the next neuron. Depending on which receptor sites have been activated, the effect in the receiving neuron is either _____, a voltage shift in a positive direction, which increases the likelihood that the neuron will fire, or _____, a voltage shift in a negative direction, which decreases the likelihood that the neuron will fire. Only when the neuron's voltage reaches a certain _____ will it fire. A single neuron either fires or does not fire. Therefore, neurons send (or fire) their messages in an _____-_____-_____ manner.

2-4. When we are born, most of our synapses have not yet _____. New learning results in increased synaptic _____. The brain's flexibility in adapting to new experiences is called _____.

2-5. Although the understanding of neurotransmitters is not complete, several neurotransmitters and their effects have been identified. For example, _____ affects neurons involved in sleep, appetite, sensory perception, temperature regulation, pain suppression, and mood. _____ influences neurons involved in muscle action, cognitive functioning, memory, and emotion. It is suspected that dopamine affects neurons that respond to _____ situations. _____ is involved with increasing heart rate and slowing intestinal activity during stress. GABA is the major _____ neurotransmitter while _____ is the major excitatory neurotransmitter in the brain. People with Alzheimer's disease lose brain cells responsible for producing _____. Those with Parkinson's disease lose brain cells that produce _____. However, determining the relationship between neurotransmitter abnormalities and _____ problems is very difficult. Substances that sometimes act as a neurotransmitter and sometimes alter the effects of neurotransmitters are _____. Endorphins reduce _____ and promote _____. Another class of chemical messengers, _____, are produced in one part of the body and affect another part of the body. They are manufactured mainly in the _____ _____. The hormone that helps regulate daily biological rhythms and promotes sleep is _____. The hormones _____ and _____ contribute to relationships by promoting attachment and trust. _____ hormones are involved in emotion and stress. The outer part of the adrenal gland produces _____, the inner part produces _____ and _____. Masculinizing hormones such as testosterone, are referred to as _____. Feminizing hormones include _____, which bring on physical changes in females at puberty, and _____, which contributes to the growth and maintenance of the uterine lining.

Terms for Review

The following is a list of the important terms from the section "Communication in the Nervous System." Make sure you are familiar with each term before taking the progress test on these terms.

neuron	acetylcholine
glia	norepinephrine
dendrites	GABA
cell body	glutamate

axon
axon terminals
myelin sheath
nerves
neurogenesis
stem cells
synaptic cleft
synapse
action potential
synaptic vesicles
neurotransmitter
receptor sites
plasticity
serotonin
dopamine

endorphins
hormones
endocrine glands
melatonin
oxytocin
vasopressin
adrenal hormones
cortisol
epinephrine
sex hormones
androgens
testosterone
estrogens
progesterone

3. Mapping the Brain

Read the section "Mapping the Brain" and then answer the following questions. If you have trouble answering any of the questions, re-study the relevant material before going on to the review of key terms and the progress tests.

3-1. The brain can be studied using several

different methods. The _____

method involves damaging or removing

sections of brain tissue from animals and

observe the effects. An alternative method

utilizes _____ that are either

pasted to the scalp or inserted into the

brain. The electrodes allow measurement

of brainwaves in a recording called an

_____. By placing a wire coil

on a person's head, a powerful magnetic

field can be generated which will stimulate

brain cell, which is known as

_____ _____

_____. Other techniques for

studying the brain involve injecting a

radioactive, _____ substance

into the brain to determine which areas of

the brain are active during certain tasks.

This is called a _____-

_____ tomography scan.

Another technique, _____

_____ imaging, utilizes

magnetic fields and radio frequencies to

produce vibrations in the nuclei of atoms

making up body organs. These vibrations

are picked up as signals that a computer

analyzes and converts into a picture. Brain

scans tell _____ things happen,

but not _____ or how they

happen.

Terms for Review

The following is a list of the important terms from the section "Mapping the Brain." Make sure you are familiar with each term before taking the progress test on these terms.

lesion method
electrode
electroencephalogram (EEG)
transcranial magnetic stimulation (TMS)
positron emission tomography (PET) scan
magnetic resonance imaging (MRI)

4. A Tour Through the Brain

Read the section "A Tour Through the Brain" and then answer the following questions. If you have trouble answering any of the questions, re-study the relevant material before going on to the review of key terms and the progress tests.

4-1. Joseph Gall was one of the first brain

researchers to propose that different brain

parts perform different tasks. This is

known as _____ of

_____. The two main structures

in the brain stem are the _____

and the _____. The medulla is

responsible for basic bodily functions such

as _____ and heart rate. The pons is involved in _____, waking, and _____. At the core of the brain stem is the _____ _____ system, which has connections with higher areas in the brain. Without it people would not be _____ or perhaps even _____.

4-2. The structure at the top of the brain stem and toward the back of the brain is called the _____ or "lesser brain." This structure plays a role in _____ and in coordinating the _____ to make movements smooth and precise. It is involved with _____ tasks, as well.

4-3. The traffic officer of the brain, deep in the brain's interior, is called the _____. This structure acts as a sensory relay center, relaying sensory messages received from the body to higher centers in the _____ for interpretation. The thalamus relays all sensory information, except _____ information, which is relayed by the _____ _____.

4-4. Underneath the thalamus is the _____, which is involved in drives such as hunger, thirst, emotion, sex, and reproduction. It also regulates body _____ and the

_____ nervous system, and contains the _____ clock. Hanging from the hypothalamus is the _____ gland, which secretes _____ that affect the endocrine glands. The functioning of this gland is governed by the _____. The set of structures that forms a border between higher and lower brain areas and that includes the hypothalamus is called the _____ _____.

4-5. A structure that plays a role in emotions involved in either approaching or withdrawing from a person or situation is the _____. It assesses _____ or threat. This structure also appears to be important in mediating _____ and _____.

4-6. A structure that has been called the "gateway to memory" is the _____. This structure enables the formation of _____ memories so that we can navigate our environment and new memories about facts and events.

4-7. The largest part of the brain is known as the _____ and is divided into two _____ _____. The two hemispheres are connected by the _____ _____, a band of neural fibers. The brain and the body operate in a contralateral fashion. The right hemisphere controls the _____ side of the body, and the left hemisphere controls the _____ side of the body. In addition, the two hemispheres control somewhat different functions, which is known as _____. The layers of neurons covering the cerebrum are known as the _____ _____. Each of the hemispheres is divided into four distinct regions called _____. The lobes that contain the visual cortex and are located at the back of the head are the _____ lobes. The lobes that contain the _____ cortex, which receives the input that allows the interpretation of bodily sensations, are the _____ lobes. The _____ lobes are at the sides of the head, just above the ears. They contain the _____ cortex, which allows the processing of sounds. Housed in the left temporal lobe is _____ area, which is important for comprehending language. Lastly, the _____ lobes, located at the front of the brain contain the _____ cortex, which initiates muscle movements. The left frontal lobe contains _____ area, which handles speech production. The frontal lobes also are involved in short-term memory tasks, making decisions and plans, thinking _____, and taking _____. The areas in the cortex that appear to be responsible for higher mental processes are called the _____ cortex. An area of the frontal lobes that is more pronounced in humans than in other animals is the

_____ cortex. This structure appears to play a role in _____ and social judgement, as evidenced by the tragic case of _____ _____, a railroad worker who had an iron rod pass clear through his head, destroying most of the prefrontal cortex.

Terms for Review

The following is a list of the important terms from the section "A Tour Through the Brain." Make sure you are familiar with each term before taking the progress test on these terms.

localization of function
brain stem
pons
medulla
reticular activating system
cerebellum
thalamus
olfactory bulb
hypothalamus
pituitary gland
limbic system
amygdala
hippocampus

cerebrum
cerebral hemispheres
corpus callosum
lateralization
cerebral cortex
occipital lobe
parietal lobe
temporal lobe
Wernicke's area
frontal lobe
Broca's area
prefrontal cortex

5. The Two Hemispheres of the Brain

Read the "The Two Hemispheres of the Brain" and then answer the following questions. If you have trouble answering any of the questions, re-study the relevant material before going on to the review of key terms and the progress tests.

5-1. The two halves of the brain are connected by the _____ _____ which allows the two hemispheres to communicate with each other. Researchers have investigated what happens when the corpus callosum is _____. Results from studies of cats with severed corpus callosums indicate that the cats responded as if they had _____ minds in _____ body. Later

63

research involved human subjects who had their corpus callosums severed as a treatment for _____. This surgery is called _____-_____ surgery. Patients who had this type of surgery afford brain researchers the ability to study the capabilities of each _____.

5-2. Results from split-brain research indicate that most people process language in the _____ hemisphere. Some researchers have concluded that the left hemisphere is _____, exerting control over the right hemisphere. Other researchers have defended the right hemisphere, noting skills at which is it superior such as _____-_____ abilities, _____ recognition, and the ability to understand facial _____. It is important to note that in everyday activities, the two hemispheres work together and that each makes a valuable contribution.

Terms for Review

The following is a list of the important terms from the section "The Two Hemispheres of the Brain." Make sure you are familiar with each term before taking the progress test on these terms.

split-brain surgery

6. Two Stubborn Issues in Brain Research

Read the section "Two Stubborn Issues in Brain Research" and then answer the following questions. If you have trouble answering any of the questions, re-study the relevant material before going on to the progress tests.

6-1. An issue relevant to research on the brain is uncovering the location of the self. Most modern brain scientists consider the mind, consciousness, and self-awareness to be products of the _____ _____. Some propose that our conscious sense of a unified self may be an _____. This is because many actions and choices occur without _____ awareness or direction.

6-2. There is evidence of a sex difference in _____, such that men appear to rely more heavily on one side of the brain and women tend to use both sides when performing some language tasks. Conclusions concerning _____ between the brains of men and women should be considered with caution. Although some researchers have noted brain differences, using these findings to help explain differences between men and women poses several problems. First, the supposed gender differences between men and women are _____. Secondly, a _____ difference does not necessarily produce a difference in _____ or performance. Lastly, sex differences in the brain could be the _____ rather than the _____ of behavioral differences.

SAMPLE ANSWERS TO *YOU ARE ABOUT TO LEARN* QUESTIONS FROM TEXTBOOK

After you have read through the chapter, go back and review the "You Are About to Learn..." statements that precede each major section. Create your own answer to each question, then compare your answers to the following sample answers. If your answers are not similar to the sample answers, review the relevant sections of the chapter more carefully.

Why do you automatically pull your hand away from something hot, "without thinking"?

This behavior is based on spinal reflex actions. These reflexes are automatic, requiring no conscious effort. Sensory nerves bring the message to the spinal cord and the spinal cord quickly sends out a command via motor nerves telling the muscles in your arm to contract. All of this takes place without input from the brain; hence one is able to do this "without thinking."

What are the major parts of the nervous system and their primary functions?

The central nervous system consists of the brain and spinal cord and receives, processes, interprets, and stores incoming sensory information. The peripheral nervous system handles the inputs and outputs of the central nervous system.

Which cells are the nervous system's "communication specialists"—and how do they "talk" to each other?

The neurons are the communication specialists. They talk to each other via chemicals called neurotransmitters. An electrical impulse travels down the length of a single neuron. When the impulse reaches the axon terminal, the synaptic vesicles open and release neurotransmitters into the synaptic cleft. Some of these neurotransmitters bind to the receptor sites on the dendrite of the next neuron. If that neuron receives enough excitatory information from incoming neurotransmitters, then an action potential will occur and an electrical impulse will be fired.

What are the functions of glial cells, the most numerous cells in the brain?

Glial cells hold neurons in place, as well as provide nutrients, insulate them, protect the brain from toxic agents, and remove cellular debris when neurons die.

Why are researchers excited about the discovery of stem cells in the brain?

New evidence points to the possibility of developing new cells in the central nervous system after infancy. Research into stem cells, immature cells that renew themselves and have the potential to develop into mature cells, offers promise for the possibility of neuron growth and regeneration in the brain.

How do learning and experience alter the brain's circuits?

New learning and experience lead to new synaptic connections, with stimulating environments producing the greatest changes. Conversely, some unused synaptic connections are lost as cells or their branches die and are not replaced.

What happens when levels of brain

The effects of neurotransmitters being too high or too low

chemicals called neurotransmitters are too low or too high?

will depend on the neurotransmitter in question. For example, low levels of serotonin and norepinephrine have been associated with depression. Abnormal GABA levels have been implicated in sleep and eating disorders and in convulsive disorders including epilepsy. The loss of brain cells responsible for producing acetylcholine has been implicated in Alzheimer's disease. The lack of the neurotransmitter dopamine plays a role in Parkinson's disease. Pinning down the relationship between neurotransmitter abnormalities and behavioral abnormalities, however, is very difficult as neurotransmitters play multiple roles.

Which brain chemicals mimic the effects of morphine by dulling pain and promoting pleasure?

Endogenous opioid peptides, more popularly known as endorphins, mimic the effects of morphine. Some function as neurotransmitters but most act primarily by altering the effects of neurotransmitters.

Which hormones are of special interest to psychologists, and why?

Melatonin helps regulate daily biological rhythms and promote sleep. Oxytocin enhances uterine contractions and promotes attachment and trust. Adrenal hormones are involved in emotion and stress. Sex hormones set in motion the physical changes. Testosterone also influences sexual arousal in both sexes. Estrogens are feminizing hormones that bring on physical changes in females at puberty, such as breast development and the onset of menstruation, and that influence the course of the menstrual cycle. Progesterone contributes to the growth and maintenance of the uterine lining in preparation for a fertilized egg, among other functions.

Why are patterns of electrical activity in the brain called "brain waves"?

In order to measure brain waves, electrodes are attached either to the scalp or inserted into the brain. The electrodes detect electrical activity in neurons in specific regions of the brain. The electrodes are connected by wires to a machine that translates the electrical activity of the brain into wavy lines (brain waves) on a piece of paper. The wave patterns vary depending on the activity in which one is engaging.

What scanning techniques reveal changes in brain activity while people listen to music or solve math problems?

The PET scan, which involves injecting a glucose-like radioactive substance into an individual, allows researchers to assess which areas of the brain are active when we engage in different activities. MRI allows us to evaluate the same types of activities using magnetic fields and radio frequencies to produce vibrations in the nuclei of atoms making up body organs (in this case, the brain). The vibrations are received as signals and analyzed by a computer and eventually converted into a picture of brain activity.

What are the limitations of brain scans as a way of understanding the brain?

Enthusiasm for new technology has produced a mountain of findings, but it has also resulted in some unwarranted conclusions about "brain centers" or "critical circuits" for this or that behavior. Currently, this technology cannot tell us why or how brain activities occur.

What are the major parts of the brain and some of their major functions?

The brain stem is responsible for non-conscious functions such as sleeping, waking, dreaming, breathing, and heart rate. The cerebellum coordinates balance and smooth, precise muscle movements. The thalamus acts as a "traffic officer." It is responsible for relaying incoming sensory information to the appropriate places in the cerebrum. The hypothalamus in emotions and drives such as fear, hunger, thirst, and reproduction. The pituitary gland produces important hormones. The amygdala regulates emotional responding. The hippocampus is considered the "gateway to memory." This structure allows us to form new memories. The cerebrum is where the higher forms of thinking take place.

Why is it a good thing that the outer covering of the human brain is so wrinkled?

The cortex or outer layers of neurons is wrinkled in order to allow for more surface space. The cortex contains almost three-fourths of all the cells in the human brain. Thus, it is important to have a large surface area. At the same time, one would not want one's skull to be too large; hence, the wrinkled surface of the cortex. This allows for a large surface area (cortex) compressed into a small container (one's skull).

How did a bizarre nineteenth-century accident illuminate the role of the frontal lobes?

The role of the prefrontal cortex was illuminated by the case of Phineas Gage. Gage was a railroad worker involved in an accident in which an iron rod entered his left cheek and exited through the top of his head destroying most of the prefrontal cortex. The accident seemed to affect mainly Gage's personality. Prior to the accident he was known as a likable fellow; yet after the accident he was ill-tempered, foul-mouthed, and undependable.

What would happen if the two cerebral hemispheres could not communicate with each other?

Studies of split-brain patients, who have had their corpus callosum cut, show that the two cerebral hemispheres have somewhat different abilities. In most people, language is processed mainly in the left hemisphere and the right hemisphere is better at spatial-visual tasks. Therefore, if the two hemispheres were "out of touch," they would feel and think differently.

Why do researchers often refer to the left hemisphere as "dominant"?

Researchers refer to the left hemisphere as dominant because it is more active during some logical, symbolic, and sequential tasks. It is also the center for language abilities in most people. Some also believe that the left hemisphere exerts control over the right hemisphere. These researchers have argued that without help from the left side, the right side's mental skills would probably be at a subhuman level.

Why are "left-brainedness" and "right-brainedness" exaggerations?

The differences between the hemispheres are relative, not absolute. In most activities the two hemispheres work together with each making a valuable contribution.

Why do some brain researchers think a unified "self" is only an

The notion of a unified self is questioned since many actions and choices occur without any direction by a conscious self.

illusion?

Some suggest that the brain consists of independent parts that deal with different aspects of thought and perception. Therefore, it is argued that the brain consists of modules and that the self is an illusion due to the verbal module constantly explaining what the other modules produce.

What are some findings and fallacies about sex differences in the brain?

Some studies have noted brain differences between men and women. Many, however, have found few consistent differences. Any brain differences found should be interpreted with caution. First, behavioral differences between men and women are based on stereotypes. Second, biological differences do not always have behavioral implications. And, sex differences in the brain could be the result rather than the cause of behavioral differences.

KEY TERMS FILL-IN-THE-BLANKS PROGRESS TEST

Fill in the blanks with the key terms from the chapter that match the definitions provided. When you have finished this progress test, check your answers with those at the end of this chapter. You should review any key terms that you do not define correctly.

1. _____ The subdivision of the peripheral nervous system that regulates the internal organs and glands.

2. _____ Neurons and supportive tissue running from the base of the brain down to the center of the back.

3. _____ Neurons that carry information to the central nervous system.

4. _____ The subdivision of the autonomic nervous system that acts as a brake, operates during relaxed states, and conserves energy.

5. _____ All portions of the nervous system outside the brain and spinal cord; including sensory and motor nerves.

6. _____ A chemical substance that is released at the synapse by a transmitting neuron and that alters the activity of a receiving neuron.

7. _____ Chemical substances, secreted by organs called glands, that affect the functioning of other organs.

8. _____ A neuron's branches that receive information from other neurons and transmit it toward the cell body.

9. _____ A bundle of nerve fibers (axons and sometimes dendrites) in the peripheral nervous system.

10. _____ Chemical substances in the nervous system that are similar in structure and action to opiates.

11. _____ A hormone secreted by the pineal gland that is involved in the regulation of daily biological rhythms.

12. _____ A fatty insulation that may surround the axon of a neuron.

13. _____ The site where transmission of a nerve impulse from one nerve cell to another occurs; it includes the axon terminal, the synaptic cleft, and the receptor sites in the membrane of the receiving cell.

14. _____ A brief change in electrical voltage that occurs when a neuron is stimulated and serves to produce an electrical impulse.

15. _____ A method for analyzing biochemical activity in the brain, using injections of a glucoselike substance containing a radioactive element.

16. _____ A method for studying body and brain tissue, using magnetic fields and special radio receivers.

17. _____ A recording or neural activity detected by electrodes.

18. _____ A structure in the brain stem responsible for certain automatic functions, such as breathing and heart rate.

19. _____ A brain structure that regulates movement and balance and is involved in the learning of certain kinds of simple responses and in some types of cognitive tasks.

20. _____ A small endocrine gland at the base of the hypothalamus that releases many hormones and regulates other endocrine glands.

21. _____ A brain structure involved in the storage of new information in memory.

22. _____ Specialization of particular brain areas for particular functions.

23. _____ A dense network of neurons found in the core of the brain stem; it arouses the cortex and screens incoming information.

24. _____ A brain structure that relays sensory messages to the cerebral cortex

25. _____ A brain structure involved in the arousal and regulation of emotion and the initial emotional response to sensory information.

26. _____ Specialization of the two cerebral hemispheres for particular operations.

27. _____ An area in the left temporal lobe involved in language comprehension.

28. _____ The procedure in which the bundle of nerve fibers connecting the two hemispheres is severed.

MULTIPLE-CHOICE PROGRESS TEST

Choose the single best answer for each of the following questions. When you have finished this progress test, check your answers with those at the end of this chapter. You should review the relevant pages in the text for the questions you do not answer correctly.

1. _____ nerves carry messages to the CNS from the PNS, and _____ nerves carry messages from the CNS to the PNS.
   a. Sensory; motor
   b. Motor; sensory
   c. Somatic; autonomic
   d. Autonomic; somatic

2. The _____ nervous system divides into the sympathetic and parasympathetic nervous systems.
   a. somatic
   b. autonomic
   c. central
   d. peripheral

3. Which of the following is NOT an action of the sympathetic nervous system, which is active during emergencies?
   a. Accelerates heartbeat
   b. Inhibits digestion
   c. Constricts pupils
   d. Stimulates sweat glands

4. Which of the following statements about glial cells is FALSE?
   a. Glial cells greatly outnumber neurons.
   b. The myelin sheath is derived from glial cells.
   c. Glial cells provide neurons with nutrients.
   d. none of the above

5. The normal path for neural transmission within a neuron is:
   a. cell body; dendrites; axon.
   b. dendrites; cell body; axon.
   c. axon; cell body; dendrites.
   d. axon; dendrites; cell body.

6. Loss of myelin surrounding axons causes _____.
   a. Alzheimer's disease
   b. epilepsy
   c. multiple sclerosis
   d. Parkinson's disease

7. Excitatory neurotransmitters _____ the probability of an action potential in the receiving neuron, and inhibitory neurotransmitters _____ this probability.
   a. increase; increase
   b. increase; decrease
   c. decrease; increase
   d. decrease; decrease

8. Which of the following statements about neural communication is FALSE?
   a. The firing of a neuron is an all-or-none event.
   b. Conduction of a neural impulse beneath the myelin sheath is impossible.
   c. Each neuron only has synaptic connections with one other neuron.
   d. none of the above

9. The major inhibitory neurotransmitter in the brain is:
   a. GABA.
   b. acetylcholine.
   c. norepinephrine.
   d. serotonin.

10. The degeneration of brain cells that produce and use _____ appears to cause the symptoms of Parkinson's disease.
    a. acetylcholine
    b. norepinephrine
    c. dopamine
    d. GABA

11. Some substances such as _____ serve as both neurotransmitters and hormones.
    a. norepinephrine
    b. melatonin
    c. endorphins
    d. L-dopa

12. Which of the following hormones helps to regulate daily biological rhythms and promotes sleep?
    a. Testosterone
    b. Epinephrine
    c. Melatonin
    d. Cortisol

13. A patient is injected with a glucose-like substance that contains a harmless radioactive element. The patient's brain is then scanned. This type of brain probe is called:
    a. an EEG.
    b. a PET scan.
    c. MRI.
    d. the lesion method.

14. "Traffic officer" is to "gateway to memory" as _____ is to _____.
    a. reticular activating system; cerebellum
    b. cerebellum; reticular activating system
    c. thalamus; hippocampus
    d. hippocampus; thalamus

15. Which of the following pairs of lobes and types of cortex is INCORRECT?
    a. Occipital lobes and visual cortex
    b. Temporal lobes and motor cortex
    c. Parietal lobes and somatosensory cortex
    d. none of the above

16. Cases such as the Phineas Gage accident indicate that the _____ lobes have something to do with personality.
    a. frontal
    b. parietal
    c. temporal
    d. occipital

17. Hormone regulation is to the _____ as the regulation of balance and muscle coordination is to the _____.
    a. hypothalamus; thalamus
    b. amygdala; medulla
    c. hypothalamus; cerebellum
    d. pituitary gland; thalamus

18. The right hemisphere is superior to the left hemisphere in all of the following EXCEPT:
    a. solving problems requiring spatial-visual ability.
    b. facial recognition.
    c. the ability to read facial expressions.
    d. explaining actions and emotions.

19. If a picture of a spoon is flashed quickly in the left visual field of a split-brain patient, then the patient can:
    a. use the right hand to identify the spoon.
    b. use the left hand to identify the spoon.
    c. say that a spoon was shown.
    d. a and c

20. Which of the following statements about sex differences in the brain is FALSE?
    a. Many supposed gender differences are actually just stereotypes, which can be misleading since the overlap between genders tends to be greater than the differences.
    b. A biological difference does not necessarily produce differences in behavior or performance.
    c. When sex differences in the brain are found to be related to behavioral differences, we know that the behavior must result from the brain difference.
    d. none of the above

72

Guided Study

1. The Nervous System: A Basic Blueprint

1-1. central
  spinal cord
  peripheral
  spinal reflexes

1-2. sensory
  Motor
  somatic
  autonomic
  voluntary
  automatic
  sympathetic
  parasympathetic

2. Communication in the Nervous System

2-1. neurons
  glial
  dendrites
  cell body
  axon
  axon terminals
  myelin sheath
  nerves

2-2. central
  stem cells
  neurogenesis

2-3. connected
  synaptic cleft
  synapse
  chemical
  action potential
  slower
  synaptic vesicles
  neurotransmitters
  receptor sites
  excitatory
  inhibitory
  threshold
  all-or-none

2-4. formed
  complexity
  plasticity

2-5. serotonin
  Acetylcholine
  novel
  norepinephrine
  inhibitory
  glutamate
  acetylcholine
  dopamine
  behavioral
  endorphins
  pain
  pleasure
  hormones
  endocrine glands
  melatonin
  oxytocin
  vasopressin
  Adrenal
  cortisol
  epinephrine
  norepinephrine
  androgens
  estrogens
  progesterone

3. Mapping the Brain

3-1. lesion
  electrodes
  electroencephalogram
  transcranial magnetic stimulation
  glucose-like
  positron emission
  magnetic resonance
  where
  why

4. A Tour Through the Brain

4-1. localization
  function
  medulla
  pons
  breathing
  sleeping
  dreaming
  reticular activating
  alert
  conscious

4-2. cerebellum
  balance
  muscles
  cognitive

4-3. thalamus
  brain
  olfactory
  olfactory bulb

4-4. hypothalamus
  temperature
  autonomic
  biological
  pituitary
  hormones
  hypothalamus
  limbic system

4-5. amygdala
  danger
  anxiety
  depression

4-6. hippocampus
  spatial
  epilepsy

4-7. cerebrum
  cerebral hemispheres
  corpus callosum
  left
  right
  lateralization
  cerebral cortex
  lobes
  occipital
  somatosensory
  parietal
  temporal
  auditory
  Wernicke's
  frontal
  motor
  Broca's
  creatively
  initiative
  association
  prefrontal
  personality
  Phineas Gage

5. The Two Hemispheres of the Brain

5-1. corpus callosum
     severed
     two
     one
     epilepsy
     split-brain
     hemisphere

5-2. left
     dominant
     spatial-visual
     facial
     expressions

6. Two Stubborn Issues in Brain Research

6-1. cerebral cortex
     illusion
     conscious

6-2. lateralization
     differences
     stereotypes
     brain
     behavior
     result
     cause

Answers to Key Terms Progress Test

1. autonomic nervous system
2. spinal cord
3. sensory nerves
4. parasympathetic nervous system
5. peripheral nervous system
6. neurotransmitter
7. hormones
8. dendrites
9. nerves
10. endorphins
11. melatonin
12. myelin sheath
13. synapse
14. action potential
15. PET scan
16. MRI
17. EEG
18. medulla
19. cerebellum
20. pituitary gland
21. hippocampus
22. localization of function
23. reticular activating system
24. thalamus
25. amygdala
26. lateralization
27. Wernicke's area
28. split-brain surgery

Answers to Multiple-Choice Progress Test

Item Number	Answers
1.	a. Sensory; motor
2.	b. autonomic
3.	c. constricts pupils
4.	d. none of the above
5.	b. dendrites; cell body; axon
6.	c. multiple sclerosis
7.	b. increase; decrease
8.	c. Each neuron only has synaptic connections with one other neuron.
9.	a. GABA.
10.	c. dopamine
11.	a. norepinephrine
12.	c. melatonin
13.	b. a PET scan
14.	c. thalamus; hippocampus
15.	b. temporal lobes and motor cortex
16.	a. frontal
17.	c. hypothalamus; cerebellum
18.	d. explaining actions and emotions.
19.	b. use the left hand to identify the spoon
20.	c. When sex differences in the brain are found to be related to behavioral differences, we know that the behavior must result from the brain difference.

CHAPTER 5

Body Rhythms and Mental States

CHAPTER OVERVIEW

The chapter opens with a definition of consciousness, the awareness of oneself and the environment. Relevant to states of consciousness is biological rhythms, which include circadian rhythms. Factors that interfere with the body's internal clock are explored next. How moods may be affected by the biological clock also is considered. Within this section is the examination of seasonal affective disorder and premenstrual syndrome.

Next, the rhythms of sleep are described. Topics in this area are the theories of why people sleep and the different stages of sleep. Differences between REM and NREM sleep are outlined. The consequences of sleep deprivation and the benefits of sleep are also addressed.

An exploration of the world of dreams follows. Lucid dreaming is defined. Then, the various theories that propose the purposes of dreams are presented. Each theory offers a competing explanation for why people dream. Possibilities suggested by these theories include fulfilling unconscious wishes, solving problems, processing information, and making sense of internal brain activity.

Hypnosis is discussed next. A description of hypnosis and the theories of hypnosis are provided. The controversial issues regarding hypnosis are examined.

The final topic is drugs that alter consciousness. The classification of some common psychoactive drugs is detailed. Four main drug types are stimulants, depressants, opiates, and psychedelics. The physiology of drugs section covers what they do to the brain's neurotransmitters, and a definition of tolerance and the possible symptoms of withdrawal are stated. Psychological concerns involved with drug use conclude the chapter.

GUIDED STUDY

1. Biological Rhythms: The Tides of Experience

Read the section "Biological Rhythms: The Tides of Experience" and then answer the following questions. If you have trouble answering any of the questions, re-study the relevant material before going on to the review of key terms and the progress tests.

1-1. A _____ rhythm is a periodic, regular fluctuation in a biological system. These rhythms are _____, generated from within rather than by external cues. Biological rhythms govern physiological aspects, such as _____ levels, urine volume, blood _____, and the responsiveness of _____ cells, as well as many other functions. A type of biological rhythm is _____ rhythms, which occur about every 24 hours. The best known rhythm of this type is the _____-_____ cycle. The clock that controls the body's circadian rhythms is located in the _____. The _____ nucleus (SCN) responds to changes in light and dark and communicates messages that cause the brain and body to adapt to these changes. The SCN regulates levels of hormones and _____ and they provide a feedback loop that influences the functioning of the SCN. An example of this system is the hormone _____, which is secreted by the _____ gland and plays a role in the regulation of the sleep-wake cycle. When people's daily routine is altered, they may experience internal _____. Crossing _____ zones, as with airplane travel, can lead to this phenomenon. Jet lag influences energy level, _____ skills, and motor _____. Another example of desynchronization happens when people work _____ that rotate frequently. Rhythms vary from one person to the next due to _____ differences.

1-2. According to folklore, people's moods change according to biological and seasonal changes. _____ _____ _____, a disorder in which a person is depressed during the winter months, may have a biological basis, but the evidence is inconsistent. Another controversial issue is whether the _____ cycle is associated with mood changes in women. It is commonly believed that in the days before menstruation, women become irritable and _____. _____ _____ is the label given to the symptoms associated with the days preceding menstruation. However, although many women experience _____ symptoms linked with menstruation, evidence of _____ symptoms associated with menstruation is rare, with fewer than _____ percent of all women predictably having such symptoms. Studies that examine the incidence of premenstrual syndrome have found the following results: no _____ differences exist in mood; no relation exists between stage of the _____ cycle and emotional symptoms.

Terms for Review

The following is a list of the important terms from the section "Biological Rhythms: The Tides of Experience." Make sure you are familiar with each term before taking the progress test on these terms.

biological rhythms
endogenous
circadian rhythms
suprachiasmatic nucleus

melatonin
internal desynchronization
seasonal affective disorder
premenstrual syndrome

2. The Rhythms of Sleep

Read the section "The Rhythms of Sleep" and then answer the following questions. If you have trouble answering any of the questions, re-study the relevant material before going on to the review of key terms and the progress tests.

2-1. Until the early 1950s, little was known about the changes that occur during sleep. The sleep cycle includes four stages of non-REM (NREM) sleep and a REM sleep stage. REM is an acronym for _____ _____ _____. The four stages of NREM sleep are: Stage 1, during which brain _____ are small and irregular indicating a state of _____ sleep; Stage 2, during which the brain emits occasional short bursts of rapid, high-peaking waves called _____ _____ and people sleep through minor noises; Stage 3, during which the brain begins to emit

_____ waves which indicate that the person will be hard to awaken; and Stage 4, during which delta waves are prominent and people are in _____ sleep. People are most likely to sleepwalk in Stage _____ sleep. Characteristics of REM sleep are very rapid, irregular brain waves, which indicate an alert brain, increases in _____ rate, _____ pressure, and _____, and _____ muscles go limp, preventing the aroused brain from producing physical movement. REM is also known as _____ _____, since the brain is very active while the body is inactive. Most _____ occurs during REM, however dreams also occur in _____ sleep. NREM dreams tends to be less _____ and more realistic compared to REM dreams. REM sleep appears necessary since people who are deprived of it spend a much _____ time than usual in REM sleep when allowed to do so.

2-2. The exact purposes of sleep are still unclear. However, during sleep the body has an opportunity to restore itself by removing waste products from _____, repairing _____, and strengthening the _____ system. And, sleep _____ directly interferes with both normal physiological and mental functioning. In chronic sleep deprivation, high levels of _____ may damage the brain cells necessary for learning and memory. And, after several days without sleep, people may _____ and have delusions. People may lose sleep due to _____ _____, a disorder in which breathing ceases for a few moments while the person is sleep, which typically awakens the person. In _____, an individual experiences irresistible and unpredictable attacks of sleepiness or actual sleep that last from 5-30 minutes. In _____ _____ disorder, the muscle paralysis typically seen during REM sleep is not present, resulting in people acting out dreams without awareness.

2-3.   A good night's sleep has many benefits. Many scientists believe that sleep plays a role in _____, in which synaptic changes associated with recently stored memories become durable and stable. Improvements in memory have been associated most closely with _____ sleep and _____-wave sleep.

Terms for Review

The following is a list of the important terms from the section "The Rhythms of Sleep." Make sure you are familiar with each term before taking the progress test on these terms.

rapid eye movement (REM)   sleep apnea
non-REM sleep   narcolepsy
alpha waves   REM behavior disorder

sleep spindles   consolidation
delta waves

3. Exploring the Dream World

Read the section "Exploring the Dream World" and then answer the following questions. If you have trouble answering any of the questions, re-study the relevant material before going on to the review of key terms and the progress tests.

3-1.   While a dream is in progress, sometimes we can become aware that we are dreaming, a phenomenon known as _____ _____. There are several theories as to why people dream. One the first theorists to take dreams seriously was _____ _____, the founder of psychoanalysis. His theory proposes that dreams serve to allow the expression of _____ wishes and desires. Therefore, because dreams provide insight into motives, desires, and conflicts that are unconsciously felt. And, Freud made a distinction between the _____, surface content we are consciously aware of, and the _____ content, hidden symbolism of dreams.

3-2.   Another theory, the _____-_____ approach to dreaming, states that dreams reflect the preoccupations of waking life. This approach is supported by findings that dreams are more likely to contain material related to a person's current concerns than would be predicted by _____. And, some psychologists see dreams as providing opportunities to

_____ problems.

3-3. The _____ approach emphasizes current concerns, but without claims about problem solving. During dreaming, parts of the cerebral cortex are involved in _____ and cognitive _____, however, we are cut off from _____ _____ and feedback. As such, the only input to the brain is its own _____.

3-4. Another theory is called the _____-_____ theory and states that dreams are the result of neurons firing spontaneously in the _____ during _____ sleep.

3-5. Freud's theory of dreams is difficult to test because no _____ rules exist for interpreting dreams. Regarding the _____-_____ function of dreams, some argue that people cannot solve problems while they are asleep. The activation-synthesis approach does not account well for dreaming that occurs _____ of REM sleep. Also, some neuropsychologists do believe that dreams reflect a person's goals and desires. At present, the _____ approach is a leading contender.

Terms for Review

The following is a list of the important terms from the section "Exploring the Dream World." Make sure you are familiar with each term before taking the progress test on these terms.

lucid dreams   problem-focused approach
manifest content   cognitive approach
latent content   activation-synthesis theory

4. The Riddle of Hypnosis

Read the section "The Riddle of Hypnosis" and then answer the following questions. If you have trouble answering any of the questions, re-study the relevant material before going on to the review of key terms and the progress tests.

4-1. A procedure in which a practitioner suggests changes in the sensations, perceptions, thoughts, feelings, or behavior of the subject refers to _____. Hypnotized people typically report that their compliance with these suggestions feels _____, without conscious control. Research on hypnosis has found that hypnotic responsiveness depends _____ on the person being hypnotized than it does on the skill of the hypnotist. And, hypnotized people _____ be forced to do things against their will. Also, feats performed under hypnosis can be performed when people are _____ to do them. In addition, hypnosis does not increase the accuracy of _____ and does not produce a literal regression to an earlier age. Finally, hypnotic suggestions have been found to be effective for many _____ and psychological

81

purposes, with its greatest success being

_____ _____.

4-2. Two competing theories of hypnosis are

_____ theories and

sociocognitive theories. Dissociation

theories argue that hypnosis involves

dissociation, a split in _____ in

which one part of the mind operates

independently of the others. This approach

points to a _____

_____ who watches but does not

participate in the hypnotic suggestion. The

_____ explanation states that the

effects of hypnosis result from an

interaction between the social

_____ of the hypnotist and the

beliefs of the subject. The hypnotized

person is basically playing a

_____, according to this

approach. A hypnotized person appears so

engrossed in the role that he or she may act

without _____ intent.

Terms for Review

*The following is a list of the important terms
from the section "The Riddle of Hypnosis."
Make sure you are familiar with each term
before taking the progress test on these terms.*

hypnosis   hidden observer
dissociation   sociocognitive explanation

5. Consciousness-Altering Drugs

*Read the "Consciousness-Altering Drugs" and
then answer the following questions. If you have
trouble answering any of the questions, re-study
the relevant material before going on to the
review of key terms and the progress tests.*

5-1. A _____ drug is a substance that

alters perception, mood, thinking, memory,

or behavior by altering the body's

biochemistry. Substances that speed up

activity in the central nervous system are

called _____. _____

slow down activity in the central nervous

system. _____ relieve pain. All

of these drugs mimic the effects of

_____. _____ drugs

interfere with normal cognitive processes,

such as the perception of _____

and space. However, _____ has

effects that can make it difficult to classify,

with some researchers placing in

psychedelic category and some researchers

stating that it doesn't belong in any of the

four categories. And, although long-term

marijuana smoking can increase the risk of

lung cancer, the drug does have some

_____ benefits. These include

reducing nausea in _____

patients, reducing the negative symptoms

of _____ _____,

decreasing the frequency of

_____ in epileptics, and it

reduces retinal swelling caused by

_____.

5-2. The effects of psychoactive drugs are due

to their influence on brain _____.

A drug may interfere with the

_____, reabsorption, or the

effects of neurotransmitters. These

biochemical changes affect cognitive and

_____ functioning. All

researchers agree that heavy or

_____ drug use can damage the

brain and result in deficits in cognitive

performance. Also, the use of some

psychoactive drugs can lead to

_____, whereby more and more

of the drug is needed to get the same effect.

And, when habitual heavy users stop taking

a drug, they may suffer severe

_____ symptoms.

5-3. Psychological effects of drugs depend on

many factors. A person's _____

with the drug affects the drug's effects.

Also, physical factors, such as body weight,

_____, emotional state, and

physical _____ for the drug need

to be considered. In addition, the

_____ setting in which the drug

is taken influences how the person

experiences the drug. And, one's

_____ about the drug's effects, as

well as the reasons for taking the drug can

alter the effects that the drug has on the

person. For example, researchers have

found a "think-drink" effect which

influences people's behaviors when they

think that they have ingested

_____, even if it wasn't

consumed.

Terms for Review

The following is a list of the important terms from the section "Consciousness-Altering Drugs." Make sure you are familiar with each term before taking the progress test on these terms.

altered states of consciousness   psychedelics
psychoactive drug   tolerance
stimulants   withdrawal
depressants   think-drink effect
opiates

SAMPLE ANSWERS TO *YOU ARE ABOUT TO LEARN* QUESTIONS FROM TEXTBOOK

After you have read through the chapter, go back and review the "You Are About to Learn..." statements that precede each major section. Create your own answer to each question, then compare your answers to the following sample answers. If your answers are not similar to the sample answers, review the relevant sections of the chapter more carefully.

How do biological rhythms affect our physiology and performance?	Biological rhythms govern our hormone levels, urine levels, blood pressure, responsiveness of brain cells to stimulation, and our sleep-wake cycle.
Why do you feel out of sync when you fly across time zones or change shifts at work?	Feeling "out of sync" occurs when people's normal routine changes and their circadian rhythms become out of phase with each other. Both jet lag and swing-shift work schedules can cause this internal desynchronization.
Why do some people get the winter blues?	Many researchers believe that the circadian rhythms of certain people are chronically out of sync during the winter. This has been labeled seasonal affective disorder. It is also suspected that SAD may result from an abnormality in melatonin.
How does culture and learning affect reports of PMS and estimates of its incidence?	Most women do not feel depressed or irritable before they menstruate. Although many women do report physical symptoms associated with the days just prior to menstruation, they rarely report emotional symptoms when carefully studied. In fact, fewer than 5 percent of women reliably report such symptoms. However, due to cultural expectations, many people reports they are being more affected by PMS than actually is the case.
What are the stages of sleep?	As you drift off into slumber, you pass through four stages: • Stage 1. Your brain waves become small and irregular, and you feel yourself drifting on the edge of consciousness, in a state of light sleep. If awakened, you may recall fantasies or a few visual images. • Stage 2. Your brain emits occasional short bursts of rapid, high-peaking waves called sleep spindles. Minor noises probably won't disturb you. • Stage 3. In addition to the waves characteristic of Stage 2, your brain occasionally emits delta waves, very slow waves with very high peaks. Your breathing and pulse have slowed down, your muscles are relaxed, and you are hard to rouse. • Stage 4. Delta waves have now largely taken over, and you are in deep sleep. It will probably take vigorous shaking or a loud noise to awaken you.
What happens when we go too long without enough sleep?	When people are sleep deprived, it affects mental flexibility, attention, and creativity. Prolonged sleep deprivation can

84

become intolerable, leading to infections, damaged brain cells necessary for learning and memory, hallucinations, delusions, and eventually death.

How do sleep disorders disrupt normal sleep?

Sleep apnea can cause a person to periodically stop breathing during sleep, causing them to awaken by choking and gasping. With narcolepsy, individuals are suddenly struck by unpredictable daytime bouts of REM sleep. In REM behavior disorder, a person's muscles are not paralyzed during REM sleep, resulting in the acting out of dreams.

What are the mental benefits of sleep?

Even a quick nap can help your mental functioning. Sleep is not a waste of time; it's an excellent use of it. Sleep can help improve memory and consolidate recently formed memories.

Why did Freud call dreams the "royal road to the unconscious"?

Freud stated that people express their unconscious wishes and desires in their dreams, which are often sexual or aggressive in nature. Freud believed that dreams provide insight into desires, motives, and conflicts of which people are unaware. Therefore, by analyzing dreams, one can take advantage of their ability to act as a roadway to the contents of the unconscious mind.

How might your dreams be related to your current problems and concerns?

Dreams may be related to one's current problems and worries since dreams are more likely to contain material related to a person's current concerns than would be predicted by chance. For example, college students, who are anxious about grades and tests, commonly report dreaming about exams and the things that could go wrong when having to take an important examination. And, although previous studies of gender differences in dream content found several differences between men's and women's dreams, recent studies of gender differences in dream content found only two gender differences, indicating that as the lives and concerns of men and women have become more similar, so have their dreams.

How might dreams be related to ordinary daytime thoughts?

The problem-focused explanation of dreaming is supported by findings that dreams are more likely to contain material related to a person's current concerns than chance would predict. For example, among college students, who are often anxious about grades and tests, test-anxiety dreams are common: the dreamer is unprepared for or unable to finish an exam, or shows up for the wrong exam, or can't find the room where the exam is being given.

Could dreams be caused by meaningless brain-stem signals?

The activation-synthesis theory proposes that dreams are caused by the activity in the brain stem, specifically the pons. The activity of the pons is synthesized or interpreted by the brain and the result is a dream.

What are common misconceptions about what hypnosis can do?

Hypnosis is typically thought to involve involuntary control. However, a hypnotist cannot force a hypnotized person to do things against his or her will. Research has found that hypnotized individuals may comply with a suggestion that is embarrassing or dangerous but they are choosing to give responsibility to the hypnotist and to cooperate. No evidence exists that hypnotized people will do anything that violates their morals, that is threatening to themselves or others, or that is beyond their normal capabilities. Further, hypnosis does not increase the accuracy of memories. Although hypnosis does sometimes increase the amount of information recalled, it also increases recall errors.

What are the legitimate uses of hypnosis in psychology and medicine?

Hypnotic suggestions have been used to reduce stress, anxiety, and severe pain; to anesthetize people; to eliminate unwanted habits; to improve study skills; to reduce nausea in chemotherapy patients; and to increase the confidence of athletes.

What are two ways of explaining what happens during hypnosis?

Dissociation theories suggest that the mind is split into two parts, a hypnotized part and a hidden observer part. Sociocognitive explanations suggest that hypnosis primarily involves playing a role and fulfilling expectations. This is not simply faking, as the person may fully play the part without conscious intent.

What are the major types of psychoactive drugs?

There are four major categories: stimulants, which speed up the central nervous system; depressants, which slow down the central nervous system; opiates, which reduce pain and produce pleasure; and psychedelics, which distort perceptions.

How do recreational drugs affect the brain?

Recreational drugs affect the brain's neurotransmitter levels. They do this by increasing or decreasing the release of neurotransmitters, preventing the reuptake of excess neurotransmitters, or blocking the effects of neurotransmitters on receiving neurons.

How do people's prior drug experiences, individual characteristics, expectations, and mental sets influence their reactions to drugs?

More experienced drug users tend to be less sensitive to drug effects, a person's metabolism can influence the effect of a drug, and expectations can alter the experience of a drug, so much that one can perceive the effects of a drug even in its absence.

KEY TERMS FILL-IN-THE-BLANKS PROGRESS TEST

Fill in the blanks with the key terms from the chapter that match the definitions provided. When you have finished this progress test, check your answers with those at the end of this chapter. You should review any key terms that you do not define correctly.

1. _____ Generated from within rather than by external cues.

2. _____ A periodic, more or less regular fluctuation in a biological system.

3. _____ A state in which biological rhythms are not in phase with one another.

4. _____ An area of the brain containing a biological clock that governs circadian rhythms.

5. _____ A disorder in which breathing briefly stops during sleep, causing the person to choke and gasp, and momentarily awaken.

6. _____ A sleep disorder involving sudden and unpredictable daytime attacks of sleepiness or lapses into REM sleep.

7. _____ Sleep periods characterized by eye movement, loss of muscle tone, and dreaming.

8. _____ Short bursts of rapid, high-peaking waves.

9. _____ The theory that dreaming results from the cortical synthesis and interpretation of neural signals triggered by activity in the lower part of the brain.

10. _____ A dream in which the person is aware of dreaming.

11. _____ The aspects of a dream that are consciously experienced during sleep and that may be remembered upon wakening.

12. _____ A procedure in which the practitioner suggests changes in the sensations, perceptions, thoughts, feelings, or behavior of the subject.

13. _____ A split in consciousness in which one part of the mind operates independently of others.

14. _____ Drugs that speed up activity in the central nervous system.

15. _____ Drugs that relieve pain and commonly produce euphoria.

16. _____ Increased resistance to a drug's effects accompanying continued use.

17. _____ Physical and psychological symptoms that occur when someone addicted to a drug stops taking it.

MULTIPLE-CHOICE PROGRESS TEST

Choose the single best answer for each of the following questions. When you have finished this progress test, check your answers with those at the end of this chapter. You should review the relevant pages in the text for the questions you do not answer correctly.

1. The body's biological clock is contained in which part of the brain?
   a. The thalamus
   b. The cerebellum
   c. The hypothalamus
   d. The prefrontal cortex

2. People's endogenous circadian rhythms last _____ than _____ hours.
   a. longer; 24
   b. shorter; 24
   c. longer; 28
   d. none of the above

3. Melatonin, a hormone that increases sleepiness and regulates circadian rhythms, is released by the:
   a. pituitary gland.
   b. pineal gland.
   c. hypothalamus.
   d. adrenal gland.

4. Jet lag and shift work can lead to:
   a. internal desynchronization.
   b. biological rhythms being out of phase with one another.
   c. seasonal affective disorder.
   d. Both a and b are correct.

5. Phototherapy is a leading treatment for:
   a. bipolar disorder.
   b. seasonal affective disorder.
   c. premenstrual syndrome.
   d. premenstrual dysphoric disorder.

6. Which of the following is typically a NREM sleep disorder?
   a. Sleep apnea
   b. REM behavior disorder
   c. Sleepwalking
   d. Narcolepsy

7. Sleep spindles usually occur during which stage of sleep?
   a. Stage 1
   b. Stage 2
   c. Stage 3
   d. Stage 4

8. People who experience _____ dreams are aware that they are dreaming and may be able to consciously control their dreams.
   a. recurring
   b. NREM
   c. REM
   d. lucid

9. Small, irregular brain waves are to Stage _____ sleep as delta waves are to Stage _____ sleep.
   a. 1; 4
   b. 2; 1
   c. 2; 3
   d. 4; 3

10. Which of the following statements regarding REM sleep is FALSE?
    a. REM sleep occurs less frequently in the latter half of a night's sleep.
    b. REM sleep has been called paradoxical sleep.
    c. REM sleep is where most dreams occur.
    d. Signs of sexual arousal in both men and women occur during REM sleep.

11. The fact that dreams cannot be reliably interpreted provides evidence against the _____ theory of dreams.
    a. activation-synthesis
    b. cognitive approach to dreams
    c. psychoanalytic
    d. problem-focused

12. Which theory of dreams is based on the idea that dreams are the brain interpretation of random neuron activity?'
    a. The activation-synthesis theory
    b. The cognitive approach
    c. The psychoanalytic theory
    d. The problem-focused approach

13. Which of the following is TRUE about hypnosis?
    a. It improves the accuracy of memories.
    b. It acts as an anesthetic for people undergoing dental work.
    c. It can lead to the reexperiencing of events in one's distant past.
    d. It has no psychological purposes.

14. The notion of the hidden observer is part of the _____ theory of hypnosis.
    a. sociocognitive
    b. behavioral
    c. Freudian
    d. dissociation

15. Which explanation of hypnosis focuses on the hypnotized individual playing a role based on the influence of the hypnotist and the individual's own expectations?
    a. Sociocognitive
    b. Humanistic
    c. Psychoanalytic
    d. Dissociation

16. Stimulants are to _____ as depressants are to _____.
    a. caffeine; marijuana
    b. cocaine; methadone
    c. amphetamines; barbiturates
    d. morphine; heroin

17. Which of the following statements about alcohol is FALSE?
    a. It stimulates the central nervous system in small doses.
    b. It can be used as an anesthetic.
    c. Large doses of alcohol can be fatal.
    d. It slows down activity in the central nervous system.

18. Which of the following statements about marijuana is TRUE?
    a. It is classified as a psychedelic drug.
    b. It can reduce retinal swelling in people with glaucoma.
    c. It reduces the physical tremors caused by multiple sclerosis.
    d. All the above are true.

19. Psychoactive drugs have which effects on the brain?
    a. They block the effects of hormones.
    b. They interfere with the release of neurotransmitters.
    c. They prevent neurotransmitters from being reabsorbed.
    d. Both b and c are true.

20. The fact that some people report drinking to try to reduce feelings of anxiety or depression provides evidence for:
    a. the importance of the environmental setting when considering a drug's effects.
    b. the importance of a person's mental set when considering a drug's effects.
    c. the importance of experience with the drug when considering a drug's effects.
    d. none of the above

Guided Study

1. Biological Rhythms: The Tides of Experience

1-1. biological
  endogenous
  hormone
  pressure
  brain
  circadian
  sleep-wake
  hypothalamus
  suprachiasmatic
  neurotransmitters
  melatonin
  pineal
  desynchronization
  time
  mental
  coordination
  shifts

1-2. seasonal affective disorder
  menstrual
  depressed
  Premenstrual syndrome
  physical
  emotional
  5
  gender
  menstrual

2. The Rhythms of Sleep

2-1. rapid eye movement
  waves
  light
  sleep spindles
  delta
  deep
  4
  alert
  heart
  blood
  breathing
  skeletal
  paradoxical sleep
  dreaming
  NREM
  vivid
  longer

2-2. muscles
  cells
  immune
  deprivation
  cortisol
  hallucinate
  sleep apnea
  narcolepsy
  REM behavior

2-3. consolidation
  REM
  slow

3. Exploring the Dream World

3-1. lucid dreams
Sigmund Freud
unconscious
manifest
latent

3-2. problem-focused
chance
resolve

3-3. cognitive
perceptual
processing
sensory input
output

3-4. activation-synthesis
pons
REM

3-5. reliable
problem-solving
outside
cognitive

4. The Riddle of Hypnosis

4-1. hypnosis
involuntary
more
cannot
motivated
memory
medical
pain management

4-2. dissociation
consciousness
hidden observer
sociocognitive
influence
role
conscious

5. Consciousness-Altering Drugs

5-1. psychoactive
stimulants
depressants
opiates
psychedelic
time
marijuana
medical
chemotherapy
multiple sclerosis
seizures
glaucoma

5-2. neurotransmitters
release
emotional
frequent
tolerance
withdrawal

5-3. experience
metabolism
tolerance
environmental
expectations
alcohol

Answers to Key Terms Progress Test

1. endogenous
2. biological rhythm
3. internal desynchronization
4. suprachiasmatic nucleus
5. sleep apnea
6. narcolepsy
7. rapid eye movement (REM) sleep
8. sleep spindles
9. activation-synthesis theory
10. lucid dream
11. manifest content
12. hypnosis
13. dissociation
14. stimulants
15. opiates
16. tolerance
17. withdrawal symptoms

Answers to Multiple-Choice Progress Test

Item Number	Answers
1.	c. hypothalamus
2.	a. longer; 24
3.	b. pineal gland
4.	d. Both a and b are correct.
5.	b. seasonal affective disorder
6.	c. sleepwalking
7.	b. Stage 2
8.	d. lucid
9.	a. 1; 4
10.	a. REM occurs less frequently in the latter half of a night's sleep.
11.	c. psychoanalytic
12.	a. activation-synthesis theory
13.	b. It acts as an anesthetic for people undergoing dental work.
14.	d. dissociation
15.	a. sociocognitive
16.	c. amphetamines; barbiturates
17.	a. It stimulates the central nervous system in small doses.
18.	d. All the above are true.
19.	d. Both b and c are true.
20.	b. the importance of a person's mental set when considering a drug's effects.

CHAPTER 6

Sensation and Perception

CHAPTER OVERVIEW

The chapter opens with the distinction between sensation and perception. The functioning of sense receptors is covered, along with types of neural coding (anatomical versus functional). Psychophysics is discussed next, which includes coverage of an absolute threshold and a difference threshold (jnd) and signal detection theory. This is followed by a description of sensory adaptation versus sensory deprivation. Lastly, sensory overload and selective attention are explained.

The visual system is covered in detail, including the structure and functioning of the eye. The psychological characteristics of hue, brightness, and saturation are related to the physical characteristics of wavelength, intensity, and complexity. The Nobel prize-winning work of Hubel and Wiesel is discussed along with two theories of color vision. The Gestalt view of perception is presented. Coverage includes discussion of Gestalt principles of perceptual organization such as figure and ground and grouping. Descriptions of other aids to perception such as the various constancies and binocular versus monocular cues to depth follow.

The properties related to the processing of sound waves are provided along with the structure and functioning of the ear. This includes descriptions of the outer, middle, and inner ear. Next, descriptions of the other senses, including taste, smell, skin senses, pain, kinesthesis, and equilibrium are given. A discussion of phantom limb pain and simple ways of treating it follows.

The perceptual abilities of the newborn are covered along with a description of methods used to test newborns. Critical periods are identified. A discussion of psychological and cultural influences on perception precedes a look at subliminal perception.

GUIDED STUDY

1. Our Sensational Senses

Read the section "Our Sensational Senses" and then answer the following questions. If you have trouble answering any of the questions, re-study the relevant material before going on to the review of key terms and the progress tests.

1-1 The detection of physical energy emitted or reflected by physical objects is _____, whereas the organization of sensory impulses into meaningful patterns is _____. The cells that detect sensory information are called _____ _____. Sense receptors convert the energy of the stimulus into an _____ _____ that travels along nerves to the brain. Johannes Müller proposed in his _____ of _____ _____ _____ that the code used by the sense receptors was anatomical. This means that the various sensory modalities exist because signals received by the sense organs stimulate different nerve pathways, which lead to specific areas of the brain. An anatomical code is not sufficient, however, to explain differences within a particular sense. On rare occasions, the stimulation of one sense consistently evokes a sensation into another resulting in a sensory crossover known as _____. Another type of code, _____, is necessary to help explain these differences. Functional coding explains perceived differences based on which cells are firing, how

_____ cells are firing, the rate of _____, and the _____ of each cell's firing.

1-2. Measurement of the sensitivity of the senses is accomplished by psychologists in the area of _____ who are concerned with how the _____ properties of a stimulus are related to the _____ experiences of them. One measurement that psychophysicists make is based on the smallest amount of energy that a person can reliably detect, which is called an _____ threshold. Another measurement studied by psychophysicists is a just noticeable difference or _____ threshold, which is the smallest difference in stimulation that a person can detect reliably. When two stimuli are compared, A and B, the difference threshold will depend on the _____ or size of A. The larger or more intense A is the _____ the change must be before one can detect a difference between them. However, due to _____ bias, there are limitations to measuring absolute and difference thresholds. Thus, researchers use methods based on _____-_____ theory for sensory measurements. This theory states that a subject's response in a detection task can be divided into a _____ process that depends on the intensity of the stimulus and a _____ process that is influenced by the observer's response bias.

1-3. When receptors or nerve cells higher up in the sensory system get tired and fire less frequently, the decline in responsiveness is called _____ _____. In _____ _____ studies, researchers investigated what would happen if the senses adapted to most incoming stimuli. Although participants responded negatively to sensory deprivation in the initial studies, later research, which used better methods, found that _____ were less dramatic and less disorienting. However, the human brain does need a minimum amount of _____ stimulation to function normally.

1-4. When sensory _____ occurs, people often cope by blocking out unimportant sights and sounds and focusing on interesting and useful information. This capacity for _____ _____ protects people from being overwhelmed by too many sensory signals. This can occur to such a degree that we may not even perceive stimuli that we are looking directly at, a phenomenon known as _____ _____.

Terms for Review

The following is a list of the important terms from the section "Our Sensational Senses." Make sure you are familiar with each term before taking the progress test on these terms.

sensation
perception
sense receptors
doctrine of specific nerve energies
synesthesia
psychophysics
absolute threshold

difference threshold
signal-detection theory
sensory adaptation
sensory deprivation
selective attention
inattentional blindness

2. Vision

Read the section "Vision" and then answer the following questions. If you have trouble answering any of the questions, re-study the relevant material before going on to the review of key terms and the progress tests.

2-1. The stimulus for vision is _____, which travels in the form of _____. The physical characteristics of light waves affect three _____ aspects of visual experience. The wavelength of light, the distance between the crests of a light wave, specifies the color or _____. The intensity or amplitude of the light wave corresponds to _____. The complexity of the wavelengths, how wide or narrow the range of wavelengths, relates to the dimension of _____.

2-2. Light waves penetrate the visual system through the eyes. The front covering of the eye is the transparent _____, which protects the eye and sends incoming light waves toward the _____, which focuses the light on the back of the eye. Muscles in the _____, the colored part of the eye, control the amount of light that enters the eye. This structure surrounds the round opening of the eye, the

_____, which changes size depending on how much light is present. The visual sense receptors are located at the back of the eye in the _____. The more numerous visual receptors are called _____. They enable sight in _____ levels of light and at _____. Rods cannot distinguish different wavelengths of light and therefore are not sensitive to _____. The less numerous visual receptors in the retina are the _____, which are located primarily in the center of the retina, the _____. Cones are sensitive to specific wavelengths of light and allow seeing _____. Unlike rods, they are not responsive to _____ levels of light. The time involved in the process of dark _____ varies for rods and cones. The rods, which are more sensitive in dim levels of illumination, take about _____ minutes, which is twice the time it takes the cones to adapt to dark conditions. Rods and cones are connected by synapses to _____ cells, which in turn communicate with neurons called _____ cells. The axons of the ganglion neurons converge to form the _____ nerve, which exits the eye at the _____ disc. As there are no rods and cones at this point on the retina, a _____ spot is produced in the field of vision.

2-3. The visual system is not a _____ recorder of the external world. Different cells in the visual system respond to different features in the environment, forming a picture of the world. For example, ganglion cells and neurons in the _____ respond to simple features in the environment, such as spots of light and dark. Special _____-_____ cells in the visual cortex respond to more complex features.

2-4. The Young-Helmholtz, or _____ theory of color vision proposes that three types of cones in the _____ work together to bring about the experience of seeing different colors. Each type of cone responds maximally to certain colors. This theory helps explain color _____ or deficiency, such as the inability to distinguish red from green. Another approach to color vision, the _____-_____ theory, focuses on how color processing works at the level of _____ cells in the retina and in neurons in the _____ and visual _____ of the brain. One pair of opponent cells is responsible for seeing red versus _____, another for _____ versus yellow, and the last for _____ versus black. The opponent process theory explains why people are susceptible to negative _____, for example, why people

97

see red after staring at the color green.

2-5. The _____ psychologists were among the first to study how people visually organize the world into meaningful units and patterns. One principle identified by the Gestalt psychologists is known as _____ and ground, which is the ability to detect where one thing begins and another ends. Other Gestalt principles that describe how the brain organizes sensory information include grouping things together that are near each other, _____; filling in the gaps in order to perceive complete forms, _____; grouping things that are alike in some way, _____; and perceiving lines and patterns in a continuous manner, _____. In order to perceive depth and distance we rely on cues that involve both eyes, _____ cues, and cues that involve only one eye, _____ cues. _____ involves the eyes turning inward when they focus on a nearby object—the closer the object the _____ the convergence. The second binocular cue is _____ _____—the slight difference in lateral separation between two objects as seen by the left eye and the right eye. For objects that are far away, people rely on _____ cues to depth perception, which include _____ and _____ perspective. The ability to perceive objects as stable or unchanging even though the sensory patterns they produce are constantly shifting is called _____ constancy. The best-studied visual constancies include: perceiving objects as having a constant shape even though the shape of the retinal image changes when one's point of view changes—_____ constancy; perceiving stationary objects as remaining in the same place even though the retinal image moves—_____ constancy; continuing to see an object as having a constant size even when its retinal image becomes smaller or larger—_____ constancy; continuing to see objects as having a relatively constant brightness even though the amount of light they reflect changes as the overall level of illumination changes—_____ constancy; and seeing an object as maintaining its hue despite the fact that the wavelength of light reaching the eyes may change—_____ constancy. Even though people regularly use all of these constancies, they occasionally can be fooled by a perceptual _____.

Terms for Review

The following is a list of the important terms from the section "Vision." Make sure you are familiar with each term before taking the progress test on these terms.

hue	Gestalt principles
brightness	proximity
saturation	closure
retina	similarity
rods	continuity
cones	binocular cues
dark adaptation	convergence
ganglion cells	retinal disparity

98

feature-detector cells   monocular cues
trichromatic theory   perceptual constancy
opponent-process theory   perceptual illusion

3. Hearing

Read the section "Hearing" and then answer the following questions. If you have trouble answering any of the questions, re-study the relevant material before going on to the review of key terms and the progress tests.

3-1. The stimulus for sound is a wave of _____ created when an object vibrates. The intensity of a wave's pressure is related to the psychological dimension of _____. The intensity of a sound is measured in _____. The frequency of a sound wave is related to the psychological experience of _____. Frequency, measured in _____, refers to the number of times per second the wave cycles through a peak and low point. The complexity of a sound wave is related to the psychological aspect of _____, the quality of a sound.

3-2. The ear is divided into three sections: outer, middle, and inner. The outer ear consists of the funnel-shaped outer ear designed to catch _____ _____. At the end of an inch-long canal is the _____, which vibrates at the same rate as the sound wave and causes three bones in the _____ ear to vibrate. These bones are the _____, the _____, and the _____. The inner ear consists of a snail-shaped structure, the

_____. The organ of _____ inside the cochlea contains the sense receptors for audition, which are the hair cells or _____. Damage to these cells can result in hearing _____. The hair cells are embedded in the _____ membrane. As the fluid in the cochlea moves, the hair cells move, initiating a signal that is passed along to the _____ nerve, which carries the message to the brain.

3-3. To understand how people perceive the auditory world, it is useful to apply _____ principles such as figure and ground, continuity, and closure. People can estimate the _____ of a sound's source by using loudness as a cue. Having two ears helps in locating the _____ from which a sound is originating.

Terms for Review

The following is a list of the important terms from the section "Hearing." Make sure you are familiar with each term before taking the progress test on these terms.

loudness   cochlea
pitch   cilia
timbre   basilar membrane
eardrum   auditory nerve
organ of Corti

4. Other Senses

Read the section "Other Senses" and then answer the following questions. If you have trouble answering any of the questions,

99

re-study the relevant material before going on to the review of key terms and the progress tests.

4-1. The sense receptors for taste or

_____ are located mainly on the

_____. _____,

elevations on the tongue, contain

_____ _____, which

are nests of taste-receptor cells. There are

four basic tastes: _____,

_____, _____, and

_____. Some researchers also

include _____, which is the taste

of monosodium glutamate. Different types

of _____ produce each of these

tastes.

4-2. The sense of smell is called

_____. The sense receptors for

smell are located in a tiny patch of

_____ membrane in the upper

part of the nasal passage, just below the

eyes. Signals from the sense receptors are

carried to the brain's olfactory

_____ by the olfactory

_____. Deficits in olfaction can

result from infection, _____,

injury, or _____.

4-3. The four skin senses include

_____ (or pressure),

_____, _____, and

_____. Scientists have had

difficulty identifying distinct

_____ for the different skin

senses.

4-4. For many years, a leading explanation of

pain was the _____-

_____ theory, which stated that

the experience of pain depends on whether

pain impulses get past a "gate" in the

_____ _____ and

reach the brain. According to this theory,

mild pressure and other kinds of

stimulation can influence the experience of

_____ by closing or opening the

gate. The brain not only responds to

incoming signals, but is also capable of

_____ pain signals. This ability

may explain the persistence of

_____ pain in the absence of

injury and disease. In one version of this,

called _____ _____,

a person continues to feel pain from an

amputated limb or removed organ. One

effective treatment involves the use of

illusion, in which a _____ is

held upright to reflect the intact limb.

4-5. _____ deals with where one's

body parts are located and when they move.

_____, the sense of balance,

relies primarily on three fluid-filled

_____ canals in the

_____ ear.

Terms for Review

The following is a list of the important terms from the section "Other Senses." Make sure you are familiar with each term before taking the progress test on these terms.

gustation	gate-control theory
papillae	phantom pain
taste buds	kinesthesis

olfaction   equilibrium
olfactory nerve   semicircular canals

5. Perceptual Powers: Origins and Influences

Read the section "Perceptual Powers: Origins and Influences" and then answer the following questions. If you have trouble answering any of the questions, re-study the relevant material before going on to the review of key terms and the progress tests.

5-1. In humans, most basic _____ abilities and many perceptual skills are _____ or develop early in life. Visual skills are shown soon after birth and _____ perception develops within the first few months. The _____ _____ is used to test an infant's perception of depth. Researchers have found that babies as young as _____ months of age refuse to crawl over the "cliff."

5-2. Although many perceptual abilities are innate, _____ also plays an important role. Researchers studying inborn perceptual abilities have used cats as subjects in experiments testing _____ periods of development. They have found that without certain early experiences, perception will be _____. For example, cats allowed to view only vertical stripes for the first few months of life seemed blind to all _____ contours later in life.

5-3. Because human beings care about what they see, hear, taste, smell, and feel, _____ factors can influence what they perceive and how they perceive it. These factors include needs, beliefs, and emotions. In particular, the perception of _____ is affected by emotion. Also, one's _____ due to previous experiences affect one's perception of the world. The tendency to perceive what one expects is called a _____ set. People's needs, beliefs, emotions, and expectations are influenced by their _____. In a study on the Müller-Lyer illusion, it was found that people living in a carpentered society were _____ susceptible to the illusion than those living in a non-carpentered society. Culture also affects perception by shaping _____, directing _____, and indicating what is and is not important.

Terms for Review

The following is a list of the important terms from the section "Perceptual Powers: Origins and Influences." Make sure you are familiar with each term before taking the progress test on these terms.

visual cliff   perceptual set
critical period

6. Perception without Awareness

Read the section "Perception without Awareness" and then answer the following questions. If you have trouble answering any of the questions, re-study the relevant material before going on to the review of key terms and the progress tests.

6-1. Behavior can be affected even by stimuli that are so weak or brief that they are below a person's absolute threshold for detecting them. In other words, the stimuli are _____. Some researchers have studied nonconscious perception by using _____, in which a person is exposed to information explicitly or subliminally and then later tested to see how performance is affected. Evidence for subliminal _____ has been inconsistent.

The following is a list of the important terms from the section "Perception without Awareness." Make sure you are familiar with each term before taking the progress test on these terms.

subliminal
priming

SAMPLE ANSWERS TO *YOU ARE ABOUT TO LEARN* QUESTIONS FROM TEXTBOOK

After you have read through the chapter, go back and review the "You Are About to Learn..." statements that precede each major section. Create your own answer to each question, then compare your answers to the following sample answers. If your answers are not similar to the sample answers, review the relevant sections of the chapter more carefully.

Why do we experience separate sensations even though they all rely on similar neural signals?

The nervous system encodes messages so that sensory neurons will interpret them differently.

What kind of code in the nervous system helps explain why a pinprick and a kiss feel different?

The first explanation for this difference was based on an anatomical coding system. This was specified in the *doctrine of specific nerve energies* by Johannes Müller and stated that different sensory modalities exist because signals received by the sense organs stimulate different nerve pathways leading to different areas of the brain. Anatomical coding, however, does not completely answer the question. Linking different skin senses to distinct nerve pathways has been difficult and the *doctrine of specific nerve energies* does not explain variations of experience within a sense. An additional kind of code, a functional code, is necessary. This coding system provides information about which cells are firing, how many cells are firing, the rate at which cells are firing, and the patterning of each cell's firing. Functional encoding may occur all along a sensory route.

How can psychologists measure the sensitivity of our senses?

Psychologists can present signals at very low intensity to study what is the minimum amount of energy that can be detected, known as absolute threshold. They can also present two similar stimuli and discover at what point people will succeed and fail at noticing a difference, known as difference threshold.

What kind of bias can influence whether you think you hear the phone ringing when you're in the shower?

According to signal-detection theory, a response bias can lead someone to think that the phone is or isn't ringing. A response bias is one's tendency to be either a yea-sayer (a gambler) or a nay-sayer (cautious and conservative.) A yea-sayer will think it's ringing; a nay-sayer will not.

What happens when people are deprived of all external sensory stimulation?

In initial studies of sensory deprivation, subjects were edgy and disoriented within a few hours. Those who participated for longer than this were confused, restless, and grouchy. Some reported having hallucinations. The methodology in these studies was questionable, and in more recent studies, the response of the subjects included hallucinations that were less dramatic and less disorienting. In fact, many people enjoy limited time periods of deprivation. It is clear, however, that the human brain requires a minimum amount of sensory stimulation in order to function normally.

Why do we sometimes fail to see an object that we're looking straight at?

Variety is the spice of life. It is also the essence of sensation, for our senses are designed to respond to change and contrast in the environment. When a stimulus is unchanging or repetitious, sensation often fades or disappears. Receptors or nerve cells higher up in the sensory system get "tired" and fire less frequently. The resulting decline in sensory responsiveness is called sensory adaptation. Such adaptation is usually useful because it spares us from having to respond to unimportant information; for example, most of the time you have no need to feel your watch sitting on your wrist. Sometimes, however, adaptation can be hazardous, as when you no longer smell a gas leak that you noticed when you first entered the kitchen.

How do the physical characteristics of light waves correspond to the psychological dimensions of vision?

Light travels in the form of waves, which affects three psychological dimensions: hue, brightness, and saturation.

What are the basics of how the eye works and how does the eye differ from a camera?

Light enters the eye through the pupil and lens and then passes through ganglion and bipolar cells to reach visual receptors. The brain then interprets incoming forms of stimulation that are sent from the optic nerve. Unlike a camera, the visual system is not a passive recorder of information. Instead of simply registering spots of light and dark, as in a photograph, neurons in the visual system construct a picture of the world by detecting its meaningful features.

How do we see colors and why can we describe a color as bluish green but not as reddish green?

Based on the opponent process theory of color vision, there are three pairs of opposing colors. These are blue/yellow, red/green, and white/black. Thus, people are able to see a bluish green color when cells responsible for these colors fire; however, as red and green represent an opposing pair, they cannot both fire at the same time so people would not be able to see a reddish green color.

How do we know how far away things are?

Binocular cues to depth and distance involve the use of both eyes and include convergence (the turning of the eyes inward when they focus on a nearby object) and retinal disparity (the slight difference in lateral separation between two objects as seen by the left eye and the right eye). When judging the depth or distance of a building in the distance, people rely on monocular cues involving one eye. Thus, if someone were blind in one eye he or she would still be able to use monocular cues, but not binocular cues.

Why do we see objects as stable even though sensory stimulation from the object is constantly changing?

Perceptual constancy allows human to perceive objects as stable and unchanging. There are multiple types of perceptual constancy. For example, size constancy depends in part on familiarity with objects and on the apparent distance of an object. As the friend approaches, one knows that she does not change in size and thus correctly perceive that she is getting closer.

104

Why are perceptual illusions valuable to psychologists?

They are valuable because they are systematic errors that provide psychologists with hints about the perceptual strategies of the mind. For example, visual illusions indicate that sometimes strategies that normally lead to accurate perceptions are overextended to situations where they do not apply. A good example is the Müller-Lyer illusion in which the brain misapplies the size-distance relationships by misjudging the distances of the two lines.

What are the basics of how we hear?

Vibrations in the air cause the eardrum to vibrate. Little hair cells in the ear sense these vibrations and send a signal along the auditory nerve to the brain, which then processes this information.

Why does a note played on a flute sound different from the same note on an oboe?

The difference is due to the timbre or complexity of the sound waves produced by each instrument. A pure tone consists of only one frequency. A flute produces relatively pure tones, whereas an oboe produces very complex sounds, not pure tones.

How can we locate the source of a sound?

Due to the fact we possess two ears, sound waves will reach one ear first and aid in localization. When the sound originates from directly above or behind the head, it is hard to localize because such sounds reach both ears at the same time. In this case, when one turns or tilts one's head, one is actively trying to overcome this problem.

What are the basics of taste, smell, and feeling?

Gustation, or our sense of taste, is the result of chemicals stimulating taste buds on the tongue. Olfaction, our sense of smell, is the result of specialized neurons in the mucous membrane of the nasal passage detecting chemical molecules. Touch, warmth, cold, and pain feelings result from sense receptors located in the skin.

Why do saccharin and caffeine taste bitter to some people but not to others?

Saccharin and caffeine taste bitter to "supertasters" for bitter substances. "Tasters," in contrast, detect less bitterness, and "nontasters" detect even less. Supertasters have more taste buds on their tongues, and papillae of a certain type are smaller, more densely packed, and look different than those in nontasters.

Why do you have trouble tasting your food when you have a cold?

A food's odor is important to a food's taste. Very subtle flavors such as vanilla and chocolate would have little taste if people also could not smell these foods. Thus, when one's nose is stuffy and one is having trouble with the sense of smell, one's sense of taste also will be inhibited.

Why is pain complicated to understand and treat?

The skin, which is the organ of touch or pressure, also senses heat, cold, and pain, not to mention itching and tickling. The ear, which is the organ of hearing, also contains receptors that account for a sense of balance. The skeletal muscles contain receptors responsible for a sense of bodily movement. All of our senses evolved to help us survive. Even pain, which

105

causes so much human misery, is an indispensable part of our evolutionary heritage, for it alerts us to illness and injury. But sensory experiences contribute immeasurably to our lives even when they are not helping us stay alive.

How do two senses inform us of the movement of our own bodies?

Kinesthesis tells us where our body parts are located and informs us when these parts are in motion. Equilibrium coordinates our sense of balance by relying on semicircular canals located in the ear.

Do babies see the world the way adults do?

Based on research findings, it appears that human infants can discriminate sizes and colors very early, possibly at birth. They can distinguish contrasts, shadows, and complex patterns when they are a few weeks old. Also, depth perception develops during the first few months. Thus, many fundamental perceptual skills are inborn or acquired shortly after birth; but not all are. In addition, perception also depends upon one's needs, beliefs, emotions, and expectations. Therefore, babies do not see the world in the same way that adults do.

What happens when people who are born blind or deaf have their sight or hearing restored?

Critical periods for sensory development also exist in human beings. When adults who have been blind from infancy have their vision restored, they may see, but often they do not see well. Their depth perception may be poor, causing them to trip constantly, and they cannot always make sense of what they see. To identify objects, they may have to touch or smell them. They may have trouble recognizing faces and emotional expressions. They may even lack size constancy and may need to remind themselves that people walking away from them are not shrinking in size. But if an infant's congenital blindness is corrected early, during a critical period during the first nine months or so, the prognosis is much better (though visual discriminations may never become entirely normal). In one study of infants who underwent corrective surgery when they were from 1 week to 9 months of age, improvement started to occur after as little as one hour of visual experience.

How do psychological and cultural factors affect perception?

People's beliefs about the world can affect their interpretations of ambiguous sensory stimuli. Hence, if a person believes that divine images can be found on everyday objects, he or she would be more likely to "see" them compared to someone who does not share this belief.

Can perception be unconscious?

Yes, people can be affected by subliminal stimuli, that is, stimuli that are so weak or brief that they are below a person's absolute threshold for detecting them.

Can "subliminal perception" tapes help you lose weight or reduce your stress?

Although subjects in some studies have demonstrated visual subliminal perception, subliminal persuasion (to lose weight or reduce stress) has not been shown. This research has found that "placebo" tapes are just as effective as subliminal tapes. Thus, subliminal tapes do not help people. To lose

106

weight or reduce stress, one would need to engage in a conscious effort to do so.

KEY TERMS FILL-IN-THE-BLANKS PROGRESS TEST

Fill in the blanks with the key terms from the chapter that match the definitions provided. When you have finished this progress test, check your answers with those at the end of this chapter. You should review any key terms that you do not define correctly.

1. _____ The detection of physical energy emitted or reflected by physical objects.

2. _____ A psychophysical theory that divides the detection of a sensory signal into a sensory process and a decision process.

3. _____ Specialized cells that convert physical energy in the environment or the body to electrical energy that can be transmitted as nerve impulses to the brain.

4. _____ The absence of normal levels of sensory stimulation.

5. _____ The process by which the brain organizes and interprets sensory information.

6. _____ The smallest quantity of physical energy that can be reliably detected by an observer.

7. _____ A process by which visual receptors become maximally sensitive to dim light.

8. _____ Vividness or purity of color; the dimension of visual experience related to the complexity of light waves.

9. _____ A theory of color perception that assumes that the visual system treats pairs of colors as opposing or antagonistic.

10. _____ Cells in the visual cortex that are sensitive to specific features of the environment.

11. _____ Visual receptors that respond to dim light but are not involved in color vision.

12. _____ The dimension of visual experience specified by color names and related to the wavelength of light.

13. _____ An erroneous or misleading perception of reality.

14. _____ The slight difference in lateral separation between two objects as seen by the left eye and the right eye.

15. _____ Neural tissue lining the back of the eyeball's interior, which contains the receptors for vision.

16. _____ Visual cues to depth or distance that can be used by one eye alone.

17. _____ The distinguishing quality of a sound; the dimension of auditory experience related to the complexity of the pressure wave.

18. _____ The sense receptors for audition that are embedded in the basilar membrane.

19. _____ The dimension of auditory experience related to the intensity of a pressure wave.

20. _____ A snail-shaped, fluid-filled organ in the inner ear, containing the organ of Corti, where the receptors for hearing are located.

21. _____ The dimension of auditory experience related to the frequency of a pressure wave.

22. _____ The theory that the experience of pain depends in part on whether pain impulses get past a neurological "gate" in the spinal cord and thus reach the brain.

23. _____ The sense of body position and movement of body parts.

24. _____ Sense organs in the inner ear that contribute to equilibrium by responding to the rotation of the head.

25. _____ Knoblike elevations on the tongue, containing the taste buds.

26. _____ A habitual way of perceiving, based on expectations.

27. _____ Perceiving and responding to messages that are below the threshold of awareness.

MULTIPLE-CHOICE PROGRESS TEST

Choose the single best answer for each of the following questions. When you have finished this progress test, check your answers with those at the end of this chapter. You should review the relevant pages in the text for the questions you do not answer correctly.

1. Our ability to perceive differences within a particular sense (e.g., differentiating red from pink) depends upon _____.
   a. the doctrine of specific nerve energies
   b. anatomical coding
   c. functional coding
   d. response bias

2. The smallest amount of energy that a person can detect 50 percent of the time is known as the _____ threshold.
   a. absolute
   b. difference
   c. attention
   d. response

3. In a signal detection task, yea-sayers will have _____ "hits" than nay-sayers when a weak stimulus is present and _____ "false alarms" when there is no stimulus present.
   a. more; more
   b. more; less
   c. less; more
   d. less; less

4. The reduction or disappearance of sensory responsiveness that occurs when stimulation is unchanging or repetitious is called _____.
   a. selective attention
   b. sensory deprivation
   c. sensory adaptation
   d. sensory overload

5. Which of the following is NOT a psychological dimension of visual experience?
   a. Hue
   b. Intensity
   c. Brightness
   d. Saturation

6. Which of the following statements about rods and cones is FALSE?
   a. There are more rods than cones.
   b. At the optic disc, there are no rods or cones.
   c. Rods are more sensitive to light than cones are.
   d. Only rods are sensitive to color.

7. Which of the following sequences represents the correct order of processing in the visual pathways?
   a. Receptor cells-bipolar cells-feature detector cells-ganglion cells-thalamus cells
   b. Bipolar cells-receptor cells-ganglion cells-thalamus cells-feature detector cells
   c. Receptor cells-bipolar cells-ganglion cells-thalamus cells-feature detector cells
   d. Thalamus cells-bipolar cells-ganglion cells-feature detector cells-receptor cells

8. According to the opponent-process theory of color vision, if one stares at a patch of red on a white screen and then the patch is taken away, one should see a _____ afterimage where the patch had been located.
   a. blue
   b. green
   c. yellow
   d. gray

9. Perceiving two groups of circles, three red circles and three blue circles, illustrates which of the following Gestalt principles of perceptual organization?
    a. Proximity
    b. Closure
    c. Continuity
    d. Similarity

10. If someone is standing between railroad tracks and staring down the tracks, the tracks appear to converge in the distance. This is an example of a _____ cue called _____.
    a. monocular; convergence
    b. binocular; convergence
    c. monocular; linear perspective
    d. binocular; linear perspective

11. The dimension of auditory experience related to the complexity of a sound wave is _____.
    a. loudness
    b. timbre
    c. pitch
    d. intensity

12. The function of the _____ in the ears is analogous to the function of the rods and cones in the eyes.
    a. cochlea
    b. cilia (hair cells)
    c. eardrum
    d. organ of Corti

13. To discriminate low-pitched sounds, we use _____; to discriminate high-pitched sounds, we use _____.
    a. the location of the activity along the basilar membrane; the frequency of the basilar membrane's activity
    b. the frequency of the basilar membrane's activity; the location of the activity along the basilar membrane
    c. the location of the activity along the basilar membrane; the location of the activity along the basilar membrane
    d. the frequency of the basilar membrane's activity; the frequency of the basilar membrane's activity

14. Which of the following statements about our sense of taste is FALSE?

a. There are at least four basic tastes— salty, sour, bitter, and sweet.
b. A different area of the tongue is sensitive to each of the four basic tastes.
c. The center of the tongue contains no taste buds.
d. Culture influences people's taste preferences.

15. With respect to the senses of the skin, which of the following statements is TRUE?
    a. The basic skin senses include pressure, heat, and pain.
    b. There is no evidence of distinct kinds of receptors for each of the four skin senses.
    c. According to the gate-control theory of pain, larger fibers that respond to pressure close the gate.
    d. According to the gate-control theory of pain, the neurological "gate" for pain is located in the thalamus.

16. Which of the following senses depends upon the three semicircular canals in the inner ear?
    a. Audition
    b. Kinesthesis
    c. Equilibrium
    d. none of the above

17. The visual cliff is a device used to test _____ perception in infants.
    a. size
    b. depth
    c. color
    d. shape

18. Which of the following psychological factors can influence what people perceive and how they perceive it?
    a. Our needs
    b. Our beliefs
    c. Our emotions
    d. All the above are answers.

19. A habitual way of perceiving based on expectations defines a:
    a. perceptual set.
    b. perceptual expectation.
    c. subliminal perception.
    d. visual illusion.

Guided Study

1. Our Sensational Senses

1-1. sensation
  perception
  sense receptors
  electrical impulse
  doctrine
  specific nerve energies
  synesthesia
  functional
  many
  firing
  pattern

1-2. psychophysics
  physical
  psychological
  absolute
  difference
  intensity
  greater
  response
  signal-detection
  sensory
  decision

1-3. sensory adaptation
  sensory deprivation
  hallucinations
  sensory

1-4. overload
  selective attention
  inattentional blindness

2. Vision

2-1. light
  waves
  psychological
  hue
  brightness
  saturation

2-2. cornea
  lens
  iris
  pupil
  retina
  rods
  low
  night
  color
  cones
  fovea
  colors
  low
  adaptation
  20
  bipolar
  ganglion
  optic
  optic
  blind

2-3. passive
  thalamus
  feature-detector

2-4. trichromatic
  retina
  blindness
  opponent-process
  ganglion
  thalamus
  cortex
  green
  blue
  white
  afterimages

2-5. Gestalt
figure
proximity
closure
similarity
continuity
binocular
monocular
Convergence
greater
retinal disparity
monocular
interposition
linear
perceptual
shape
location
size
brightness
color
illusion

3. Hearing

3-1. pressure
loudness
decibels
pitch
hertz
timbre

3-2. sound waves
eardrum
middle
hammer
anvil
stirrup
cochlea
Corti
cilia
loss
basilar
auditory

3-3. Gestalt
distance
direction

4. Other Senses

4-1. gustation
tongue
papillae
taste buds
salty
sour
bitter
sweet
umami
chemicals

4-2. olfaction
mucous
bulb
nerve
disease
smoking

4-3. touch
warmth
cold
pain
receptors

4-4. gate-control
spinal cord
feelings
pain
generating
chronic
phantom pain
mirror

4-5. kinesthesis
equilibrium
semicircular
inner

5. Perceptual Powers: Origins and Influences

5-1. sensory
inborn
depth
visual cliff
six

5-2. experience
critical
impaired

5-3. psychological
expectations
pain
expectations
perceptual
culture
more
stereotypes
attention

6. Perception without Awareness

6-1. subliminal
priming
persuasion

Answers to Key Terms Progress Test

1. sensation
2. signal detection theory
3. sense receptors
4. sensory deprivation
5. perception
6. absolute threshold
7. dark adaptation
8. saturation
9. opponent-process theory
10. feature detectors
11. rods
12. hue
13. perceptual illusion
14. retinal disparity
15. retina
16. monocular cues
17. timbre
18. hair cell (cilia)
19. loudness
20. cochlea
21. pitch
22. gate-control theory of pain
23. kinesthesis
24. semicircular canals
25. papillae
26. perceptual set
27. subliminal perception

Answers to Multiple-Choice Progress Test

Item Number	Answers
1.	c. functional coding
2.	a. absolute threshold
3.	a. more; more
4.	c. sensory adaptation
5.	b. intensity
6.	d. Only rods are sensitive to color.
7.	c. receptor cells-bipolar cells-ganglion cells-thalamus cells-feature detector cells
8.	b. green
9.	d. similarity
10.	c. monocular; linear perspective
11.	b. timbre
12.	b. cilia (hair cells)
13.	b. the frequency of the basilar membrane activity; the location of the activity along the basilar membrane
14.	b. A different area of the tongue is sensitive to each of the four basic tastes
15.	c. According to the gate-control theory of pain, larger fibers that respond to pressure close the gate.
16.	c. equilibrium
17.	b. depth
18.	d. All the above are answers.
19.	a. perceptual set

CHAPTER 7

Thinking and Intelligence

CHAPTER OVERVIEW   The chapter opens with a discussion of the elements of cognition. This includes explanations of such terms as prototype, propositions, cognitive schemas, and mental images. Subconscious and nonconscious processes are covered and related to implicit learning and mindlessness. Formal versus informal reasoning is considered next. This involves a description of deductive versus inductive reasoning, algorithms versus heuristics, dialectical reasoning, and reflective judgment. Barriers to rational reasoning such as using the affect and availability heuristics, avoiding loss, fairness bias, hindsight bias, confirmation bias, and mental sets are explained. The need for cognitive consistency as studied by research on cognitive dissonance is explored. Also, how cognitive biases can be overcome is outlined.

A definition of intelligence is provided as well as the debate over its definition. The field of intelligence testing is explored. The discussion of the psychometric approach includes aptitude tests, and intelligence quotients. The Stanford-Binet Intelligence Scale, the Wechsler Adult Intelligence Scale (WAIS), and the Wechsler Intelligence Scale for Children (WISC) are described. Stereotype threat is discussed. Recent cognitive theories of intelligence also are introduced. These include Sternberg's triarchic theory and a discussion of emotional intelligence.

Next, the origins of intelligence are considered. The heritability of intelligence is discussed with respect to twin and adoption studies. Included here is a description of how to interpret intellectual differences within groups versus between groups. Several environmental factors impacting intelligence are presented. In addition, the effects of attitudes and motivation on intelligence are emphasized through the description of a study comparing Asian and American children. The last section contains a discussion of animal intelligence. The area of cognitive ethology is introduced and various studies on language in animals are described.

GUIDED STUDY

1. Thought: Using What We Know

Read the section "Thought: Using What We Know" and then answer the following questions. If you have trouble answering any of the questions, re-study the relevant material before going on to the review of key terms and the progress tests.

1-1. Thinking involves the _____ manipulation of internal representations of objects, activities, and situations. One type of mental representation that groups objects, relations, activities, abstractions, or qualities having common properties is a _____. _____ concepts are those that have a moderate number of instances and tend to be easier to acquire. An especially representative example of a concept is called a _____. One way in which people represent the relationship of concepts to one another is through the use of _____, units of meaning which express singular ideas. Propositions are linked together in networks of knowledge, associations, beliefs, and expectations called _____ _____. Another important aspect of thinking is the use of _____ images especially visual images.

1-2. Not all mental processing takes place at a conscious level. _____ processes lie outside of awareness but can be brought into consciousness with little effort. _____ processes on the other hand remain outside of awareness, but can affect behavior. Insight and _____

involve several stages of mental processing. Solving problems may rely on _____ learning, which occurs when people acquire knowledge about something without being aware of how they did so and without being able to state exactly what was learned. Thinking that takes place at a conscious level when one is not thinking very hard or analyzing what one is doing is called _____. Although this type of thinking helps complete more tasks, it also can lead to errors (e.g., driving carelessly while on "automatic pilot").

Terms for Review

The following is a list of the important terms from the section "Thought: Using What We Know." Make sure you are familiar with each term before taking the progress test on these terms.

concept	mental image
basic concepts	subconscious processes
prototype	nonconscious processes
proposition	implicit learning
cognitive schema	mindlessness

2. Reasoning Rationally

Read the section "Reasoning Rationally" and then answer the following questions. If you have trouble answering any of the questions, re-study the relevant material before going on to the review of key terms and the progress tests.

2-1. Purposeful mental activity that involves operating on information in order to reach conclusions is referred to as _____. When the information to solve a problem is specified clearly and there is one correct answer to the problem, the problem involves _____ reasoning. Some formal reasoning problems may be solved by applying an _____, a set of procedures guaranteed to produce a solution. When a conclusion necessarily follows from certain propositions or premises, _____ reasoning is being used. However, when the premises provide support for a conclusion, but the conclusion may be false, _____ reasoning is involved.

2-2. Algorithms do not provide solutions to all problems. Contrary to formal reasoning problems, _____ reasoning problems may have no clear, correct solution. Sometimes it helps to apply a general rule, a _____, which suggests a course of action without guaranteeing an optimal solution. A person must also be able to evaluate opposing points of view. This involves the ability to use _____ _____.

2-3. Kitchener and King have studied people's ability to use _____ judgment, which involves their ability to evaluate and integrate evidence, consider _____ interpretations, and reach a conclusion that can be defended as most _____. According to these researchers people in the early stages of reflective thought are said to be _____, they assume a correct answer always exists and that it can be obtained directly through the senses. During the _____-_____ stages people recognize that some things cannot be

known with absolute certainty but they are not sure how to deal with these situations. Lastly, when an individual becomes capable of _____ judgment, they understand that although some things can never be known with certainty, some judgments are more valid than others are.

Terms for Review

The following is a list of the important terms from the section "Reasoning Rationally." Make sure you are familiar with each term before taking the progress test on these terms.

reasoning	heuristic
formal reasoning problems	dialectical reasoning
algorithm	reflective judgment
deductive reasoning	prereflective stages
inductive reasoning	quasi-reflective stages
informal reasoning problems	reflective stages

3. Barriers to Reasoning Rationally

Read the section "Barriers to Reasoning Rationally" and then answer the following questions. If you have trouble answering any of the questions, re-study the relevant material before going on to the review of key terms and the progress tests.

3-1. One barrier to thinking rationally is people's tendency to exaggerate or underestimate the _____ of very events. One reason people do this is they rely on the _____ heuristic, which involves estimating probability based on emotions. People also do this when they rely on the _____ heuristic, which involves a tendency to judge the probability of an event by how easy it is to think of examples or instances of the event.

3-2. Another bias is that people tend to avoid or minimize _____ when making decisions. When a choice is presented in terms of the risk of losing something, people will be more _____ than when the same choice is presented in terms of gain, a phenomenon known as _____ _____.

3-3. Another bias occurs when people will accept irrational loss if they perceive that gains are not being shared in a relatively equal manner, known as _____ _____. The field of _____ _____ was developed to study how economic decisions are not always rational.

3-4. According to psychologists, the statement "I knew it all along" is evidence of the _____ _____. This is a tendency to overestimate one's ability to have _____ an event once the outcome is known.

3-5. Another barrier occurs when humans pay more attention to information that confirms what they believe and find fault with evidence to the contrary, thereby employing the _____ _____.

3-6. Problem _____ can be more efficient by using the same heuristic, strategy, or rule that has worked in the past. This is referred to as a _____ _____. Mental sets also can lead people to hold on to old assumptions, hypotheses, and strategies, keeping them from better or more rapid _____.

3-7. When in a state of _____ due to holding two cognitions that are incompatible or a belief that is incongruent with the person's behavior, Festinger said people are in a state of _____ _____. Three conditions that may arouse dissonance are: (1) when one needs to justify a choice or decision that was freely made, known as _____ dissonance; (2) when one's actions violate the _____ of oneself; and (3) when one needs to justify the _____ put into reaching a goal or making a choice, referred to as the _____ of effort.

3-8. The fact that people's decisions and judgments are not always rational has consequences for all aspects of life. Most people tend to recognize bias in others and then fail to see bias in their own behavior, known as bias _____ _____. Also, when people understand a _____, they may be able to reduce or eliminate it.

Terms for Review

The following is a list of the important terms from the section "Barriers to Reasoning Rationally." Make sure you are familiar with each term before taking the progress test on these terms.

affect heuristic
availability heuristic
framing effect
fairness bias
behavioral economics
hindsight bias

confirmation bias
mental set
cognitive dissonance
postdecision dissonance
justification of effort

4. Measuring Intelligence: The Psychometric Approach

Read the section "Measuring Intelligence: The Psychometric Approach" and then answer the following questions. If you have trouble answering any of the questions, re-study the relevant material before going on to the review of key terms and the progress tests.

4-1. There is disagreement among psychologists regarding the definition of _____. The traditional approach to studying intelligence that focuses on how well people perform on standardized aptitude tests is the _____ approach. Researchers use a statistical technique, _____ _____, to identify which basic abilities underlie intelligence. Psychologists disagree over whether intelligence is based on one factor, a _____, or whether it is determined by multiple factors. The first intelligence test was developed by _____ _____ in 1904. This test measured a child's _____ age. Later, others developed a scoring system that uses a formula in which a child's mental age is divided by a child's _____ age to yield an _____ _____. There were problems, however, in the derivation of intelligence quotients, and intelligence test scores now are computed from tables based on established

norms. Binet's test was revised by _____ _____ and named the _____-Binet Intelligence Scale. Another set of intelligence tests was developed by David _____. The first was the _____, which was designed for adults. This was followed by the _____, constructed for children. Some problems with intelligence testing involve the use of the tests to _____ people rather than to help slow learners achieve average performance. Negative cultural stereotypes can depress people's scores on intelligence tests since members of stereotyped groups can experience _____ _____, which occurs when people believe that if they do not do well, they will confirm the stereotypes about their group.

Terms for Review

The following is a list of the important terms from the section "Measuring Intelligence: The Psychometric Approach." Make sure you are familiar with each term before taking the progress test on these terms.

intelligence
psychometrics
factor analysis
g factor
Alfred Binet
mental age

intelligence quotient (IQ)
Stanford-Binet Intelligence Scale
Wechsler Adult Intelligence Scale (WAIS)
Wechsler Intelligence Scale for Children (WISC)
stereotype threat

5. Dissecting Intelligence: The Cognitive Approach

Read the section "Dissecting Intelligence: The Cognitive Approach" and then answer the following questions. If you have trouble answering any of the questions, re-study the relevant material before going on to the review of key terms and the progress tests.

5-1. An alternative view to the psychometric approach to intelligence is the _____ approach, that emphasizes the strategies people use when thinking about problems and arriving at solutions. One cognitive theory, the _____ theory of intelligence, was proposed by _____ _____. According to Sternberg, there are _____ aspects to intelligence. _____ intelligence, typically measured by IQ tests, involves the information processing strategies people use when thinking intelligently about a problem. Some of these operations require knowledge and awareness of one's own cognitive processes, _____. The second aspect of intelligence according to Sternberg is _____ intelligence. This refers to how well one can _____ skills to new situations. The third aspect of intelligence is _____ intelligence. This involves the _____ application of intelligence and _____ knowledge—action-oriented strategies for success that usually are not formally taught but are inferred by observing others. One nonintellectual intelligence may correspond to what some psychologists call _____ intelligence, which is the ability to identify one's own and others' emotions, express one's

emotions clearly, and to _____ one's own and others' emotions.

Terms for Review

The following is a list of the important terms from the section "Dissecting Intelligence: The Cognitive Approach." Make sure you are familiar with each term before taking the progress test on these terms.

cognitive approach
triarchic theory of intelligence
componential intelligence
metacognition

experiential intelligence
contextual intelligence
tacit knowledge
emotional intelligence

6. The Origins of Intelligence

Read the section "The Origins of Intelligence" and then answer the following questions. If you have trouble answering any of the questions, re-study the relevant material before going on to the review of key terms and the progress tests.

6-1. Behavioral geneticists study the _____ of intelligence, that is, the proportion of the total variance in a trait that is attributable to genetic differences among individuals within the group. Heritability estimates for intelligence in children and adolescents are about _____ or _____. For adults, the estimates are higher, from _____ to _____. Twin studies have shown that identical twins reared _____ are more similar in their intelligence scores than are fraternal twins reared _____. Although genetics can explain some _____ differences in intelligence levels, genes do not provide an accurate explanation for differences _____ groups.

6-2. There are several ways in which the

_____ can reduce mental ability. These include poor _____ care; _____; exposure to _____; and _____ family circumstances. Factors in the environment that can raise mental performance include providing mental _____ at home.

6-3. _____-_____ accounted for more than twice as much variance in student grades and achievement than did IQ. Self-discipline and motivation to work hard depend on _____ about intelligence and achievement, which are strongly influenced by _____ values. One study comparing American school children to Asian school children found that the Asian children far _____ the Americans on a broad battery of mathematical tests. These differences could not be accounted for by educational _____ or _____ ability in general. The researchers found instead that Asians and Americans were very different in their attitudes and _____. Overall, American parents believe that mathematical ability is _____ and have _____ standards for their children's performance. They also found that American students do not _____ education as much as Asian students do.

Terms for Review

The following is a list of the important terms from the section "The Origins of Intelligence." Make sure you are familiar with each term before taking the progress test on these terms.

heritability

7. Animal Minds

Read the section "Animal Minds" and then answer the following questions. If you have trouble answering any of the questions, re-study the relevant material before going on to the review of key terms and the progress tests.

7-1. The study of cognitive processes in nonhuman animals is _____ _____. Cognitive ethologists argue that some animals can _____ future events, make _____, and coordinate their activities with others. One of the most controversial questions is whether any animal have a system of beliefs about the way one's own mind and the minds of others work, known as _____ of _____.

7-2. In a variety of studies, researchers have attempted to teach animals to use _____, that is, combine meaningless elements to convey meaning. Chimpanzees have communicated with geometric plastic shapes, by punching symbols on a computer-monitored keyboard, and by using American _____ Language. Today, better-controlled experiments have established that with training, chimps can acquire the ability to use _____ to refer to

_____. In further studies, _____ have been taught to respond to requests made in two artificial languages and one researcher has even taught an African _____ _____ to count, classify, and compare objects.

7-3. Scientists are concerned, however, about the tendency to falsely attribute human qualities to nonhuman beings, _____. On the other hand, others warn of _____, the tendency to think that human beings have nothing in common with other animals.

Terms for Review

The following is a list of the important terms from the section "Animal Minds." Make sure you are familiar with each term before taking the progress test on these terms.

cognitive ethology   anthropomorphism
theory of mind   anthropodenial

SAMPLE ANSWERS TO *YOU ARE ABOUT TO LEARN* QUESTIONS FROM TEXTBOOK

After you have read through the chapter, go back and review the "You Are About to Learn..." statements that precede each major section. Create your own answer to each question, then compare your answers to the following sample answers. If your answers are not similar to the sample answers, review the relevant sections of the chapter more carefully.

What are the basic elements of thought?

One type of element of cognition is a *concept*, which is a mental category that groups objects, relations, activities, abstractions, or qualities having a common property. Types of concepts include basic concepts, which have a moderate number of instances as well as *prototypes*, which is an especially representative example of a concept. Concepts can be combined into a unit that expresses a single idea, which is known as a *proposition*. Cognitive schemas are integrated mental networks of knowledge, beliefs, and expectations concerning a particular topic or aspect of the world. Finally, a mental image is a cognitive representation that resembles the thing it is meant to represent.

Does the language you speak affect the way you think?

In many languages, speakers must specify whether an object is linguistically masculine or feminine (in Spanish, for example, *la cuenta*, the bill, is feminine but *el cuento*, the story, is masculine). It seems that labeling a concept as masculine or feminine affects the attributes that native speakers ascribe to it. A German speaker will describe a key (masculine in German) as hard, heavy, jagged, metal, serrated, and useful, whereas a Spanish speaker is more likely to describe a key (feminine in Spanish) as golden, intricate, little, lovely, shiny, and tiny. German speakers will describe a bridge (feminine in German) as beautiful, elegant, fragile, peaceful, pretty, and slender, whereas Spanish speakers are more likely to describe a bridge (masculine in Spanish) as big, dangerous, long, strong, sturdy, and towering.

How do subconscious thinking, nonconscious thinking, and mindlessness help us--and also cause us trouble?

These processes help us be more efficient in everyday life by reducing the amount of effort we have to expend on considering the details relevant to constant demands of life. However, these processes can also lead to mishaps or more serious consequences as we are lead into poor decisions. For example, mindlessness keeps people from recognizing when a change in context requires a change in behavior.

Why is it that algorithms and logic can't solve all of our problems?

Logic cannot solve all of life's problems because for informal reasoning problems, there may be no clearly correct solution. In informal reasoning problems, many approaches, viewpoints, or possible solutions may compete, and one may have to decide which one is most reasonable, based on what one knows.

What is the difference between deductive and inductive reasoning?

With deductive reasoning, the conclusion will always be true if given a set of true observations or propositions. With inductive reasoning, the conclusion is probably true but may possibly be false.

Why are heuristics and dialectical reasoning important in solving real-life problems?

Heuristics are a fast and easy way of solving problems with incomplete information by simply relying on rules of thumb that have been successful in the past. Dialectical reasoning is useful when we must compare and contrast opposing sources of information. Dialectical reasoning is what juries are supposed to use to arrive at a verdict. This involves considering arguments for and against the defendant's guilt. Dialectical reasoning is the ability to evaluate opposing points of view.

How does cognitive development affect the ways in which people reason and justify their views?

During the prereflective stages of reasoning, people assume that a correct answer always exists and that it can be obtained from either their senses or authority figures. Later on, people engage in quasi-reflective thinking, whereby everyone has a right to their own opinion and all opinions are created equal. Ultimately, it is best if people use reflective thinking in which some judgments are better than others because of their coherence, their fit with the evidence, their usefulness, etc.

How do biases in reasoning impair the ability to think rationally and critically?

Bias prevents us from accurately judging the probability of events, making decisions based on content rather than how offers are worded, causing unnecessary personal loss, carefully estimating our predictive capabilities, and ignoring important evidence.

Why do people worry more about vivid but rare disasters than about dangers that are far more likely?

One reason is the use of the availability heuristic, the tendency to judge the probability of an event by how easy it is to think of examples or instances. Catastrophes stand out in people's minds and are therefore more available than other kinds of negative events. Thus, people incorrectly think that the likelihood of dying in an airplane crash (a very available event because such crashes always make the headlines) is greater than for other less available but more probable dangers (e.g., dying from disease).

How does that way a decision is framed affect the choices that people make?

In general, people try to avoid or minimize risks and losses when they make decisions. So when a choice is framed in terms of the risk of losing something, they will respond more cautiously than when the same choice is framed in terms of gain. They will choose a ticket that has a 10 percent chance of winning a raffle rather than one that has a 90 percent chance of losing.

Why is it that people often value fairness above rational self-interest?

People often adhere to fairness bias, which means they will prefer a complete and irrational loss of all resources for everyone involved rather than feel like resources were split up in a relatively unequal manner.

How will the need to justify the expenditure of time, money, and effort affect how people think about a group they joined or a product they bought?

One will become more loyal to the group as a result of having to justify the effort put into reaching the goal of joining the group. To reduce cognitive dissonance, one has to make the cognition (deciding to undergo the hazing) consistent with the cognition about the group that did the hazing. The cognition that one decided to go through the hazing is dissonant with the cognition that one hates the group. Therefore, one must really like this group. This mental reevaluation is called the justification of effort and is one of the most popular methods of reducing dissonance.

What are the two sides of the debate regarding whether a single thing called "intelligence" actually exists?

Some psychologists argue that there is a general ability, or g factor, that underlies intelligence and this single attribute can account for success. Other psychologists argue it is not sensible to measure one type of intelligence and that there are many different types and domains of intelligence.

How did the original purpose of intelligence testing change when IQ tests came to America?

The original purpose of intelligence testing in France was to identify children with learning problems, not to rank all children. In America, IQ tests became widely used not to bring slow learners up to the average, but to categorize people in school and the armed services according to their presumed "natural ability." The testers overlooked the fact that all people do not share the same background and experience.

What are the difficulties of designing intelligence tests that are free of cultural influence?

Several test-makers have tried to construct culture-free and culture-fair intelligence tests but with little success. Culture affects performance. Cultural values affect a person's attitude toward taking tests, comfort while being tested, motivation, rapport with the test-giver, competitiveness, and experience in solving problems independently rather than with others. Moreover, cultures differ in the problem-solving strategies they emphasize.

Which kinds of intelligence are not measured by standard IQ tests?

IQ tests do not access experiential intelligence, or the ability to transfer skills to new settings. Also, IQ tests neglect contextual intelligence, or one's ability to accurately judge the requirements of different situations in which one is put.

What is the meaning of "emotional intelligence" and why might it be as important as IQ?

Emotional intelligence (EQ) is the ability to identify one's own and other people's emotions accurately, express one's emotions clearly, and regulate emotions in oneself and others. It is important because people with high EQ use their emotions to motivate themselves, to spur creative thinking, and to deal empathically with others. People with low EQ often are unable to identify their own emotions, express emotions inappropriately, and have problems interpreting nonverbal signals from others.

What are some reasons that Asian children perform much better in school than American students do?

Research has shown that Asians and Americans vary widely in their attitudes, expectations, and efforts. For example, Americans are far more likely to believe that ability is innate and that if one doesn't have it, there's no point in trying. American parents have far lower standards for their

127

children's performance than Asian parents do. American students do not value education as much as Asian students do and are more complacent about mediocre work. These factors then account for the differences in academic performance.

Can animals think?

Cognitive ethologists argue that some animals can anticipate future events, make plans and choices, and coordinate their activities with those of their comrades. The versatility of these animals in meeting new challenges in the environment also suggests to these researchers that the animals are capable of thought. Other scientists are not so sure, noting that even complex behavior can be genetically prewired.

Are there some animal species that can master aspects of human language?

Several researchers have used visual symbol systems or American Sign Language to teach primates language skills, and some animals (even some nonprimates) seem able to use simple grammatical ordering rules to convey meaning. However, scientists are still divided as to how to interpret these findings, and they are trying to avoid anthropomorphism and anthropodenial.

KEY TERMS FILL-IN-THE-BLANKS PROGRESS TEST

Fill in the blanks with the key terms from the chapter that match the definitions provided. When you have finished this progress test, check your answers with those at the end of this chapter. You should review any key terms that you do not define correctly.

1. _____ Mental processes occurring outside of conscious awareness but accessible to consciousness when necessary.

2. _____ An especially representative example of a concept.

3. _____ An integrated mental network of knowledge, beliefs, and expectations concerning a particular topic or aspect of the world.

4. _____ A unit of meaning that is made up of concepts and expresses a single idea.

5. _____ A general rule that suggests a course of action or guides problem solving but does not guarantee an optimal solution.

6. _____ The drawing of conclusions or inferences from observations, facts, or assumptions.

7. _____ Reasoning when the information needed for drawing a conclusion or a solution is specified clearly, and there is a single right (or best) answer.

8. _____ Reasoning when a conclusion probably follows from certain propositions or premises, but it could conceivably be false.

9. _____ A problem-solving strategy guaranteed to produce a solution even if the user does not know how it works.

10. _____ A process in which opposing facts or ideas are weighed and compared, with a view to determining the best solution or to resolving differences.

11. _____ The tendency to look for or pay attention only to information that confirms one's own belief.

12. _____ A state of tension that occurs when a person simultaneously holds two cognitions that are psychologically inconsistent, or when a person's belief is incongruent with his or her behavior.

13. _____ The tendency to judge the probability of a type of event by how easy it is to think of examples or instances.

14. _____ The tendency to overestimate one's ability to have predicted an event once the outcome is known.

15. _____ A measure of mental development expressed in terms of the average mental ability at a given age.

16. _____ A statistical method for analyzing the intercorrelations among various measures or test scores.

17. _____ A measure of intelligence originally computed by dividing a person's mental age by his or her chronological age and multiplying by 100.

18. _____ The knowledge or awareness of one's own cognitive processes.

19. _____ A general intellectual ability assumed by some theorists to underlie specific mental abilities and talents.

20. _____ A burden of doubt a person feels about his or her performance, due to negative stereotypes about his or her group's abilities.

21. _____ Strategies for success that are not explicitly taught but that instead must be inferred.

22. _____ A theory of intelligence that emphasizes information-processing strategies, the ability to transfer skills to new situations, and the practical application of intelligence.

23. _____ A statistical estimate of the proportion of the total variance in some trait that is attributable to genetic differences among individuals within a group.

24. _____ The study of cognitive processes in nonhuman animals.

Choose the single best answer for each of the following questions. When you have finished this progress test, check your answers with those at the end of this chapter. You should review the relevant pages in the text for the questions you do not answer correctly.

1. Which of the following is the correct ordering of units of thought from simplest to most complex?
   a. concepts-propositions-cognitive schemas
   b. propositions-concepts-cognitive schemas
   c. cognitive schemas-concepts-propositions
   d. cognitive schemas-propositions-concepts

2. Intuition is described in the text as an orderly process involving two stages. The first stage involves _____ processes.
   a. subconscious
   b. nonconscious
   c. Freud's unconscious
   d. conscious

3. Deducing that the conclusion *I am mortal* must necessarily follow from the premises *All human beings are mortal* and *I am a human being* is an example of _____ reasoning.
   a. dialectical
   b. informal
   c. deductive
   d. inductive

4. Which of the following is NOT a characteristic of informal reasoning?
   a. There are typically several possible answers that vary in quality.
   b. Established methods often exist for solving the problem.
   c. Some premises are implicit and some are not supplied at all.
   d. none of the above

5. According to King and Kitchener, people who assume that a correct answer always

exists and that it can be obtained directly through the senses are in the _____ stages of reflective thought.
   a. prereflective
   b. quasi-reflective
   c. reflective
   d. dialectical

6. When people overestimate the frequency of deaths from tornadoes and underestimate the frequency of deaths from asthma, they are most likely _____.
   a. using the availability heuristic
   b. using dialectical thinking
   c. demonstrating hindsight bias
   d. demonstrating confirmation bias

7. If a doctor says that there is a 10 percent chance of survival given Treatment X and a 90 percent chance of dying given Treatment Y, people usually choose Treatment _____ because _____.
   a. X; this alternative is framed in terms of gain
   b. Y; this alternative is framed in terms of gain
   c. X; they are using the availability heuristic
   d. Y; they are using the availability heuristic

8. The difficulty that people have with the 9-dot problem given in the text illustrates the barrier of _____.
   a. cognitive dissonance
   b. the confirmation bias
   c. the hindsight bias
   d. a mental set

9. Which of the following conditions is NOT one under which someone is likely to try to reduce cognitive dissonance?
   a. when one feels that one has freely

made a decision

b. when what one does, does not violate one's self concept

c. when one puts a lot of effort into a decision only to find the results less than one had hoped for

d. none of the above

10. Which of the following developed the Stanford-Binet Intelligence Test?
   a. Binet
   b. Terman
   c. Wechsler
   d. Sternberg

11. Using the IQ formula, an eight-year-old child with a mental age of a six-year-old child would have an IQ of _____.
   a. 50
   b. 75
   c. 100
   d. 125

12. Which of the following statements about intelligence testing is FALSE?
   a. Rather than using the IQ formula, intelligence test scores today are computed from tables based on established norms.
   b. Attempts to design culture-free and culture-fair intelligence tests have not been very successful.
   c. To eliminate earlier-observed sex differences on the Stanford-Binet intelligence test, the items leading to these differences were deleted.
   d. None of the above is false.

13. The psychometric approach to intelligence is to the cognitive approach to intelligence as _____ is to _____.
   a. Terman; Sternberg
   b. Sternberg; Terman
   c. Binet; Terman
   d. Terman; Binet

14. According to the triarchic theory of intelligence, _____ intelligence refers to how well someone transfers skills to new situations.
   a. componential
   b. emotional

c. contextual

d. experiential

15. IQ scores are distributed on a normal curve with an average score of 100 and 68 percent of the scores between _____.
   a. 55 and 145
   b. 70 and 130
   c. 85 and 115
   d. 100 and 130

16. Which of the following statements about emotional intelligence (EQ) is FALSE?
   a. People who have low EQs are unable to identify their own emotions.
   b. People who have low EQs misread nonverbal signals from others.
   c. People who have high EQs use their emotions to motivate themselves and to spur creative thinking.
   d. None of the above is false.

17. Which of the following statements about heritability and intelligence test scores is FALSE?
   a. The kind of intelligence that produces high IQ scores is highly heritable.
   b. For adults, the estimates of heritability are higher than for children and adolescents.
   c. If intellectual differences within each of two groups are due to genetics, then the differences between the groups must also be due to genetics.
   d. None of the above is false.

18. Which of the following statements about environmental deficits that hinder intellectual development is FALSE?
    a. Lead can damage the nervous system, producing lower IQ scores.
    b. The average IQ gap between severely malnourished and well-nourished children is less than 5 points.
    c. On average, each family risk factor reduces a child's IQ score by four points.
    d. None of the above is false.

19. Based on the results of the study of the "Termites," which of the following factors led to success?
    a. high IQ
    b. high EQ
    c. motivation
    d. logical thinking

20. Which of the following statements about Asians and Americans is FALSE?
    a. American parents have far lower standards for their children's school performance than Asian parents do.
    b. American parents and children are far more likely than Asians to believe that mathematical ability is innate.
    c. American students do not value education as much as Asian students do.
    d. None of the above is false.

Guided Study

1. Thought: Using What We Know

1-1. mental
concept
Basic
prototype
propositions
cognitive schemas
mental

1-2. Subconscious
Nonconscious
intuition
implicit
mindlessness

2. Reasoning Rationally

2-1. reasoning
formal
algorithm
deductive
inductive

2-2. informal
heuristic
dialectical reasoning

2-3. reflective
alternative
reasonable
prereflective
quasi-reflective
reflective

3. Barriers to Reasoning Rationally

3-1. probability
affect
availability

3-2. risk
cautious
framing effect

3-3. fairness bias
behavioral economics

3-4. hindsight bias
predicted

3-5. confirmation bias

3-6. solving
mental set
solutions

3-7. tension
cognitive dissonance
postdecision
view
effort
justification

3-8. blind spot
bias

4. Measuring Intelligence: The Psychometric Approach

4-1. intelligence
psychometric
factor analysis
g factor
Alfred Binet
mental
chronological
intelligence quotient
Lewis Terman
Stanford
Wechsler
WAIS
WISC
categorize
stereotype threat

5. Dissecting Intelligence: The Cognitive Approach

5-1. cognitive
triarchic
Robert Sternberg
three
Componential
metacognition
experiential
transfer
contextual
practical
tacit
emotional
regulate

6. The Origins of Intelligence

6-1. heritability
.40
.50
.60
.80
apart
together
individual
between

6-2. environment
prenatal
malnutrition
toxins
stressful
enrichment

6-3. self-discipline
attitudes
cultural
outperformed
resources
intellectual
efforts
innate
lower
value

7. Animal Minds

7-1. cognitive ethology
anticipate
plans
theory
mind

7-2. language
Sign
symbols
objects
dolphins
gray parrot

7-3. anthropomorphism
anthropodenial

Answers to Key Terms Progress Test

1. subconscious processes
2. prototype
3. cognitive schema
4. proposition
5. heuristic
6. reasoning
7. formal reasoning
8. inductive reasoning
9. algorithm
10. dialectical reasoning
11. confirmation bias
12. cognitive dissonance
13. availability heuristic
14. hindsight bias
15. mental age
16. factor analysis
17. intelligence quotient
18. metacognition
19. g factor
20. stereotype threat
21. tacit knowledge
22. triarchic theory of intelligence
23. heritability
24. cognitive ethology

Item Number	Answers
1.	a. concepts-propositions-cognitive schemas
2.	b. nonconscious
3.	c. deductive
4.	b. Established methods often exist for solving the problem.
5.	a. prereflective
6.	a. using the availability heuristic
7.	a. X; this alternative is framed in terms of gain
8.	d. a mental set
9.	b. when what one does, does not violate one's self concept
10.	b. Terman
11.	b. 75
12.	d. None of the above is false.
13.	a. Terman; Sternberg
14.	d. experiential
15.	c. 85 and 115
16.	d. None of the above is false.
17.	c. If intellectual differences within each of two groups are due to genetics, then the differences between the two groups must also be due to genetics.
18.	b. The average IQ gap between severely malnourished and well-nourished children is less than 5 points.
19.	c. motivation
20.	d. None of the above is false.

CHAPTER 8

Memory

CHAPTER OVERVIEW

The chapter begins with a discussion of the accuracies and inaccuracies of memory. This involves consideration of the reconstructive nature of memory, source misattribution, flashbulb memories, and the conditions of confabulation. The section on memory and the power of suggestion covers the topics of eyewitness testimony and children's testimony.

Next, various methods of measuring memory are examined, including recall versus recognition tests of memory. The different types of memory tests are related to explicit versus implicit memory. Then, different models of memory are presented including the information-processing models. Coverage of these models necessitates explanations of sensory memories, short-term memory, and long-term memory. The limitations and functioning of each of these memory constructs are considered. Key distinctions such as procedural versus declarative memory and semantic versus episodic memory are introduced and explained. Also, the serial position effect is defined and related to the different memory storage areas.

The biological factors involved in memory are then considered, including a discussion of how neurons and synapses are altered, long-term potentiation, and consolidation. The role of various brain structures in memories, with the hippocampus in particular, are detailed. How hormones and emotional states influence the intensity and recall of memories are covered.

Mechanisms for remembering information are presented next. These include effortful encoding, elaborative rehearsal, deep processing, and mnemonic strategies. Then, theories of forgetting such as decay theory, replacement, interference, cue-dependent forgetting, and repression are described. The last section provides a discussion of autobiographical memories, including topics such as childhood amnesia and personal narratives.

GUIDED STUDY

1. Reconstructing the Past

Read the section "Reconstructing the Past" and then answer the following questions. If you have trouble answering any of the questions, re-study the relevant material before going on to the review of key terms and the progress tests.

1-1. The capacity to retain and retrieve information and the structures that account for this capacity refers to _____. The idea that memory is not like replaying a videotape but more like watching a few unconnected frames and trying to figure out what happened in the rest of the scene was put forth by _____, who concluded that memory is largely a _____ process. When attempting to _____ events, people may have difficulty separating their original experiences from what they added after the fact. This phenomenon is referred to as _____ _____.

1-2. The vivid recollections of surprising, shocking, or tragic events are called _____ memories. Research has indicated, however, that these memories are not as _____ as once thought and are vulnerable to reconstruction.

1-3. The reconstructive nature of memory makes it subject to _____, which is most likely to occur under certain circumstances. These conditions are (1) one has thought about the imagined event _____ times; (2) the image of the event contains a lot of _____, and (3) the event is _____ to imagine.

Terms for Review

The following is a list of the important terms from the section "Reconstructing the Past." Make sure you are familiar with each term before taking the progress on these terms.

memory	flashbulb memories
reconstructive process	confabulation
source misattribution	

2. Memory and the Power of Suggestion

Read the section "Memory and the Power of Suggestion" and then answer the following questions. If you have trouble answering any of the questions, re-study the relevant material before going on to the review of key terms and the progress tests.

2-1. Since the accounts of _____ play a vital role in the justice system, the accuracy of their memory is critical to consider. Because memory is _____, eyewitness testimony is not always reliable. For example, in a classic study by Loftus and Palmer on _____ questions, subjects' estimates of the _____ of two cars involved in an accident varied depending on the way the questions were phrased. Leading questions, _____ comments, and _____ information also affect people's memories for their own experiences. In fact, researchers have induced people to "recall" complicated events from their lives that

_____ actually happened.

2-2. Memory research on the power of _____ is relevant when considering the accuracy of children's memories. Child _____ _____ cases depend on the reliability of children's memories. After a review of the studies, researchers conclude that, children, like adults, can be _____ in their recall. However, also like adults, they can be _____ by leading questions and suggestions. A child is more likely to give a false report when the interviewer strongly believes that the child has been _____ and then uses _____ techniques.

3. In Pursuit of Memory

Read the section "In Pursuit of Memory" and then answer the following questions. If you have trouble answering any of the questions, re-study the relevant material before going on to the review of key terms and the progress tests.

3-1. Explicit memory involves _____, intentional recollection of an event or piece of information. This type of memory can be measured using tests that require retrieval of information, _____ tests, or tests that require identification of information, _____ tests. Examples of recall tests include fill-in-the-blank and _____ tests, whereas examples of recognition tests include _____-_____ and multiple-choice tests.

In general, _____ tests are easier than _____ tests. When information learned previously affects people's thoughts and actions even though they do not consciously remember it, they are said to be using _____ memory. One way to examine implicit memory is to use the method of _____ in which information is presented to people and later they are tested to see if the information affected their performance on another type of task. Another way to measure implicit memory is to use the _____ method, or savings method, devised by Hermann _____. This method requires relearning information learned at an _____ time. If one relearns the information _____ than it was learned initially, something must be remembered from the prior learning experience.

3-2. The _____-_____ models of memory use computer analogies to illustrate memory processes. According to these models, people have the capability to encode, _____, and retrieve information. In most information-processing models, storage occurs in _____ interacting memory systems. First a sensory _____ keeps incoming sensory information for a very brief amount of time. Then, _____-_____ memory holds a limited amount of

140

information for about _____ seconds. Finally _____-_____ memory can store information indefinitely. This model is often called the _____-_____ _____. A more recent model of memory, the _____ _____ _____ (PDP) model, proposes that knowledge is represented as connections among many interacting processing units, distributed in a vast network, and all operating in parallel.

Terms for Review

The following is a list of the important terms from the section "In Pursuit of Memory." Make sure you are familiar with each term before taking the progress test on these terms.

explicit memory	information-processing
recall	models
recognition	sensory register
implicit memory	short-term memory
priming	long-term memory
relearning method	parallel distributed processing

4. The Three-Box Model of Memory

Read the section "The Three-Box Model of Memory" and then answer the following questions. If you have trouble answering any of the questions, re-study the relevant material before going on to the review of key terms and the progress tests.

4-1. According to the three-box model of memory, the entryway of memory is the _____ _____. As there are many _____, this memory area is comprised of many subsystems. Visual images are stored for a maximum of a _____ second.

Auditory information is held for about _____ seconds or so. The information stored in the sensory register is highly _____ and if it is considered important, it then continues on to the next memory storage area.

4-2. After the sensory register, information that is kept enters _____-_____ memory (STM), which holds information for approximately _____ seconds. Then, this material is either transferred to _____-_____ memory (LTM) or it decays and is no longer available. In people with certain types of brain damage, like H.M., explicit memories do not get into long-term memory, even though _____-_____ memory is functioning. STM often is described as a "leaky bucket" because it has a very limited _____ of approximately _____ items. To hold more material in STM, several pieces of information are _____ into meaningful units that may be composed of smaller units. Some psychologists have suggested that STM also functions as _____ memory because of its active role in the retrieval and interpretation of information.

4-3. The third box in the three-box model of memory is _____-_____ memory (LTM). As

141

there is a vast amount of information stored in LTM, it must be _____ in some manner. For example, it may be organized according to _____ categories. This idea was supported by the case of M. D., who had a series of _____ that left him with the inability to identify fruits or _____. Many models of long-term memory see it containing a _____ of interrelated _____ and propositions. Also, material in LTM is categorized based on the way words _____ or look. For example, when trying to retrieve information that is on the _____ of the _____ (TOT), people frequently recall not only words with similar _____, but also words that _____ similar. The contents of LTM are stored based on information regarding "knowing how" to do something, _____ memories, and information regarding "knowing that," _____ memories. Procedural memories are considered to be _____ and declarative memories are considered to be _____. One type of declarative memory is _____ memories, which are memories of general knowledge, including _____ and rules. The other type of declarative memory contains memories of personally experienced events, and is called _____ memories. The three-box model helps explain the

_____-_____ effect. This is the tendency for better recall of items at the beginning of the list, the _____ effect, and for the items at the end of the list, the _____ effect. According to the three-box model, the information at the beginning of the list is remembered because it has the best chance of getting into _____-_____ _____, and the information at the end of the list is remembered because it is still in _____-_____ _____.

Terms for Review

The following is a list of the important terms from the section "The Three-Box Model of Memory." Make sure you are familiar with each term before taking the progress test on these terms.

sensory register	procedural memories
short-term memory	declarative memories
chunk	semantic memories
working memory	episodic memories
long-term memory	serial-position effect
semantic categories	primacy effect
tip-of-the-tongue states	recency effect

5. The Biology of Memory

Read the section "The Biology of Memory" and then answer the following questions. If you have trouble answering any of the questions, re-study the relevant material before going on to the review of key terms and the progress tests.

5-1. With short-term memory, neurons _____ alter their ability to release neurotransmitters, whereas long-term memory involves _____ structural changes in the brain. These changes involve a long-lasting increase in the strength of synaptic responsiveness,

known as _____-
_____ _____. Over
time, memories become more durable and
stable, a process called _____.

5-2. The _____ is involved in the
formation, consolidation, and retrieval of
memories of fearful and other emotional
events. However, the brain structure most
strongly associated with many aspects of
memory is _____. Different
parts of the brain are involved in encoding
different kinds of memories, as evidenced
by people who cannot form lasting
declarative memories, but still form lasting
_____ memories.

5-3. _____ is released by the
_____ glands during stress and
emotional arousal, which can enhance
memory. Arousal tells the brain that an
event or information is important enough to
_____ and _____ for
future use. However, _____
arousal can interfere with memory.

Terms for Review

*The following is a list of the important terms
from the section "The Biology of Memory."
Make sure you are familiar with each term
before taking the progress test on these terms.*

long-term potentiation
consolidation

6. How We Remember

*Read the section "How We Remember" and then
answer the following questions. If you have
trouble answering any of the questions, re-study
the relevant material before going on to the
review of key terms and the progress tests.*

6-1. In order to remember information well, it
has to be _____ accurately.
Some information will be encoded
_____ without effort, but most
information requires _____
encoding, involving selecting and labeling

the main points, and _____
them with personal or previously known
information.

6-2. _____ is an important technique
for keeping information in STM and for
increasing the chances of retention in LTM.
Without _____, the contents in
_____ memory quickly fade.
There are two types of rehearsal, the rote
repetition of material, _____
rehearsal, and associating new items of
information with knowledge that has
already been stored, _____
rehearsal. The latter type of rehearsal is
better for _____ retention.
Also, it is important to process information
for meaning, _____ processing.
This is a better approach than
_____ processing, which is
simply processing information based on
_____ or sensory features of a
stimulus.

6-3. Simply just reading and rereading a text
book is an inefficient study technique
because it is a _____ strategy,
which is inferior to _____
rehearsing and recalling the material.
Reading a text, closing the book, writing
down everything down, and then rereading
to see what you recalled and forgotten is
known as the _____-
_____-_____
strategy.

6-4. Cognitive psychologists have found that _____ _____ is necessary if a memory is going to undergo consolidation. This is why _____ testing has a large, significant benefit.

6-5. Another strategy for improving memory is to use formal strategies and tricks for encoding, storing, and retaining information called _____. Mnemonics can involve rhymes, _____, visual images, or _____ associations. The best mnemonics require _____ material actively and thoroughly. This can be achieved by _____ it and making the material _____.

Terms for Review

The following is a list of the important terms from the section "How We Remember." Make sure you are familiar with each term before taking the progress test on these terms.

effortful encoding
rehearsal
maintenance rehearsal
elaborative rehearsal
deep processing

shallow processing
read-recite-review strategy
retrieval practice
mnemonics

7. Why We Forget

Read the section "Why We Forget" and then answer the following questions. If you have trouble answering any of the questions, re-study the relevant material before going on to the review of key terms and the progress tests.

7-1. There are several explanations of _____. One view, the _____ theory, holds that memories fade with time if they are not retrieved occasionally. This theory alone, however, cannot explain all forgetting in _____ memory.

7-2. Another theory states that new information can _____ old information. This view was supported by a study in which subjects were misled by the use of _____ questions so that their original perceptions had seemingly been "erased" by the _____ information.

7-3. A third theory posits that forgetting occurs because similar items of information _____ with one another in either storage or _____. This interference can happen in both STM and _____ and is likely when people have to recall isolated _____. When new information interferes with old information, _____ interference has taken place. When old information interferes with new information, _____ interference has occurred.

7-4. When trying to remember, people often rely on retrieval _____. When memory fails due to a lack of cues, people experience _____-_____ forgetting. Cues that were present when a new fact or event was learned are usually

144

the best _____ aids, for example the external environment in which the learning occurred. A _____ or physical state also can act as a memory cue. This is called _____-_____ memory. There also is evidence that _____, or one's emotional state, may serve as a retrieval cue.

7-5. Forgetting may occur due to _____, which is memory loss for important personal, often painful, information. This loss may be due to _____ factors or, less commonly, is psychogenic. One explanation of _____ amnesia is based on what Freud referred to as _____. The involuntary pushing of threatening or upsetting information into the _____ is difficult to test since it is hard to identify or distinguish from other forms of forgetting. This issue is controversial because people can have _____ memories of events that never occurred. Only rarely have _____ memories been corroborated by objective evidence, making it often impossible to determine their accuracy.

Terms for Review

The following is a list of the important terms from the section "Why We Forget." Make sure you are familiar with each term before taking the progress test on these terms.

decay theory
retroactive interference
proactive interference
retrieval cues
cue-dependent forgetting
state-dependent memory

mood-congruent memory
amnesia
psychogenic amnesia
traumatic amnesia
repression

8. Autobiographical Memories

Read the section "Autobiographical Memories" and then answer the following questions. If you have trouble answering any of the questions, re-study the relevant material before going on to the review of key terms and the progress tests.

8-1. Most people have no _____ memories for events that happened before the first _____ or _____ year of life. This is referred to as _____ or infantile _____. Freud thought that childhood amnesia was due to _____. Biological psychologists however, feel that childhood amnesia is due to the fact that _____ areas involved in the formation or storage of events are not well developed until a few years after birth. There are also _____ explanations for childhood _____. These include (1) lack of a sense of _____, (2) impoverished _____, (3) a focus on the _____, and (4) differences between early and later cognitive _____.

8-2. A person's _____ or "life story" organizes the events of his or her life and gives them _____. Life stories are to some degree works of

_____ and imagination. And, adult memories indicate as much about the _____ as they do about the past, providing themes or cognitive schemas that guide what people remember and what they forget, as well as their _____ of others.

Terms for Review

The following is a list of the important terms from the section "Autobiographical Memories." Make sure you are familiar with each term before taking the progress test on these terms.

childhood amnesia
narrative

146

SAMPLE ANSWERS TO *YOU ARE ABOUT TO LEARN* QUESTIONS FROM TEXTBOOK

After you have read through the chapter, go back and review the "You Are About to Learn..." statements that precede each major section. Create your own answer to each question, then compare your answers to the following sample answers. If your answers are not similar to the sample answers, review the relevant sections of the chapter more carefully.

Why does memory not work like a camera, and how does it work?

Unlike a movie camera, human memory is highly selective and largely a reconstructive process. It is more like watching a few unconnected frames and then figuring out what the rest of the scene must have been like rather than replaying a film of an event. People add, delete, and change elements in ways that help them make sense of information and events.

Why do errors creep into our memories of surprising or shocking events?

Surprising and shocking events sometimes result in very detailed memories known as flashbulb memories. Despite their intensity, flashbulb memories are not always complete or accurate records of the past. Like other memories, they often grow dim with time. Facts tend to get mixed with a little fiction. Even with flashbulb memories, remembering is an active process, one that involves not only dredging up stored information but also putting two and two together to reconstruct the past.

Why does having strong feelings about a memory not mean that the memory is accurate?

Emotional reactions to an imagined event can resemble those that would have occurred in response to a real event, and so they can be misleading. This means that strong feelings about an event, no matter how strongly they are held, are not a reliable cue to the event's reality.

Can your memories of an event be affected by the way someone questions you about it?

Yes, they certainly can. Eyewitness accounts are heavily influenced by the way in which questions are put to the witness. Research has shown differences in eyewitness accounts due to the particular words used in the questions asked by the researchers. People have even been induced by leading questions to reconstruct complicated personal events that never happened.

Can children's testimony about sexual abuse be trusted?

Children, like adults, can be accurate in what they report. However, also like adults, they can be suggestible, especially in response to biased interviewing by adults. For example, children's testimony may not be accurate when they are asked leading questions that blur the line between fantasy and reality, when they are bribed to give the "correct" answer, or when they are pressured to conform to what they believe other children have said. In sum, such conditions may lead to suggestibility and thus the testimony cannot be trusted.

In general, which is easier: a multiple-choice item or a short-

A multiple-choice item calls for recognition whereas a short-answer essay item requires recall. Although multiple-choice

answer essay item?

items can be difficult when the false items closely resemble the correct alternative, under most conditions recognition is easier than recall. Thus, multiple-choice items usually are easier than short-answer essay items because they only require recognition and not recall.

Can you know something without knowing that you know it?

Sometimes information affects thoughts and actions even though it is not consciously or intentionally remembered. This is a phenomenon known as implicit memory. To get at this subtle sort of knowledge, researchers must rely on indirect methods, such as priming in which people show that they know more than they know that they know.

Why is the computer often used as a metaphor for the mind?

Many cognitive psychologists liken the mind to an information processor, along the lines of a computer, though it is more complex. This metaphor is often used because both the computer and the mind encode, store, and retrieve information. In a computer, when something is typed on the keyboard, the machine encodes the information into an electronic language, stores it on a disk, and retrieves it when it is needed. Similarly, in information-processing models of memory, people encode information by converting it to a form that the brain can understand, store the information, and retrieve it later when they need to use it. Some cognitive scientists, however, have pointed out a crucial difference between the mind and the computer. Most computers process instructions sequentially and work on a single stream of data whereas the human brain performs many operations in parallel. Because of this difference, recent information-processing models of the mind assume parallel distributed processing.

How do the three "boxes" in the three-box model of memory operate?

The first box, the sensory register, holds images for a very short period of time. The second box, short-term memory, can hold memory for slightly longer and is often used to hold retrieved information. The third box, the long-term memory, holds memory and has no practical limits.

Why is short-term memory like a leaky bucket?

Short-term memory has been called a "leaky bucket" because information in short-term memory is in such a fragile state that if a person is distracted, the information is forgotten (it has leaked from the bucket). If the bucket did not leak, however, it would overflow quickly because the capacity of short-term memory is very limited.

When a word is on the tip of your tongue, what errors are you likely to make in recalling it?

When a word is on the tip of the tongue, people are likely to come up with incorrect words that are similar in meaning to the right one or incorrect guesses that have the correct number of syllables, the correct stress pattern, the correct first letter, or the correct prefix or suffix. This is because information in long-term memory is organized not only by semantic groupings but also in terms of the way words look and sound.

What's the difference between "knowing how" and "knowing that"?	Memories of "knowing how" are procedural memories, which are implicit. Once skills and habits are well learned, they do not require much conscious processing. Memories of "knowing that" are declarative memories, which are explicit and thus require conscious processing. Declarative memories come in two types—episodic memories (personal recollections) and semantic memories (general knowledge).
What are the change occur in the brain when you store a short-term versus a long-term memory?	In short-term memory, neurons in the brain will temporarily alter their ability to release neurotransmitters. When memories are stored long-term, however, there is a lasting structural change in the neurons.
Where in the brain are memories for facts and events are stored?	The amygdala helps with memory formation, consolidation, and retrieval involved in fearful and other emotional events. The frontal lobes also has active areas during short-term and working memory tasks. However, the hippocampus seems to play the biggest role and is critical for forming long-term declarative memories.
Which hormones can improve memory?	Memories tend to be more vivid when involving emotional and arousing events. Part of this may be due to the hormones released by the adrenal gland during stressful and emotional arousal. These hormones, including epinephrine and norepinephrine, have been shown to be involved in memory formation and retrieval in research studies.
What's wrong with trying to memorize in a rote fashion when you're studying—and what's a better strategy?	Maintenance rehearsal (memorizing in a rote fashion) is fine for keeping information in short-term memory, but it will not always lead to long-term retention. A better strategy is elaborative rehearsal. This involves associating new items of information with material that already has been stored or with other new facts. People also should engage in the related strategy of deep processing, or the processing of meaning.
Memory tricks are fun—but are they always useful?	No, they are not always useful. For ordinary memory tasks, such tricks are often no more effective than rote rehearsal, and sometimes they are actually worse. Most memory researchers do not use such mnemonics themselves.
What would be the problem with remembering everything?	If we did not forget things and retained all things equally, our recall would be much less efficient as we would need to constantly sort through unnecessary and trivial memories to access the relevant and important memories.
What are some major reasons we forget even when we'd rather not?	New information might wipe out old information, just like taping over material on an audiocassette or videotape will obliterate the original material. This is the assumption of the replacement theory of memory. The interference theory can also explain the forgetting of information. For example, old information can interfere with the ability to remember new information.
Why are many researchers	Skeptical researchers argue that although real abuse occurs,

149

skeptical about claims of "repressed" and "recovered" memories?

false memories of victimization are encouraged by therapists who are unaware of the power of suggestion and the dangers of confabulation. These researchers also point out that repeated experiences of trauma are more likely to be remembered than forgotten, even when the victims wish they could forget. Only rarely have "recovered" memories been corroborated by objective evidence, so it is difficult to determine their accuracy. In addition, most research psychologists are skeptical of the whole concept of repression, which they consider vague and poorly defined.

Why are the first few years of life a mental blank?

People experience childhood amnesia in that they cannot remember any events from earlier than the third or fourth year of their lives. Freud thought that childhood amnesia was due to repression, but biological researchers argue that it occurs because brain areas involved in the formation or storage of events are not well developed until a few years after birth. Cognitive explanations include lack of a sense of self, differences between early and later cognitive schemas, inadequate encoding, and a focus on the routine.

Why have human beings been called the storytelling animal?

People have been called the "storytelling animal" because they compose stories or narratives about their lives and live by the stories they tell. People compose narratives to explain and make sense of their lives. These narratives provide a unifying theme that organizes and gives meaning to life's events. However, since narratives rely heavily on memory and memories are reconstructed and constantly shifting in response to present needs, beliefs, and experiences, narratives are a work of interpretation and imagination. And, narrative themes guide what is remembered and what is forgotten.

KEY TERMS FILL-IN-THE-BLANKS PROGRESS TEST

Fill in the blanks with the key terms from the chapter that match the definitions provided. When you have finished this progress test, check your answers with those at the end of this chapter. You should review any key terms that you do not define correctly.

1. _____ The inability to remember events and experiences that occurred during the first two or three years of life.

2. _____ Confusion of an event that happened to someone else with one that happened to you, or a belief that you remember something when it never actually happened.

3. _____ The ability to retrieve and reproduce from memory previously encountered material.

4. _____ A method for measuring implicit memory in which a person reads or listens to information and is later tested to see whether the information affects performance on another type of task.

5. _____ Conscious, intentional recollection of an event or of an item of information.

6. _____ A method for measuring retention that compares the time required to relearn material with the time used in the initial learning of the material.

7. _____ Unconscious retention in memory, as evidenced by the effect of a previous experience or previously encountered information on current thoughts or actions.

8. _____ A memory system that accurately but very briefly registers sensory information before the information fades or moves into short-term memory.

9. _____ Memories of facts, rules, concepts, and events ("knowing that").

10. _____ A meaningful unit of information; it may be composed of smaller units.

11. _____ Memories of general knowledge, including facts, rules, concepts, and propositions.

12. _____ The tendency for recall of the first and last items on a list to surpass recall of items in the middle of the list.

13. _____ In the three-box model of memory, the memory system involved in the long-term storage of information.

14. _____ Memories for the performance of actions or skills ("knowing how").

15. _____ Association of new information with already stored knowledge and analysis of the new information to make it memorable.

16. _____ Strategies and tricks for improving memory, such as the use of a verse or a formula.

17. _____ In the encoding of information, the processing of meaning rather than simply the physical or sensory features of a stimulus.

18. _____ Rote repetition of material in order to maintain its availability in memory.

19. _____ Forgetting that occurs when previously stored material interferes with the ability to remember similar, more recently learned material.

20. _____ The theory that information in memory eventually disappears if it is not accessed; it applies more to short-term than to long-term memory.

21. _____ In psychoanalytic theory, the involuntary pushing of threatening or upsetting information into the unconscious.

22. _____ The tendency to remember something when the rememberer is in the same physical or mental state as during the original learning or experience.

MULTIPLE-CHOICE PROGRESS TEST

Choose the single best answer for each of the following questions. When you have finished this progress test, check your answers with those at the end of this chapter. You should review the relevant pages in the text for the questions you do not answer correctly.

1. Which of the following statements about human memory is TRUE?
   a. Human memory works like a tape recorder.
   b. Human memory usually allows recalling information by rote.
   c. Human memory is largely a reconstructive process.
   d. Both a and b are true.

2. The inability to distinguish what was originally experienced from what one heard or was told about an event later is called _____.
   a. motivated forgetting
   b. confabulation
   c. priming
   d. cue-dependent forgetting

3. Confabulation for the memory of an event is most likely to occur when:
   a. one has thought about the imagined event often.
   b. the image of the event is not very detailed.
   c. the event is difficult to image.
   d. one focuses on what actually happened and not one's emotional reactions to the event.

4. Which of the following statements about human memory is FALSE?
   a. Researchers have been able to induce people to "recall" personal events that never actually happened to them.
   b. Because of their vividness, flashbulb memories are always complete and accurate records of the past.
   c. Eyewitness memory is heavily influenced by the way in which questions are put to the witnesses.
   d. None of the above is false.

5. In the Loftus and Palmer classic study of leading questions, which of the following words led to the highest estimate of speed for the question, "About how fast were the cars going when they _____ each other?"
   a. smashed
   b. bumped
   c. collided
   d. contacted

6. Essay exams are to multiple-choice exams as _____ is to _____.
   a. long-term memory; short-term memory
   b. short-term memory; long-term memory
   c. recall; recognition
   d. recognition; recall

7. The _____ method is a way to measure implicit memory.
   a. recall
   b. recognition
   c. relearning
   d. mnemonic

8. Which of the following is not a characteristic of long-term memory?
   a. Contains sensory information
   b. Unlimited capacity
   c. Permanent storage
   d. Organized and indexed information

9. Which of the following types of memory has the most limited capacity?
   a. Sensory memory

b. Short-term memory
c. Episodic memory
d. Semantic memory

10. Which memory system could be described as momentary photographic memory?
   a. Short-term memory
   b. Long-term memory
   c. Sensory register
   d. Working memory

11. The difficulty with amnesic patients like H. M. is with the flow of information:
   a. from the sensory register to short-term memory.
   b. from short-term to long-term memory.
   c. from long-term to short-term memory.
   d. from the sensory register to long-term memory.

12. The acronym PBS is _____ chunk(s); the date 1776 is _____ chunk(s).
   a. 1; 1
   b. 1; 4
   c. 3; 1
   d. 3; 4

13. Recalling "Siam" or "sarong" when one is trying to recall "sampan" is an example of:
   a. a reminiscence bump.
   b. a TOT state.
   c. the serial position effect.
   d. source amnesia.

14. "Knowing how" is to "knowing that" as _____ memory is to _____ memory.
   a. declarative; procedural
   b. procedural; declarative
   c. semantic; episodic
   d. episodic; semantic

15. The tendency for recall of the first and last items on a list to surpass recall of items in the middle of the list is called _____.
   a. parallel distributed processing
   b. the serial position effect
   c. chunking
   d. cue-dependent forgetting

16. Which of the following leads to better long-term memory?
   a. Maintenance rehearsal
   b. Elaborative rehearsal
   c. Rote repetition
   d. Memorization

17. When new information interferes with the recall of similar material that was stored previously, _____ has occurred.
   a. decay
   b. retroactive interference
   c. proactive interference
   d. amnesia

18. Someone who has driven only cars with 5-speed manual transmissions, and then buys a car with an automatic transmission, is likely to have problems driving the new car due to:
   a. decay.
   b. retroactive interference.
   c. proactive interference.
   d. motivated forgetting.

19. Which type of forgetting is related to the Freudian notion of repression?
   a. cue-dependent forgetting
   b. retroactive interference
   c. proactive interference
   d. psychogenic amnesia

20. Which of the following has been proposed to explain childhood amnesia?
   a. Brain areas involved in the formation or storage of events are not developed until a few years after birth.
   b. People lack a sense of self during the first few years of life.
   c. Young children rely on cognitive schemas that differ from the schemas used later on in life.
   d. All have been proposed.

ANSWERS

Guided Study

1. Reconstructing the Past

1-1. memory
Bartlett
reconstructive
recall
source misattribution

1-2. flashbulb
accurate

1-3. confabulation
many
details
easy

2. Memory and the Power of Suggestion

2-1. eyewitnesses
reconstructive
leading
speed
suggestive
misleading
never

2-2. suggestion
sexual abuse
accurate
influenced
molested
suggestive

3. In Pursuit of Memory

3-1. conscious
recall
recognition
essay
true-false
recognition
recall
implicit
priming
relearning
Ebbinghaus
earlier
faster

3-2. information-processing
store
three
register
short-term
thirty
long-term
three-box model
parallel distributed processing

4. The Three-Box Model of Memory

4-1. sensory register
senses
half
two
accurate

4-2. short-term
    thirty
    long-term
    short-term
    capacity
    seven
    chunked
    working

4-3. long-term
    organized
    semantic
    strokes
    vegetables
    network
    concepts
    sound
    tip
    tongue
    meanings
    sound
    procedural
    declarative
    implicit
    explicit
    semantic
    facts
    episodic
    serial-position
    primacy
    recency
    long-term memory
    short-term memory

5. The Biology of Memory

5-1. temporarily
    lasting
    long-term potentiation
    consolidation

5-2. amygdala
    hippocampus
    procedural

5-3. Hormones
    adrenal
    encode
    store
    extreme

6. How We Remember

6-1. encoded
    automatically
    effortful
    associating

6-2. Rehearsal
    rehearsal
    short-term
    maintenance
    elaborative
    long-term
    deep
    shallow
    physical

6-3. passive
    actively
    read-recite-review

6-4. retrieval practice
    repeated

6-5. mnemonics
    formulas
    word
    encoding
    chunking
    meaningful

7. Why We Forget

7-1. forgetting
decay
long-term

7-2. replace
leading
misleading

7-3. interfere
retrieval
LTM
facts
retroactive
proactive

7-4. cues
cue-dependent
retrieval
mental
state-dependent
mood

7-5. amnesia
organic
psychogenic
repression
unconscious
false
recovered

8. Autobiographical Memories

8-1. autobiographical
third
fourth
childhood
amnesia
repression
brain
cognitive
amnesia
self
encoding
routine
schemas

8-2. narrative
meaning
interpretation
present
judgments

Answers to Key Terms Progress Test

1. childhood (infantile) amnesia
2. confabulation
3. recall
4. priming
5. explicit memory
6. relearning method
7. implicit memory
8. sensory register
9. declarative memories
10. chunk
11. semantic memories
12. serial-position effect
13. long-term memory (LTM)
14. procedural memories
15. elaborative rehearsal
16. mnemonics
17. deep processing
18. maintenance rehearsal
19. proactive interference
20. decay theory
21. repression
22. state-dependent memory

Item Number	Answers
1.	c. Human memory is largely a reconstructive process.
2.	b. confabulation
3.	a. one has thought about the imagined event often.
4.	b. Because of their vividness, flashbulb memories are always complete and accurate records of the past.
5.	a. smashed
6.	c. recall; recognition
7.	c. relearning
8.	a. contains sensory information
9.	b. short-term memory
10.	c. sensory register
11.	b. from short-term to long-term memory.
12.	a. 1; 1
13.	b. a TOT state
14.	b. procedural; declarative
15.	b. the serial position effect
16.	b. elaborative rehearsal
17.	b. retroactive interference
18.	c. proactive interference
19.	d. psychogenic amnesia
20.	d. All have been proposed.

CHAPTER 9

Learning and Conditioning

CHAPTER OVERVIEW

The chapter opens with definitions of learning, behaviorism, and conditioning. Then, classical conditioning is discussed. This includes mention of Pavlov and his original research in physiology in addition to the principles of classical conditioning he developed. Terms essential to classical conditioning such as unconditioned stimulus, unconditioned response, conditioned stimulus, and conditioned response are illustrated. Basic principles of classical conditioning also are covered, including extinction, spontaneous recovery, higher-order conditioning, stimulus generalization, and stimulus discrimination. Various examples of classical conditioning in real life are presented. These include learned fears and taste aversions.

Next, operant conditioning procedures are compared to classical conditioning procedures. Thorndike is discussed along with the basic premises put forth by Skinner. Primary and secondary reinforcers and punishers are defined. A description of the differences between positive and negative reinforcement and positive and negative punishment follows. Various principles of operant conditioning are presented including extinction, spontaneous recovery, stimulus generalization, stimulus discrimination, and continuous versus intermittent (partial) schedules of reinforcement. The steps involved with shaping a behavior are given. And, the biological limits on learning are outlined. Examples of operant conditioning in real life are explored, including coverage of applied behavior analysis and possible problems with both the use of punishment and with the provision of rewards.

The section on learning and the mind looks at latent learning. Also, the differences between social-cognitive learning theories and the learning theories previously described are noted. This includes a description of the cognitive aspects of social learning theories, observational learning, and the effects of models, for example those in the media, on behavior.

GUIDED STUDY

1. Classical Conditioning

Read the section "Classical Conditioning" and then answer the following questions. If you have trouble answering any of the questions, re-study the relevant material before going on to the review of key terms and the progress tests.

1-1. A relatively permanent change in behavior that occurs because of experience is referred to by psychologists as _____. Two types of learning that behaviorists study are _____ conditioning and _____ conditioning. The person who first researched classical conditioning was _____. He called the food in the mouth an _____ stimulus and salivation to the food an _____ response because neither one requires any learning. According to Pavlov, learning occurs when a _____ stimulus is presented shortly before the presentation of the unconditioned stimulus. The neutral stimulus then becomes a _____ stimulus and elicits a _____ response. The procedure by which a neutral stimulus becomes a _____ stimulus eventually became known as _____ conditioning, or Pavlovian, or _____ conditioning.

1-2. Conditioned _____ may not last forever. When the conditioned stimulus continuously is presented without the _____ stimulus, the conditioned response will eventually disappear through the process of _____. The reappearance of the conditioned response during extinction is referred to as _____ recovery. A neutral stimulus can be paired with a conditioned stimulus and become a _____ stimulus itself through the procedure of _____-_____ conditioning. When a stimulus similar to the conditioned stimulus produces a _____ _____, the organism is displaying stimulus _____. The opposite of this process, stimulus _____, occurs when different responses are made to stimuli that resemble the conditioned stimulus in some way.

1-3. For classical conditioning to be effective, the neutral stimulus, which will become the conditioned stimulus, must _____ the unconditioned stimulus. When explanations for behavior involve factors such as "information seeking," "preconceptions," and "representations of the world," it is likely that the explanation is coming from a _____ view of behavior.

161

Terms for Review

The following is a list of the important terms from the section "Classical Conditioning." Make sure you are familiar with each term before taking the progress test on these terms.

learning
behaviorism
conditioning
unconditioned stimulus (US)
unconditioned response (UR)
classical conditioning

extinction
spontaneous recovery
higher-order conditioning
stimulus generalization
stimulus discrimination

2. Classical Conditioning in Real Life

Read the section "Classical Conditioning in Real Life" and then answer the following questions. If you have trouble answering any of the questions, re-study the relevant material before going on to the review of key terms and the progress tests.

2-1. One of the first psychologists to recognize the significance of Pavlovian conditioning was John B. _____. For example, classical conditioning plays an important role in people's _____ responses to objects, events, and places. And, this explains why television commercials associate products with _____, _____ people, or other appealing sounds and images.

2-2. Classical conditioning also can help explain how people acquire fears and _____. In a classic study, Watson and Rayner conditioned an 11-month-old boy to fear a white _____ by pairing it with a loud noise. In a later study, Watson and Jones reversed a _____ of rabbits in a 3-year-old boy through the process of

_____, which involves pairing a conditioned stimulus with a stimulus that elicits a response that is _____ with an unwanted conditioned response.

2-3. Also, classical conditioning helps to understand people's _____ preferences. When a food is paired with falling ill, for example, people typically become _____ to dislike that food.

2-4. And, classical conditioning explains why cancer patients _____ their nausea and vomiting to other stimuli besides the chemotherapy. Cancer patients can acquire a classically conditioned response to anything _____ with their chemotherapy. On the other hand, _____ can lead to improved health since they may be associated with real drugs.

Terms for Review

The following is a list of the important terms from the section "Classical Conditioning in Real Life." Make sure you are familiar with each term before taking the progress test on these terms.

phobia
counterconditioning

3. Operant Conditioning

Read the section "Operant Conditioning" and then answer the following questions. If you have trouble answering any of the questions, re-study the relevant material before going on to the review of key terms and the progress tests.

3-1. Unlike classical conditioning, _____ conditioning is the process by which a response becomes more or less likely to occur, depending on its _____. One of the first psychologists to study operant conditioning was Edward _____, who placed cats in a _____ _____ in order to observe how they learned to escape from the box. The general principle that behavior is controlled by its consequences, that the correct response is "stamped in" by satisfying consequences, was established by Thorndike and elaborated on by B. F. _____. Skinner called his approach _____ _____ and argued that to understand behavior focus should be on factors _____ of the individual.

3-2. Certain consequences strengthen a response or make it more likely to occur and involves the use of _____. Another type of consequence weakens a response or makes it less likely to occur and involves _____. Reinforcers that satisfy biological needs, like food, are _____ reinforcers, whereas reinforcers that are learned are _____ reinforcers, like money. Punishers that are inherently punishing, such as pain, are _____ punishers and punishers that are learned are _____ punishers, such as criticism. In addition, there are distinctions between _____ and _____ reinforcement and positive and negative _____. When using _____ reinforcement, something pleasant follows a response. However, when using _____ reinforcement, a behavior is strengthened by the _____ of something unpleasant. When using _____ punishment, a response is followed by something _____; but when using _____ punishment, a response is followed by the _____ of something pleasant. All reinforcers _____ the likelihood of a response, whereas all punishers _____ the likelihood of a response.

Terms for Review

The following is a list of the important terms from the section "Operant Conditioning." Make sure you are familiar with each term before taking the progress test on these terms.

operant conditioning	secondary reinforcers
reinforcement	secondary punishers
punishment	positive reinforcement
primary reinforcers	negative reinforcement
primary punishers	

4. The Principles of Operant Conditioning

Read the section "The Principles of Operant Conditioning" and then answer the following questions. If you have trouble answering any of the questions, re-study the relevant material before going on to the review of key terms and the progress tests.

4-1. A commonly used tool in research on operant conditioning is the _____ box. Research using this tool has helped clarify the techniques and applications of operant conditioning. For example, a response learned through operant conditioning procedures may be stopped or undergo _____ by withholding the reinforcer. Also, _____ recovery after a rest period may occur. Similar to _____ conditioning, a response may generalize to stimuli that resemble original stimuli, as in stimulus _____. Or, it may not, as in stimulus _____. When an animal or person learns to respond to a stimulus only in the presence and not respond in the present of other stimuli, the stimulus controlling the response is called a _____ stimulus. The procedure of _____ reinforcement involves reinforcing a response every time it occurs, whereas the procedure of _____ reinforcement involves reinforcing only some responses. _____ reinforcement leads to the fastest learning, but _____ reinforcement leads to responding that is more resistant to extinction. An operant conditioning procedure in which successive _____ of a desired response are reinforced is called _____. Not any response, however, can be _____. There are limitations due to _____ constraints. Often an animal's behavior will drift back to _____ behavior, known as instinctive _____.

Terms for Review

The following is a list of the important terms from the section "The Principles of Operant Conditioning." Make sure you are familiar with each term before taking the progress test on these terms.

Skinner box	continuous reinforcement
extinction	intermittent reinforcement
spontaneous recovery	shaping
stimulus generalization	successive approximations
stimulus discrimination	instinctive drift
discriminative stimulus	

5. Operant Conditioning in Real Life

Read the section "Operant Conditioning in Real Life" and then answer the following questions. If you have trouble answering any of the questions, re-study the relevant material before going on to the review of key terms and the progress tests.

5-1. The use of operant and classical conditioning techniques in real world settings is called behavior modification or _____ _____ _____. Behavior modification has had some enormous _____, although it does sometimes require careful implementation. For example, although _____ can be effective when it follows an unwanted behavior and is applied consistently, it can fail when misused. There are several reasons this occurs. First, punishment is often administered _____ or mindlessly. Second, the recipient of punishment often responds with _____, fear, or

164

_____. Third, the effects of punishment are often _____. Fourth, most misbehavior is hard to punish _____. Fifth, punishment conveys little _____. Lastly, an action intended to be punishing may instead be _____ due to the fact that it brings _____. An alternative to punishment is to combine _____ of undesirable acts with the _____ of alternative ones.

5-2. Giving people _____ also may affect behavior in unwanted ways when used inappropriately. For example, rewards must not be dispensed _____, or they may become meaningless. And, psychologists have found that reinforcers that come from an outside source, _____ reinforcers, may undermine the pleasure of doing something for its own sake when delivered incorrectly. Therefore, they should be used in ways that do not weaken the impact of _____ reinforcers, which are inherently related to the activity being reinforced and involve enjoyment of the task and the satisfaction of accomplishment.

Terms for Review

The following is a list of the important terms from the section "Operant Conditioning in Real Life." Make sure you are familiar with each term before taking the progress test on these terms.

behavior modification   extrinsic reinforcers
applied behavior analysis   intrinsic reinforcers

6. Learning and the Mind

Read the section "Learning and the Mind" and then answer the following questions. If you have trouble answering any of the questions, re-study the relevant material before going on to the review of key terms and the progress tests.

6-1. Edward _____ studied _____ learning in rats, which is learning that is not immediately _____ in an overt response and occurs without obvious _____. Much of human learning also remains _____ until circumstances allow or require its expression.

6-2. Social-cognitive learning theories differ from traditional behavioral theories in that they emphasize that learning is acquired by _____ other people in a _____ context. These theories also study the effects of mental _____, such as expectations and beliefs, on behavior and _____. Observational learning or _____ conditioning involves learning by watching a _____ behaving in certain ways and experiencing the consequences. In a study on observational learning, Albert _____ had children watch a film of two adults playing together. One of the adults acted _____ towards the other and took all of the toys. When the children were allowed to play with the same toys, those that had seen the film acted more _____ than did those who had not viewed the film. This and

165

hundreds of other _____ studies
of children, teenagers, and adults
corroborate the general finding that
observing _____ does increase
_____. Thankfully however,
children do, of course, _____
positive models.

Terms for Review

*The following is a list of the important terms
from the section "Learning and the Mind."
Make sure you are familiar with each term
before taking the progress test on these terms.*

latent learning
social-cognitive theories
observational learning

SAMPLE ANSWERS TO *YOU ARE ABOUT TO LEARN* QUESTIONS FROM TEXTBOOK

After you have read through the chapter, go back and review the "You Are About to Learn..." statements that precede each major section. Create your own answer to each question, then compare your answers to the following sample answers. If your answers are not similar to the sample answers, review the relevant sections of the chapter more carefully.

Why would a dog salivate when it sees a light bulb or hears a buzzer?

The dog would salivate because the sight of the light bulb and the sound of the buzzer have become conditioned stimuli for the salivary response. This means that they were paired with an unconditioned stimulus for the salivary response (e.g., food in the dog's mouth) using the classical conditioning procedure. The conditioned salivary responses that were achieved would be like those Pavlov observed in his dogs.

What are four important features of classical conditioning?

One important feature of classical conditioning is the presence of an unconditioned stimulus that elicits the second important feature of an unconditioned response. These stimuli and responses are called unconditioned because they do not require a learning history. Other important features include a conditioned stimulus that elicits a conditioned response. These stimuli and responses are called conditioned because they depend upon a learning history of the individual organism.

What is learned in classical conditioning?

In classical conditioning, people and animals learn to react to the conditioned stimuli in a manner similar to the stimuli they were originally paired with. It is critical that the neutral stimulus precede the stimulus it is being paired with. Some theorists have argued that this is because the stimulus must signal information.

Why do advertisers often include pleasant music and gorgeous scenery in ads for their products?

Because people like the music and scenery, the advertisers are hoping that these feelings will be associated with their products. In classical conditioning terms, the music and scenery are unconditioned stimuli for internal responses associated with pleasure; and the products become conditioned stimuli for similar responses.

How would classical conditioning explain your irrational fear of heights or mice?

The irrational fear of heights had been classically conditioned through some earlier experiences in life. The objects of the phobic response (e.g., mice) have come to serve as conditioned stimuli for the fear response. Such phobias can be treated with counterconditioning and other exposure therapies.

How might you be conditioned to like certain tastes and odors and be turned off by others?

Preferred tastes and odors may have a history of being paired with other pleasurable stimuli, so that those tastes and odors become conditioned stimuli. A similar process exists for acquiring dislikes and distastes. For example, as with taste aversion, many people have learned to dislike a food after eating it and then falling ill, even though the two events were unrelated. The food (in this case, licorice) becomes a conditioned stimulus for nausea or for other symptoms produced by the illness.

How can sitting in a doctor's office make you feel sick and how can placebos make you feel better?

Unpleasant reactions to a treatment in the doctor's office can generalize to a wide range of stimuli, including the office, waiting room, and even the sound of the nurse's voice. All of these stimuli may become conditioned stimuli for nausea. With placebos, real drugs that produce improvement have been paired with expectations of improvement, such that the expectations alone become conditioned stimuli that elicit improvements.

How is technology helping researchers understand the biological basis of classical conditioning?

Research has shown that a particular gene is associated with reactivity in the amygdala and that people with this gene more readily acquired a conditioned startle response. Further, impaired cognitive control in the prefrontal cortex influences resistance to extinction.

How do the consequences of your actions affect your future behavior?

The principle of reinforcement demonstrates that certain consequences can increase the future frequency of behavior whereas the principle of punishment demonstrates that certain consequences can decrease the future frequency of behavior.

What do praising a child and quitting your nagging have in common?

They both involve reinforcement. Giving praise would be an example of positive reinforcement (the presentation of something pleasant), and quitting one's nagging is an example of negative reinforcement (the removal of something unpleasant).

What are the four important features of operant conditioning?

One important feature is that operant conditioning is subject to extinction, in that the response will weaken if the consequences that usually follow a behavior are stopped. Another important feature is stimulus generalization and discrimination, in which a response tends to occur in presence of stimuli similar to stimuli in which it has been previously reinforced (generalization) or the response does not occur (discrimination). A third important feature is learning on a schedule, in which different methods of delivering a reinforcer will produce different patterns of behavior. Finally, shaping is another important feature, in which the form of the response changes over time due to the reinforcement of successive approximations to a desired behavior.

Why is it not always a good idea to reinforce a response every time it occurs?

A response is more likely to persist longer, even in the absence of reinforcement, if it has a history of being reinforced intermittently. Thus, if you want a response to last, you should not reinforce the response every time it occurs.

How can operant principles account for superstitious behavior?

Coincidental reinforcement might account for some human superstitions, such as good-luck charms. Intermittent reinforcement may make the response particularly resistant to extinction. If coincidental reinforcement occurs occasionally, the superstitious behavior may continue indefinitely.

What does it mean to shape behavior?

One way of creating new behaviors is to use shaping, which involves reinforcing successive approximations to the final desired behavior.

What are some biological limits on operant conditioning?

Operant conditioning cannot create just any behavior in all organisms, no matter how careful the training is. For example, there are some behaviors that organisms are biologically incapable of and many animals tend to revert back to instinctual behaviors over time.

How can operant principles be applied to many real-world problems?

Operant conditioning has successfully taught toilet training skills, communication skills to autistic children, eliminated unwanted habits, and fostered desired habits.

When does punishment work and why does it sometimes fail?

Punishment works when it is delivered consistently and immediately. However, people often administer punishment inappropriately and mindlessly when rage prevents them from thinking through what they are doing and how they are doing it. The recipient of punishment often responds with anxiety, fear, or rage. The effects of punishment are sometimes temporary, depending heavily on the presence of the punishing person or circumstances. Most misbehavior is hard to punish immediately. Punishment conveys little information. An action intended to punish may instead be reinforcing because it brings attention. Because of these drawbacks, attempts to punish may go awry.

What are some effective alternatives to punishment?

Instead of punishing undesired behavior, one could focus on reinforcing desired behavior and combined this with the extinction of undesired behavior.

How might reinforcement be misused?

Reinforcement is sometimes given indiscriminately and not as a consequence for appropriate behavior. Under such circumstances, it stops functioning as reinforcement and may actually weaken behavior.

Why does paying children for good grades sometimes backfire?

Extrinsic reinforcement (in this case, the payment), if the child focuses on it exclusively, can undermine the pleasure of doing something (getting good grades) for its own sake. One possibility why extrinsic reinforcement hinders intrinsic motivation is that when people are paid for an activity, they interpret it as work. Another possibility is that extrinsic rewards are seen as controlling, and therefore may reduce a person's sense of autonomy and choice. A third, more behavioral explanation is that extrinsic reinforcement sometimes raises the rate of responding above some optimal, enjoyable level. Then the activity really does become work.

Can you learn something without any obvious reinforcement?

Yes, this is referred to as latent learning, which is a form of learning that is not immediately expressed in an overt response and occurs without obvious reinforcement. Much of human learning remains latent until circumstances allow or require it to be expressed. The knowledge learned may allow people to be creative and flexible in reaching their goals.

Why do two people often learn different lessons from exactly the same experience?

Social learning theorists would say this is due to the importance of people's perceptions in what they learn, perceptions of the models they observe, and also perceptions of themselves. Individuals also bring different knowledge and assumptions to an event, and they notice and pay attention to different aspects of a situation. Thus, all of these individual differences result in people learning different lessons from exactly the same experience.

Can we learn by simply watching instead of doing?

Yes, various behaviors can be acquired through observational learning—learning by watching what others do and the consequences that follow for these other people. For example, watching violence on TV does make some people more aggressive. However, it is important to remember that the more aggressive a person is to begin with, the more likely the person is to seek out violent media and be affected by what they see.

KEY TERMS FILL-IN-THE-BLANKS PROGRESS TEST

Fill in the blanks with the key terms from the chapter that match the definitions provided. When you have finished this progress test, check your answers with those at the end of this chapter. You should review any key terms that you do not define correctly.

1. _____ The classical conditioning term for a stimulus that elicits a reflexive response in the absence of learning.

2. _____ A relatively permanent change in behavior (or behavioral potential) due to experience.

3. _____ The reappearance of a learned response after its apparent extinction.

4. _____ The tendency to respond differently to two or more similar stimuli; in classical conditioning, it occurs when a stimulus similar to the CS fails to evoke the CR.

5. _____ The classical-conditioning term for a reflexive response elicited by a stimulus in the absence of learning.

6. _____ The process by which a previously neutral stimulus acquires the capacity to elicit a response through association with a stimulus that already elicits a similar or related response.

7. _____ In classical conditioning, the process of pairing a conditioned stimulus with a stimulus that elicits a response that is incompatible with an unwanted conditioned response.

8. _____ The process by which a stimulus or event strengthens or increases the probability of the response that it follows.

9. _____ A stimulus that is inherently punishing.

10. _____ In operant conditioning, the tendency for a response that has been reinforced (or punished) in the presence of one stimulus to occur (or be suppressed) in the presence of other, similar stimuli.

11. _____ A stimulus that has acquired reinforcing properties through association with other reinforcers.

12. _____ During operant learning, the tendency for an organism to revert to instinctive behavior.

13. _____ A reinforcement procedure in which a response is followed by the removal, delay, or decrease in intensity of an unpleasant stimulus; as a result, the response becomes stronger or more likely to occur.

14. _____ The process by which a response becomes more likely to occur or less so, depending on its consequences.

15. _____ An operant-conditioning procedure in which successive approximations of a desired response are reinforced.

16. _____ A reinforcement schedule in which a particular response is sometimes but not always reinforced.

17. _____ The application of conditioning techniques to teach new responses or to reduce or eliminate maladaptive or problematic behavior.

18. _____ Reinforcers that are not inherently related to the activity being reinforced, such as money, prizes, and praise.

19. _____ A process in which an individual learns new responses by observing the behavior of another (a model) rather than through direct experience; sometimes called vicarious conditioning.

20. _____ Theories that emphasize how behavior is learned and maintained through observation and imitation of others, positive consequences, and cognitive processes, such as plans, expectations, and beliefs.

21. _____ A form of learning that is not immediately expressed in an overt response; it occurs without obvious reinforcement.

MULTIPLE-CHOICE PROGRESS TEST

Choose the single best answer for each of the following questions. When you have finished this progress test, check your answers with those at the end of this chapter. You should review the relevant pages in the text for the questions you do not answer correctly.

1. In Pavlov's classical conditioning research, the ticking of a metronome is to salivation as _____ is to _____.
   a. unconditioned stimulus (US); unconditioned response (UR)
   b. unconditioned response (UR); unconditioned stimulus (US)
   c. conditioned stimulus (CS); conditioned response (CR)
   d. conditioned response (CR); conditioned stimulus (CS)

2. For effective classical conditioning to occur, the stimulus to be conditioned must reliably _____ the unconditioned stimulus.
   a. precede
   b. follow
   c. occur simultaneously with
   d. All of the above are equally effective procedures.

3. Disappearance of the conditioned response is to reappearance of the conditioned response as _____ is to _____.
   a. stimulus generalization; stimulus discrimination
   b. stimulus discrimination; stimulus generalization
   c. extinction; spontaneous recovery
   d. spontaneous recovery; extinction

4. In classical conditioning, _____ occurs when a stimulus similar to the CS fails to evoke the CR.
   a. acquisition
   b. spontaneous recovery
   c. stimulus generalization
   d. stimulus discrimination

5. Classical conditioning is likely involved in _____.
   a. learning to like and dislike various foods
   b. acquiring emotional responses to music
   c. developing a tolerance to addictive drugs
   d. all of the above

6. For Little Albert, the loud noise was the _____ and the rat was the _____.
   a. CS; US
   b. US; CS
   c. CS; CR
   d. US; UR

7. Which of the following is NOT the same as the others?
   a. Pavlovian conditioning
   b. Operant conditioning
   c. Classical conditioning
   d. Respondent conditioning

8. In classical conditioning, a procedure in which a neutral stimulus becomes a CS through association with an already established CS is called _____.
   a. generalization
   b. higher-order conditioning
   c. discrimination
   d. spontaneous recovery

9. An emphasis on the environmental consequences of a behavior is at the heart of _____ conditioning.
   a. operant
   b. respondent
   c. Pavlovian
   d. classical

10. Increasing the probability of the response it follows is to decreasing the probability of the response it follows as _____ is to _____.
    a. positive reinforcement; negative reinforcement
    b. negative punishment; positive reinforcement
    c. negative reinforcement; positive punishment
    d. positive punishment; positive reinforcement

11. Frederick's parents took away his favorite toy because he bit his classmate and now he bites his classmates less often. His parents used _____ to change his behavior.
    a. positive reinforcement
    b. negative reinforcement
    c. positive punishment
    d. negative punishment

12. Which of the following could NEVER be a primary reinforcer?
    a. Food
    b. Water
    c. A grade of A+
    d. A comfortable air temperature

13. Which of the following is TRUE regarding the differences between classical and operant conditioning?
    a. Classical conditioning involves voluntary behavior and operant conditioning involves reflexive behavior.
    b. Operant conditioning emphasizes consequences whereas classical conditioning emphasizes antecedents.
    c. Both classical and operant conditioning involve reflexive behavior.
    d. Both classical and operant conditioning emphasize environmental consequences.

14. For rapid learning and greater resistance to extinction, the use of _____ reinforcement should be followed by the use of _____ reinforcement.
    a. continuous; continuous
    b. continuous; intermittent
    c. intermittent; continuous
    d. partial; intermittent

15. The reinforcement of successive approximations of a desired response is involved in _____.
    a. counterconditioning
    b. higher-order conditioning
    c. shaping
    d. instinctive drift

16. Reinforcers that are inherently related to the activity being reinforced, such as enjoyment of the task and the satisfaction of accomplishment are called _____.
    a. intrinsic reinforcers
    b. extrinsic reinforcers
    c. positive punishers
    d. negative punishers

17. Which of the following is a reason that punishment fails?
    a. The recipient often responds with anxiety, fear, or rage.
    b. The effectiveness depends heavily on the presence of the punishing person or circumstances.
    c. Punishment conveys little information.
    d. All the above are reasons.

18. Observational learning is sometimes called _____ conditioning.
    a. classical
    b. operant
    c. vicarious
    d. higher-order

19. A form of learning that is not immediately expressed in an overt response and occurs without obvious reinforcement is:
    a. behavior modification.
    b. shaping.
    c. latent learning.
    d. instinctive drift.

Guided Study

1. Classical Conditioning

1-1. learning
classical
operant
Pavlov
unconditioned
unconditioned
neutral
conditioned
conditioned
conditioned
classical
respondent

1-2. responses
unconditioned
extinction
spontaneous
conditioned
higher-order
conditioned response
generalization
discrimination

1-3. precede
cognitive

2. Classical Conditioning in Real Life

2-1. Watson
emotional
music
attractive
images

2-2. phobias
rat
phobia
counterconditioning
incompatible

2-3. taste
conditioned

2-4. generalize
associated
placebos

3. Operant Conditioning

3-1. operant
consequences
Thorndike
"puzzle box"
Skinner
"radical behaviorism"
outside

3-2. reinforcement
punishment
primary
secondary
primary
secondary
positive
negative
punishment
positive
negative
removal
positive
unpleasant
negative
removal
increase
decrease

4. The Principles of Operant Conditioning

4-1. Skinner
    extinction
    spontaneous
    classical
    generalization
    discrimination
    discriminative
    continuous
    intermittent (partial)
    Continuous
    intermittent (partial)
    approximations
    shaping
    trained
    biological
    instinctive
    drift

5. Operant Conditioning in Real Life

5-1. applied behavior analysis
    successes
    punishment
    immediately
    inappropriately
    anxiety
    rage
    temporary
    immediately
    information
    reinforcing
    attention
    extinction
    reinforcement

5-2. rewards
    indiscriminately
    extrinsic
    intrinsic

6. Learning and the Mind

6-1. Tolman
    latent
    expressed
    reinforcement
    latent

6-2. observing
    social
    processes
    learning
    vicarious
    model
    Bandura
    aggressively
    aggressively
    experimental
    aggression
    aggressiveness
    imitate

176

Answers to Key Terms Progress Test

1. unconditioned stimulus
2. learning
3. spontaneous recovery
4. stimulus discrimination
5. unconditioned response
6. classical conditioning
7. counterconditioning
8. reinforcement
9. primary punisher
10. stimulus generalization
11. secondary reinforcer
12. instinctive drift
13. negative reinforcement
14. operant conditioning
15. shaping
16. intermittent (partial) schedule of reinforcement
17. behavior modification
18. extrinsic reinforcers
19. observational learning
20. social-cognitive theories
21. latent learning

Answers to Multiple-Choice Progress Test

Item Number	Answers
1.	c. conditioned stimulus (CS); conditioned response (CR)
2.	a. precede
3.	c. extinction; spontaneous recovery
4.	d. stimulus discrimination
5.	d. all of the above
6.	b. US; CS
7.	b. operant conditioning
8.	b. higher-order conditioning
9.	a. operant
10.	c. negative reinforcement; positive punishment
11.	d. punishment
12.	c. a grade of A+
13.	b. Operant conditioning emphasizes consequences whereas classical conditioning emphasizes antecedents.
14.	b. continuous; intermittent
15.	c. shaping
16.	a. intrinsic reinforcers
17.	d. All the above are reasons.
18.	c. vicarious
19.	c. latent learning

CHAPTER 10

Behavior in Social and Cultural Context

CHAPTER OVERVIEW   The chapter opens with a discussion of social norms and social roles. Classic studies investigating these issues are described, including the Milgram obedience study and the Zimbardo prison study. The power of roles and the question of why people obey is raised and analyzed. The process of entrapment is explored. Next social influences on beliefs are examined within the context of attribution theory. The differences between situational and dispositional attributions are addressed. In addition, common errors in attribution are covered, including the fundamental attribution error, various self-serving biases, and the just-world hypothesis. The origin of attitudes is covered next. This includes a description of cognitive dissonance theory and persuasion techniques.

The issue of conformity is investigated within Asch's famous line-length judgment experiment. A discussion of groupthink and strategies to avoid it follow. The concept of diffusion of responsibility is explained with respect to deindividuation. Situations in which conformity is avoided and persons dissent or act altruistically are described. The concept of social identity is presented as it applies to ethnic identity, acculturation, ethnocentrism, and stereotypes. Finally, the coverage of group-conflict and prejudice includes the identification of possible solutions to these problems.

GUIDED STUDY

1.   Roles and Rules

Read the section "Roles and Rules" and then answer the following questions. If you have trouble answering any of the questions, re-study the relevant material before going on to the review of key terms and the progress tests.

1-1. The fields of _____ psychology and cultural psychology study human behavior by emphasizing the social and cultural environment. Rules about how people are supposed to act from one situation to another are referred to as social _____. A given social position that is governed by a set of _____ for proper behavior is called a _____.

1-2. The Milgram study on _____ looked at the influence of norms and social roles on behavior in a situation in which participants, playing the role of _____, were asked to comply with a request to deliver supposed _____ _____ whenever the "learner," who was actually a _____ of Milgram, made an error. Participants were told that the experiment was on the effects of _____ on learning, when in reality it was on obedience. Milgram found that about _____-_____ of the participants obeyed to the fullest extent. In later experiments, Milgram identified situations in which fewer participants _____. These included (1) having the _____ leave the room, (2) having the _____ in the room, (3) having two experimenters issuing _____ demands, (4) having an ordinary _____ issuing the orders, and (5) having the participant work with _____ who refused to go further. Some criticisms of the Milgram obedience study are that it was _____ because participants were unaware of the true nature of the experiment and that participants may have suffered _____ pain.

1-3. In an experiment investigating the power of roles, _____ and Haney randomly _____ college students to the roles of prisoners and _____. They found that both groups fell very easily into their respective _____. In fact, within a short time the _____ became distressed, helpless, and panicky and the _____ typically took on one of three roles. Some were _____, others were tough but _____, and about a _____ of the guards were _____. The experiment was supposed to last for _____ weeks but was discontinued after only _____ days due to the rapid and alarming _____ of healthy students.

1-4. Most people follow orders because of the obvious _____ for disobedience.

180

Social psychologists have identified several factors that lead people to obey even when they would rather not. One factor is _____, the process by which individuals increase their commitment to a course of action in order to _____ their investment in it.

Terms for Review

The following is a list of the important terms from the section "Roles and Rules." Make sure you are familiar with each term before taking the progress test on these terms.

norms   culture
role   entrapment

2. Social Influences on Beliefs and Behavior

Read the section "Social Influences on Beliefs and Behavior" and then answer the following questions. If you have trouble answering any of the questions, re-study the relevant material before going on to the review of key terms and the progress tests.

2-1. Researchers in the area of social _____ study how people's _____ of themselves and others affect their _____ and how the social environment affects thoughts, _____, and values. Two topics examined in this area are explanations people make about _____ and _____ formation. How people make explanations about their own and others' behavior is explained in _____ theory. Attributions typically fall into two categories, a _____ attribution, which is based on the environment, and a _____ attribution, which is

based on an internal trait or _____ in the person. A common error committed when making attributions about another's behavior is the _____ _____ error. This is the tendency to attribute the behavior of others to _____ factors. This error is more frequently made in _____ nations. Westerners do not always make dispositional attributions. For example, when explaining their own behavior, they tend to reveal a _____-_____ bias, taking credit for their _____ actions but letting the _____ account for their failures and harmful actions. Further, people tend to biased to believe that they are better, smarter, and kinder than _____. People are influenced by the need to believe that the _____ is fair and that good people are rewarded and bad people _____, which is called the _____-_____ _____. This can lead to the phenomenon of _____ the victim, a _____ attribution. When something bad happens to another person, it is reassuring to think that they must have done something to _____ it.

2-2. An _____ is a belief about people, groups, ideas, or activities. Some attitudes are _____, they consciously shape people's decisions, and

181

some are implicit. Another influence on attitudes is people's behavior, due to _____ _____, which is a state of tension that occurs when a person simultaneously holds two thoughts that are _____, or when a person's attitude is incongruent with his or her _____. Some attitudes are formed due to social influence and may be altered as a result of persuasion. For example, people tend to feel more positive about something if they are familiar with it, which is termed the _____ effect. Further, when statements are _____, people eventually began to believe them, which is called the _____ effect. Researchers have also investigated whether genetics influence attitudes. For example, they have found that religious _____ is not heritable, but _____ does have a genetic component. Some methods used to alter attitudes involve a type of "brainwashing". These methods of indoctrination involve several processes, including (1) subjecting the person to _____, (2) explaining the person's _____ by one _____ attribution, (3) a new _____ and promise of _____ are offered, and (4) the person's access to information is severely _____.

Terms for Review

The following is a list of the important terms from the section "Social Influences on Beliefs

and Behavior." Make sure you are familiar with each term before taking the progress test on these terms.

social cognition
attribution theory
situational attribution
dispositional attribution
fundamental attribution error

just-world hypothesis
cognitive dissonance
familiarity effect
validity effect

3. Individuals in Groups

Read the section "Individuals in Groups" and then answer the following questions. If you have trouble answering any of the questions, re-study the relevant material before going on to the review of key terms and the progress tests.

3-1. Something that people in groups do is _____, acting or forming attitudes due to real or _____ group _____. In a set of classic experiments, _____ had students in a group make a simple judgment about the length of three lines. He found that all but _____ percent of the participants conformed at some time during the study and went along with the group's unanimous, but obviously incorrect judgment.

3-2. When working in a group, the tendency for all members to think alike and to suppress _____ is called _____. According to Janis, groupthink occurs when a group's need for total _____ overpowers its need to make the _____ decision. Symptoms of groupthink include (1) an _____ of invulnerability, (2) _____-_____, (3) pressure on _____ to conform,

182

and (4) and an illusion of _____.
Creating group norms that encourage and
reward the expression of doubt and
_____ can help prevent
groupthink.

3-3. When people do not offer help to someone
in need it may be due to _____
of responsibility, which can result in
_____ apathy. In the most
extreme case of diffusion of responsibility,
members of a group lose all awareness of
their _____ and sense of self,
which is called _____. People
are more likely to feel deindividuated in a
_____ city or when wearing a
_____ or mask. Although
considered a reason for _____
violence, deindividuation also can lead
people to become more _____.
Therefore, its effects depend on the norms
of the _____ situation.

3-4. Individuals can commit acts of dissent and
_____, the willingness to take
selfless and dangerous action on behalf of
others, due to personal _____ or
_____ influences. Social
psychologists have identified several
factors involved when people decide to
behave _____. These include
(1) the individual perceives the need for
_____ or help, (2) cultural
_____ encourage you to take
action, (3) the individual has an

_____, and (4) the individual
becomes _____.

Terms for Review

*The following is a list of the important terms
from the section "Individuals in Groups." Make
sure you are familiar with each term before
taking the progress test on these terms.*

groupthink   bystander apathy
diffusion of responsibility deindividuation

4. Us Versus Them: Group Identity

*Read the section "Us Versus Them: Group
Identity" and then answer the following
questions. If you have trouble answering any of
the questions, re-study the relevant material
before going on to the review of key terms and
the progress tests.*

4-1. According to social psychologists,
everyone develops a social
_____, which is the part of one's
self-concept that is based on his or her
_____ with a nation,
_____ or political group,
occupation or other _____
_____. One's _____
identity involves identification with a
_____ or ethnic group. It also
may be based on _____,
identification with the dominant culture.

4-2. The belief that one's own ethnic group,
nation, or religion is superior to all others is
known as _____. The us-them
distinctions people make are reinforced
when groups are _____ against
each other. In one experiment, Muzafer
Sherif created a _____ between

two groups of _____

_____ that resulted in the boys

acting _____ toward outgroup

members.   Later, Sherif replaced

competition with a policy of

_____ in reaching

_____ goals by having the boys

pool their resources in order to reach a

shared outcome. This was successful in

decreasing the boys' hostility since it

reduced their tendency to think in terms of

_____versus _____.

4-3. Conflicts can result from _____,

summary impressions of a group of people

in which all members of the group are

viewed as sharing a common trait.

Although stereotypes can make decision

making more _____, there are

three ways in which they distort reality: (1)

they _____ differences between

groups, (2) they produce _____

_____, and (3) they

_____ differences within other

groups. And, negative stereotypes can lead

to _____.

Terms for Review

*The following is a list of the important terms
from the section "Us Versus Them: Group
Identity." Make sure you are familiar with each
term before taking the progress test on these
terms.*

social identity   ethnocentrism
ethnic identity   stereotype
acculturation

5. Group Conflict and Prejudice

*Read the section "Group Conflict and
Prejudice" and then answer the following
questions. If you have trouble answering any of
the questions, re-study the relevant material
before going on to the review of key terms and
the progress tests.*

5-1. Negative _____ are involved

with prejudice, a strong, _____

dislike or hatred of a group. Prejudice has

many causes, including _____,

_____, _____, and

cultural/national causes. A psychological

function is that prejudice offers a way for

people to use the target group as a

_____, blaming the group for all

their problems. Prejudice also increases

when people are in direct_____

for jobs. Prejudice is often used to state

that enemies _____ to be

harmed because they are less than human.

5-2. In order to measure unconscious or

_____ prejudice, researchers

have developed several different

techniques. One way involves

_____ _____ , or the

reluctance to get "too close" to another

group. Another is to assess what people do

when they are _____ or

_____ . Measure of

_____ activity have also proved

useful. A more controversial method is the

_____ _____

_____ (IAT), which measures

response rates between racial features and

positive or negative words.

5-3. Social psychologists have identified four conditions that must be met before conflict and _____ can be lessened. First, both sides must have many _____ to work and socialize together. According to the _____ hypothesis, prejudice tends to decline with more exposure to another group's rules, food, customs, and attitudes. Second, both sides must have _____ _____ status, economic opportunities, and _____. Third, _____ and _____ institutions must provide moral, legal, and economic support to both sides. Finally, both sides must _____, working together for a _____ goal. An example of this is the _____ method of building cooperation, which has successfully reduced intergroup tension and competition in schools.

Terms for Review

The following is a list of the important terms from the section "Group Conflict and Prejudice." Make sure you are familiar with each term before taking the progress test on these terms.

prejudice   Implicit Association Test
social distance   contact hypothesis

SAMPLE ANSWERS TO *YOU ARE ABOUT TO LEARN* QUESTIONS FROM TEXTBOOK

After you have read through the chapter, go back and review the "You Are About to Learn..." statements that precede each major section. Create your own answer to each question, then compare your answers to the following sample answers. If your answers are not similar to the sample answers, review the relevant sections of the chapter more carefully.

How do social rules regulate behavior and what is likely to happen when you violate them?

Social norms are rules about how people are supposed to act. They include social conventions, explicit laws, and unspoken cultural standards. They make interactions with other people predictable and orderly. They are enforced by threats of punishment if people violate them. Thus, if a norm is violated, one will be punished according to the law, or informally by other people, in that one will be made to feel guilty or inadequate.

How does the power of roles and situations make people behave in ways they never would have predicted for themselves?

Two studies illustrate the power of roles and situations in determining our behavior. The obedience research by Stanley Milgram demonstrated that about two-thirds of the participants obeyed orders to inflict high levels of shock to another person. More than 1,000 participants at several American universities eventually participated in the Milgram study. Most of them, men and women equally, inflicted what they thought were dangerous amounts of shock to another person. Researchers in other countries also have found high percentages of such obedience. Milgram concluded that this obedience was more a function of the situation than of the particular personalities of the participants. The Stanford Prison Experiment demonstrated similar control by the environmental context. Philip Zimbardo, who designed the prison study, would argue that all one needs to do is put the college students into the role of prison guards, and some of the students would become sadistic prison guards. About a third of the guards in the prison study became tyrannical and abusive. Zimbardo believes that the results of the prison study demonstrate that roles transform people.

How can people be "entrapped" into violating their moral principles?

Entrapment is a process in which individuals increase their commitment to a course of action in order to justify their investment in it. The first steps of entrapment pose no difficult choices with respect to one's moral principles, but one step leads to another. Before it is realized, one has become committed to a course of action that poses moral problems, and it is hard to free oneself. For example, in Milgram's study, once participants had given a 15-volt shock, they had committed themselves to the experiment. Unless they resisted authority soon afterwards, they were likely to go on to administer what they believed were dangerously strong shocks. At that point, it was difficult to explain a sudden decision to quit.

186

What are two general ways that people explain their own or other people's behavior and why does it matter?

People tend to either use situational attributions, in which the environment is blamed or credited for one's actions or they use dispositional attributions, in which the blame or credit is placed on an internal trait or characteristic. It matters because people often miss out on the relevant controlling variables due to the type of attribution they make. For example, one of the most common mistakes people make when explaining the behaviors of others is to overestimate personality factors and underestimate the influence of the situation. This tendency is called the fundamental attribution error. People are especially likely to overlook situational attributions when they are distracted or preoccupied. It especially is prevalent in Western nations, where middle-class people tend to believe that individuals are responsible for their own actions.

What three self-serving biases influence how people think about themselves and the world?

The first bias is a tendency to select the most flattering and forgiving attributions of their lapses. The second is the general belief of people to think they are better, smarter, and kinder than other people. The third bias is the just-world hypothesis, in which attributions are affected by the need to believe the world is fair and that justice prevails, and that good people are rewarded and bad people are punished. This leads to a dispositional attribution called blaming the victim. Thus, victims of tragedy or crime are blamed for having deserved what happened to them.

Why do most people believe outright lies and nonsensical statements if they are repeated often enough?

Repeat something often enough, even the basest lie, and eventually the public will believe it. Its formal name is the validity effect. It works so well because it employs a well-established relationship—people tend to feel more positive toward things to which they are repeatedly exposed.

Do fundamental political and religious attitudes have a genetic component?

Specific religious and political affiliations are not heritable. However, religiosity, the depth of a person's religious feelings, does have a genetic component. Similarly, political conservatism also has a genetic component.

Why do people in groups often go along with the majority even when the majority is dead wrong?

Some do so because they identify with group members and want to be like them in dress, attitudes, or behavior. Some want to be liked and know that disagreeing with a group can make them unpopular. Some believe the group has knowledge or abilities that are superior to their own. And some go along to keep their jobs, win promotions, or win votes.

How can "groupthink" lead to bad decisions?

In situations in which groupthink occurs, the group believes that it can do no wrong. It has an illusion of invulnerability. There is no self-censorship. Dissenters decide to keep quiet in order not to rock the boat, offend their friends, or risk being ridiculed. There is direct pressure on dissenters to conform, either by the leader or other group members. By discouraging dissent, leaders and group members create an illusion of unanimity. Thus, without the presence of any dissent or doubt, such conformity can lead to bad decisions.

How do crowds create "bystander apathy" and unpredictable violence?

One is more likely to get help when there are only a few strangers in the area. When there are many people around the scene of an emergency, people fail to take action because they believe that someone else will do so. This is a process called diffusion of responsibility—in which responsibility for helping is spread among many people, and individuals fail to take action because they believe that someone else will do so. An extreme version of this, deindividuation, occurs when people lose their sense of individuality to a group, increasing the probability of going along with the group, including events such as mob violence.

What conditions increase dissent, help others at risk to themselves, or blow the whistle on wrongdoers?

These actions of dissent, altruism, and disobedience are in part a matter of personal convictions and conscience. There are also many external influences leading to such actions. The individual perceives the need for intervention or help. The individual must decide to take responsibility and that the costs of doing nothing outweigh the costs of getting involved. Having an ally also helps. Lastly, a person may become entrapped. Once having taken the initial step of getting involved, most people will increase their commitment to taking action. Thus, certain social conditions make dissent, altruism, and disobedience more likely to occur.

In what different ways do people balance their ethnic identity and acculturation in a multicultural society?

Four outcomes are possible, depending on whether ethnic identity is strong or weak and whether identification, or acculturation, with the larger culture is strong or weak. People who are bicultural have strong ties both to their ethnicity and to the larger culture. Those who choose assimilation have weak ties to their ethnic identity but a strong sense of acculturation. Ethnic separatists have a strong sense of ethnic identity but weak feelings of acculturation. And some people feel marginal, connected to neither their ethnicity nor the dominant culture.

What causes ethnocentrism, us-them thinking, and how can we decrease it?

Ethnocentrism occurs when one believes that his or her culture, nation, or religion is superior to all others. As in Sherif's Robbers Cave study, creating interdependence in reaching mutual goals will reduce "us-them" thinking. The reason is that cooperation causes people to think of themselves as members of one large group instead of members of a group opposed to another.

How do stereotypes benefit us, and how do they distort reality?

Stereotypes benefit people by helping them process new information and retrieve memories. They allow the organization of experience, making sense of differences among individuals and groups, and the prediction of how people will behave. In brief, they allow people to make efficient decisions. Stereotypes, however, also distort reality in three ways. First, they exaggerate differences between groups, making the stereotyped group seem odd, unfamiliar, or dangerous. Second, they produce selective perception;

188

people tend to see only what fits the stereotype and to reject any perceptions that do not fit. Third, they underestimate differences within other groups. Stereotypes create the impression that all members of other groups are the same.

What are the four causes and functions of prejudice?

Prejudice can have a psychological cause, especially when people want to inflate their self-esteem or find a scapegoat. Social causes also exist, in which prejudice occurs simply due to conforming to group standards. There are also economic causes of prejudice, in which conflict and dislike increase when resources are scarce and competition is high. Finally, cultural and national causes foster prejudice when negative attitudes can be used to justify poor treatment of other cultures and nations.

What are four indirect ways of measuring prejudice?

Social distance, how willing an individual is to get close to a member of another group, is one measure. Measuring what people do during times of stress and anger is another method. Measure of brain activity, such as fMRI and PET scans, have been used to measure prejudice. Last, prejudice can be measured through tests of implicit attitude, such as the controversial Implicit Association Test.

What four conditions are necessary for prejudice and conflict to be reduced?

In order for prejudice and conflict to be overcome, the four conditions must first be met: (1) Both sides must have many opportunities to work and socialize together, (2) both sides must have equal legal status, economic opportunities, and power, (3) authorities and community institutions must provide moral, legal, and economic support for both sides, and (4) both sides must cooperate, working together for a common goal.

Fill in the blanks with the key terms from the chapter that match the definitions provided. When you have finished this progress test, check your answers with those at the end of this chapter. You should review any key terms that you do not define correctly.

1. _____ A given social position that is governed by a set of norms for proper behavior.

2. _____ A gradual process in which individuals escalate their commitment to a course of action to justify their investment of time, money, or effort.

3. _____ Rules that regulate human life, including social conventions, explicit laws, and implicit cultural standards.

4. _____ The theory that people are motivated to explain their own and other people's behavior by attributing causes of that behavior to a situation or a disposition.

5. _____ The tendency of people to feel more positive toward a person, item, product, or other stimulus the more familiar they are with it.

6. _____ The tendency of people to believe that a statement is true simply because it has been repeated many times.

7. _____ The notion that many people need to believe that the world is fair and that justice is served; that bad people are punished and good people rewarded.

8. _____ The tendency, in explaining other people's behavior, to overestimate personality factors and underestimate the influence of the situation.

9. _____ An area in social psychology concerned with social influences on thought, memory, perception, and other cognitive processes.

10. _____ In close-knit groups, the tendency for all members to think alike for the sake of harmony and to suppress disagreement.

11. _____ In groups or crowds, the loss of awareness of one's own individuality.

12. _____ In groups, the tendency of members to avoid taking responsibility for actions or decisions, assuming that others will do so.

13. _____ The willingness to take selfless or dangerous action on behalf of others.

14. _____ A person's identification with a racial, religious, or ethnic group.

15. _____ The process by which members of minority groups come to identify with and feel part of the mainstream culture.

16. _____ The part of a person's self-concept that is based on his or her identification with a nation, ethnic group, gender, or other social affiliation.

17. _____ A summary impression of a group, in which a person believes that all members of the group share a common trait or traits (positive, negative, or neutral).

18. _____ The belief that one's own ethnic group, nation, or religion is superior to all others.

19. _____ Consists of a negative stereotype and a strong, unreasonable dislike or hatred of a group.

MULTIPLE-CHOICE PROGRESS TEST

Choose the single best answer for each of the following questions. When you have finished this progress test, check your answers with those at the end of this chapter. You should review the relevant pages in the text for the questions you do not answer correctly.

1. In Milgram's original study on obedience, every single subject administered some shock to the learner, and about _____ of all participants obeyed to the fullest extent.
   a. one-fourth
   b. one-half
   c. two-thirds
   d. three-fourths

2. Which of the following statements about the findings of Milgram's obedience studies is FALSE?
   a. When the experimenter left the room, people were more likely to disobey.
   b. When two experimenters issued conflicting demands to continue the experiment or to stop at once, no one kept inflicting shock.
   c. When the subject worked with peers who refused to go further, they were more likely to disobey.
   d. None of the above is false.

3. Which of the following statements about Zimbardo's prison study is FALSE?
   a. The college student volunteers chose which role they wanted, prisoner or guard.
   b. About a third of the guards became tyrannical, and the study was stopped after only six days.
   c. According to Zimbardo, this study illustrated the power of roles to transform people.
   d. None of the above is false.

4. In the Milgram obedience studies, some people became so fixated on the "learning task" that they shut out any moral concerns about the learner's demands that he be let out. This illustrates _____.
   a. legitimization of the authority
   b. routinization
   c. the rules of good manners
   d. entrapment

5. Which of the following is a process in which individuals increase their commitment to a course of action in order to justify their investment in it?
   a. Validity effect
   b. Groupthink
   c. Deindividuation
   d. Entrapment

6. A strong ethnic identity paired with strong acculturation leads to a _____ identity.
   a. bicultural
   b. assimilated
   c. separatist
   d. marginal

7. Reading about Milgram's obedience findings and thinking that the participants were sadistic is a good example of the _____.
   a. just-world hypothesis
   b. validity effect
   c. fundamental attribution error
   d. diffusion of responsibility

8. Which of the following leads to a dispositional attribution called "blaming the victim"?
   a. Just-world hypothesis
   b. Entrapment
   c. Acculturation
   d. Cohort effect

9. The formal name for the effectiveness of a repeated message is _____.
   a. the validity effect
   b. the cohort effect
   c. entrapment
   d. acculturation

10. Which of the following is NOT a characteristic of brainwashing?
    a. The person is offered a new identity and is promised salvation.
    b. The person is subjected to entrapment.
    c. The person's access to information is not controlled.
    d. None of the above is the answer.

11. Which of the following statements about the experimental findings on conformity is FALSE?
    a. In America, conformity has increased since Asch's work in the 1950s.
    b. In Asch's conformity study, the majority of participants went along with the inaccurate group at least some of the time.
    c. Regardless of culture, everyone conforms under some circumstances and for similar reasons.
    d. None of the above is false.

12. Which of the following is NOT a symptom of groupthink?
    a. An illusion of invulnerability
    b. Self-censorship
    c. No pressure on dissenters to conform
    d. An illusion of unanimity

13. Deindividuation is likely to occur:
    a. in a large city rather than a small town.
    b. when signs of individuality are covered by masks or uniforms.
    c. in a mob rather than in an intimate group.
    d. All the above are answers.

14. Which of the following social and situational factors has a higher probability of leading a person to independent action?
    a. The individual does not perceive the need for intervention.

b. The situational risks are high.
c. The individual decides that the cost of getting involved outweighs the cost of doing nothing.
d. The individual has an ally.

15. The belief that one's own culture or ethnic group is superior to all others is called:
    a. self-serving bias.
    b. ethnocentrism.
    c. social identity.
    d. acculturation.

16. Stereotypes distort reality by:
    a. exaggerating differences between groups.
    b. producing selective perception.
    c. underestimating differences within other groups.
    d. All the above are answers.

17. Which of the following is NOT a condition that will lead to lessening conflict and prejudice between groups?
    a. Both sides have equal legal status, economic opportunities, and power.
    b. Authorities endorse egalitarian norms and provide moral support for both sides.
    c. Both sides have opportunities to work and socialize together, formally and informally.
    d. None of the above is an answer.

Guided Study

1. Roles and Rules

1-1. social
norms
norms
role

1-2. obedience
"teacher"
electric shocks
confederate
punishment
two-thirds
obeyed
experimenter
victim
conflicting
person
peers
unethical
emotional

1-3. Zimbardo
assigned
guards
roles
prisoners
guards
nice
fair
third
tyrannical
two
six
transformation

1-4. consequences
entrapment
justify

2. Social Influences on Beliefs

2-1. cognition
perceptions
relationships
beliefs
behavior
attitude
attribution
situational
dispositional
motive
fundamental attribution
dispositional
Western
self-serving
good
situation
others
world
punished
just-world hypothesis
blaming
dispositional
deserve

2-2. attitude
explicit
cognitive dissonance
inconsistent
behavior
familiarity
repeated
validity
affiliation
religiosity
entrapment
problems
simple
identity
salvation
controlled

3. Individuals in Groups

3-1. conform
imagined
pressure
Asch
twenty

3-2. dissent
groupthink
agreement
wisest
illusion
self-censorship
dissenters
unanimity
dissent

3-3. diffusion
bystander
individuality
deindividuation
large
uniform
mob
friendly
specific

3-4. altruism
convictions
external
courageously
intervention
norms
ally
entrapped

4. Us Versus Them: Group Identity

4-1. identity
identification
religious
social affiliation
ethnic
racial
acculturation

4-2. ethnocentrism
competing
competition
Boy Scouts
hostile
interdependence
mutual
"us"
"them"

4-3. stereotypes
efficient
exaggerate
selective perception
underestimate
prejudice

5. Group Conflict and Prejudice

5-1. stereotypes
unreasonable
psychological
social
economic
competition
deserve

5-2. implicit
social distance
stressed
angry
brain
Implicit Association Test

5-3. prejudice
opportunities
contact
equal legal
power
authorities
community
cooperate
common
jigsaw

Answers to Key Terms Progress Test
1. role
2. entrapment
3. social norms
4. attribution theory
5. self-serving bias
6. validity effect
7. just-world hypothesis
8. fundamental attribution error
9. social cognition
10. groupthink
11. deindividuation
12. diffusion of responsibility
13. altruism
14. ethnic identity
15. acculturation
16. social identity
17. stereotype
18. ethnocentrism
19. prejudice

Item Number	Answers
1.	c. two-thirds
2.	d. None of the above is false.
3.	a. The college student volunteers chose which role they wanted, prisoner or guard.
4.	b. routinization
5.	d. entrapment
6.	a. bicultural
7.	c. fundamental attribution error
8.	a. just-world hypothesis
9.	a. the validity effect
10.	c. The person's access to information is not controlled.
11.	a. In America, conformity has increased since Asch's work in the 1950s.
12.	c. no pressure on dissenters to conform
13.	d. All the above are answers.
14.	d. The individual has an ally.
p15.	b. ethnocentrism
16.	d. All the above are answers.
17.	d. None of the above is an answer.

CHAPTER 11

Psychological Disorders

CHAPTER OVERVIEW

The chapter opens with a description of the criteria for defining a mental disorder. This includes having a harmful dysfunction, in which behavior or an emotion is harmful to oneself or others and dysfunctional because it is not performing its evolutionary function. Means of diagnosing and classifying mental disorders are discussed next. The Diagnostic and Statistical Manual of Mental Disorders is described, and possible problems with the use of the manual, such as the danger of overdiagnosis and the power of labels, are outlined. Projective tests such as the Rorschach Inkblot Test and more objective means such as the Minnesota Multiphasic Personality Inventory also are used to measure and diagnose mental disorders. The reliability and validity of these measures are mentioned.

Anxiety disorders that are covered include generalized anxiety disorder, posttraumatic stress disorder, panic disorder, phobia, and obsessive-compulsive disorder. The symptoms of mood disorders, including major depression and bipolar disorder, are discussed. The vulnerability-stress model for depression is explained. Personality disorders, borderline and antisocial, are explained. Causes of antisocial personality disorder are explored.

Coverage of drug abuse and addiction involves examining both the biological model and the learning model of substance abuse. Criticisms of each model are offered. Dissociative identity disorder, formerly termed multiple personality disorder, is described and critiqued. Finally, schizophrenic disorders are discussed. In addition, various explanations of schizophrenia are provided.

GUIDED STUDY

1. Defining and Diagnosing Mental Disorders

Read the section "Defining and Diagnosing Mental Disorders" and then answer the following questions. If you have trouble answering any of the questions, re-study the relevant material before going on to the review of key terms and the progress tests.

1-1. The term abnormal behavior differs from the term _____ disorder in several respects. Also, having a mental disorder does not mean that one is _____, which is a legal term. Determining a mental disorder involves the consideration of _____ dysfunction, that is, is the behavior or emotional state harmful to oneself or others and _____ because it is not performing its _____ function. A mental disorder is defined broadly as any condition that causes a person to _____, is _____-_____, seriously impairs a person's ability to _____ or get along with others, or _____ others or the _____.

1-2. The main diagnostic tool used by clinicians is the _____ and _____ _____ of _____ Disorders (DSM). The manual lists the _____ of each disorder, as well as other available information. Although a valuable resource, it has several _____. First, there is a danger of _____ since the DSM may encourage the overuse of diagnostic categories. Second, there is the problem of diagnostic _____. Third, there is the problem of confusing serious mental disorders with _____ problems. The last limitation is that the DSM manual gives the illusion of _____ when diagnosis remains very subjective. Advantages of the DSM include the inclusion of _____-_____ _____ for symptoms that are specific to the culture in which they occur.

1-3. One type of test used in the assessment of mental disorder, a _____ test, is designed to reveal _____ motives, feelings, and conflicts. These tests involve the interpretation of _____ stimuli. They lack _____ and _____, meaning that they fail to measure what they claim to measure. One of the most popular projective tests consists of symmetrical abstract patterns and is called the _____ _____ test. The most widely used _____ test for assessing mental disorders is the _____ _____ _____ _____ (MMPI). Objective tests or _____ are standardized objective _____ requiring written responses and usually include _____ on which people are

198

asked to _____ themselves.

Terms for Review

The following is a list of the important terms from the section "Defining and Diagnosing Mental Disorders." Make sure you are familiar with each term before taking the progress test on these terms.

insanity
harmful dysfunction
mental disorder
Diagnostic and Statistical Manual of Mental Disorders
culture-bound syndromes
projective tests
objective tests
Minnesota Multiphasic Personality Inventory

2. Anxiety Disorders

Read the section "Anxiety Disorders" and then answer the following questions. If you have trouble answering any of the questions, re-study the relevant material before going on to the review of key terms and the progress tests.

2-1. When fear and anxiety are present without any apparent danger, the individual may be suffering from an _____ disorder. When anxiety is continuous and _____, an individual may be experiencing _____ anxiety disorder. This constant feeling of foreboding and dread must occur on the majority of days for _____ months or longer and cannot be brought on by _____ causes. People who have lived through particularly harrowing experiences may suffer from

_____ _____

_____ (PTSD) and symptoms often include the presence of recurrent, intrusive _____, a sense of

_____, and increase physiological _____. In addition to having experienced a traumatic event, cognitive and _____ functioning appears to be implicated in people's tendency to develop PTSD. Another kind of anxiety disorder is _____ disorder and is characterized by recurring attacks of intense fear or panic, often with feelings of impending _____ or death. The physiological symptoms of this disorder make many sufferers feel like they are having a _____

_____.

2-2. An exaggerated and unrealistic fear of a specific situation, activity, or thing is a _____. One type of phobia, a _____ phobia, deals with situations in which individuals fear that others will observe them. The most disabling fear disorder is _____, which involves the basic fear of being away from a _____ place or person. It is often set off by a _____ attack.

2-3. Recurrent, persistent thoughts called _____ and repetitive, ritualized behaviors called _____ are the defining characteristics of

_____-_____ disorder (OCD.) People often find the obsessions frightening or _____. The most common compulsions are

_____ _____,
counting, touching, and _____.

Terms for Review

The following is a list of the important terms from the section "Anxiety Disorders." Make sure you are familiar with each term before taking the progress test on these terms.

anxiety disorders
generalized anxiety disorder
posttraumatic stress disorder
panic disorder
phobia
social phobia
agoraphobia
obsessive-compulsive disorder

3. Mood Disorders

Read the section "Mood Disorders" and then answer the following questions. If you have trouble answering any of the questions, re-study the relevant material before going on to the review of key terms and the progress tests.

3-1. In the DSM, _____ disorders involve disturbances in emotion ranging from extreme depression to extreme _____. People who experience emotional, behavioral, and _____ changes _____ enough to disrupt their usual lives suffer from _____ depression. Some symptoms include despair and _____, loss of satisfaction or _____ in usual activities, and loss of energy. This disorder afflicts at least _____ as many women as men, but it probably is _____ in men.

3-2. At the opposite pole from depression is _____, an abnormally high state of _____. People in this state often get into _____, making impulsive and rash decisions. When people experience at least one episode of _____ alternating with episodes of _____, they suffer from _____ disorder, formerly called _____-_____ disorder.

3-3. Many researchers emphasize a _____-_____ _____ to explain depression in which a person's vulnerabilities interact with stressful events. There are several contributing factors to depression, including _____ predispositions; violence, childhood physical _____, and parental _____; losses of important _____; and _____ habits. This last factor is reflected by the fact that many depressed individuals tend to _____, brooding about everything that is wrong in their lives and persuading themselves that no one cares about them.

Terms for Review

The following is a list of the important terms from the section "Mood Disorders." Make sure you are familiar with each term before taking the progress test on these terms.

mood disorders   bipolar disorder
major depression   vulnerability-stress model

4. Antisocial/Psychopathic Personality Disorder

Read the section "Antisocial/Psychopathic Personality Disorder" and then answer the following questions. If you have trouble answering any of the questions, re-study the relevant material before going on to the review of key terms and the progress tests.

4-1. Rigid personality patterns that cause great _____ or an inability to get along with others characterize _____ disorders. _____ personality disorder involves a history of intense but unstable _____ in which they alternate between idealizing the partner and devaluing the partner. A personality disorder that is characterized by a lack of remorse despite use deceit and manipulation is known as _____. When this behavior occurs over a person's lifetime, the DSM labels such individuals with _____ _____ _____ (APD). Possible causes for APD include, (1) abnormalities in the _____ _____ system, (2) impaired _____ _____ functioning, (3) _____ influences, and _____ events.

Terms for Review

The following is a list of the important terms from the section "Antisocial/Psychopathic Personality Disorder." Make sure you are familiar with each term before taking the progress test on these terms.

personality disorders
borderline personality disorder
psychopathy
antisocial personality disorder

5. Drug Abuse and Addiction

Read the section "Drug Abuse and Addiction" and then answer the following questions. If you have trouble answering any of the questions, re-study the relevant material before going on to the review of key terms and the progress tests.

5-1. According to the DSM, substance abuse is "a _____ pattern of substance use leading to clinically significant _____ or distress." The _____ model of drug addiction asserts that the primary causes of addiction are the person's _____ and _____ predisposition. It is usual for people to assume that biological factors cause addiction. However, it is also possible that _____ can results from the _____ of _____. For example, a person's abuse of drugs may cause changes in the _____.

5-2. Contrary to the biological model, the _____ model of drug addiction examines the roles that the environment, learning, and _____ play in drug abuse and addiction. Four findings are relevant to the consideration of these factors. First, addiction rates vary according to _____ practices. When children are taught to drink responsibly and moderately, there is a far lower rate of _____. Secondly,

201

policies of total _____ tend to _____ rates of addiction rather than _____ them. Thirdly, not all addicts have _____ symptoms when they stop taking a drug. Lastly, _____ does not depend on the aspects of the drug alone, but also on the _____ for taking it.

5-3. Although they are both helpful, the views of the biological and _____ models of drug addiction are quite _____. For example, proponents of the _____ model believe that once an individual is an alcoholic, he or she is _____ an alcoholic. Proponents of the _____ model, however, state that some problem drinkers can learn to drink _____.

6-1. _____ identity disorder, formerly called _____ _____ disorder (MPD), is a controversial disorder marked by the appearance within one person of two or more distinct _____, each with its own _____, memories, and traits. One explanation for this disorder is that it originates in _____ as a means of coping with _____ events. Many people, however, are _____ about MPD and feel that clinicians may actually be _____ the disorder in their clients through the power of _____. An alternative explanation of MPD is provided by the _____ explanation. This view states that MPD is an _____ form of the ability all people have to present different aspects of their _____ to others.

Terms for Review

The following is a list of the important terms from the section "Drug Abuse and Addiction." Make sure you are familiar with each term before taking the progress test on these terms.

substance abuse
biological model
learning model

6. Dissociative Identity Disorder

Read the section "Dissociative Identity Disorder" and then answer the following questions. If you have trouble answering any of the questions, re-study the relevant material before going on to the review of key terms and the progress tests.

Terms for Review

The following is a list of the important terms from the section "Dissociative Identity Disorder." Make sure you are familiar with each term before taking the progress test on these terms.

dissociative identity disorder
sociocognitive explanation

7. Schizophrenia

Read the section "Schizophrenia" and then answer the following questions. If you have trouble answering any of the questions, re-study the relevant material before going on to the review of key terms and the progress tests.

7-1. Schizophrenia is a type of _____, an extreme mental condition that involves distorted perceptions of _____ and an inability to function in most aspects of life. People with schizophrenia do not have a _____ or _____ personality. The most common positive symptoms include (1) bizarre _____, (2) _____, (3) disorganized, incoherent _____ that consists of a jumble of ideas and symbols linked in a meaningless way called word _____, (4) grossly _____ and inappropriate _____, and _____ cognitive abilities. Some schizophrenics completely withdraw into a private world and are immobile for hours in a condition called a _____ stupor.

7-2. The brains of individuals diagnosed with schizophrenia often show reduced volumes of gray matter in the _____ cortex and _____ lobes, as well as disrupted _____ between neurons. Most individuals with schizophrenia also show enlargement of the _____, which are spaces in the brain filled with _____ fluid. Researchers have identified three contributing factors to schizophrenia, including _____ predispositions, _____ problems or birth complications, and biological events during _____.

Terms for Review

The following is a list of the important terms from the section "Schizophrenia." Make sure you are familiar with each term before taking the progress test on these terms.

schizophrenia
psychosis

SAMPLE ANSWERS TO *YOU ARE ABOUT TO LEARN* QUESTIONS FROM TEXTBOOK

After you have read through the chapter, go back and review the "You Are About to Learn..." statements that precede each major section. Create your own answer to each question, then compare your answers to the following sample answers. If your answers are not similar to the sample answers, review the relevant sections of the chapter more carefully.

Why is insanity not the same thing as having a mental disorder?

Insanity is a legal term that means that a person is unaware of the consequences of his or her actions or was unable to control his or her behavior. One could be diagnosed with a mental disorder and yet not be considered insane.

How do mental disorders differ from normal problems?

Unlike normal problems, mental disorders involve behavior or an emotional state that is harmful to oneself or others and is dysfunctional because it is not performing its evolutionary function.

Why is the standard professional guide to the diagnosis of mental disorders so controversial?

It is controversial because it has extraordinary impact worldwide, but it has limitations. These limitations include the danger of overdiagnosis, the power of diagnostic labels to influence the perceptions of clinicians and the behavior of clients, the possible confusion of serious mental disorders with normal problems, and the illusion of objectivity and universality.

How reliable are projective tests like the popular Rorschach Inkblot Test?

Projective tests such as the Rorschach Inkblot Test have both low reliability and low validity when they are used for assessment or diagnosis. In brief, such tests give inconsistent results and fail to measure what they claim to measure. Thus, some recommend that they should not be used to diagnose mental illnesses.

What is the difference between ordinary anxiety and an anxiety disorder?

Ordinary anxiety is attached to some dangerous, unfamiliar, or stressful situation. It is adaptive because it energizes and motivates people to cope with the situation. In individuals who may be suffering from an anxiety disorder, however, anxiety is detached from any apparent danger, or it doesn't dissipate when the danger has passed.

Why is the most disabling of all phobias known as the "fear of fear"?

The fundamental fear in agoraphobia is of being away from a safe place or person and being trapped in a crowded public place, where escape might be difficult or where help might be unavailable if the person has a panic attack. Agoraphobia usually begins with a panic attack that has no relation with previous events. The attack is so frightening that the person begins to avoid situations that he or she thinks may provoke another panic attack. Because many of the actions associated with this phobia arise as a mistaken effort to avoid a panic attack, it is sometimes known as the "fear of fear."

Why do some people recover quickly after a trauma whereas others develop posttraumatic stress disorder?

One theory is that certain people have a genetic predisposition to develop this disorder. This vulnerability to the disorder does not manifest itself until the person is exposed to a severe trauma. Other people who do not have this predisposition recover more readily from the traumatic experience.

How can you tell whether you have major depression or just the blues?

Major depression involves emotional, behavioral, and cognitive changes severe enough to disrupt a person's usual functioning. Emotionally healthy people who are sad or grieving do not see themselves as completely worthless and unlovable, and they know at some level that their sadness or grief will pass. But depressed people have low self-esteem and interpret losses as signs of personal failure and conclude that they will never be happy again.

What are the four contributing factors in depression?

The contributing factors of depression are a genetic predisposition, abuse and neglect, losses of important relationships, and cognitive habits.

How do some people think themselves into depression?

Some people may have a pessimistic explanatory style, which leads to depression. They believe that nothing good will ever happen to them, that the future is bleak, and that they cannot do anything to change it. It also is possible that such people have a ruminating response style. A person with this response style tends to brood endlessly about her or his negative feelings.

What do a charming, but heartless tycoon and a remorseless killer have in common?

They both may have antisocial personality disorder. People with this disorder are without conscience and have no regard for the rights of others. They lack empathy and the ability to feel remorse or sorrow for immoral actions, which include lying, stealing, manipulating others, and sometimes violence.

Why are some people seemingly incapable of feeling guilt and shame?

The inability of some people to feel guilt and shame suggests an abnormality in the central nervous system. Some researchers believe these people share a genetic predisposition, which involves a lack of impulse control. Other possible causes include parental rejection or neglect, being physically abused in childhood, and living in a subculture that rewards and fosters ruthlessness.

In what ways might genes contribute to alcoholism?

Genes could contribute to a type of alcoholism by contributing to traits or temperaments that predispose a person to become alcoholic. Or they may affect biochemical processes in the brain and make some people more susceptible to alcohol or cause them to respond to it differently than others do.

Why is alcoholism more common in some cultures than others?

Alcoholism is much more likely to occur in societies that forbid children to drink but condone drunkenness in adults (as in Ireland) than in societies that teach children how to drink responsibly and moderately but condemn adult drunkenness (as in Italy).

Why don't policies of abstinence from alcohol reduce problem drinking?

According to the learning model of addiction, because people are denied the opportunity to learn to drink moderately, they drink excessively when given the chance to drink. And, when a substance is forbidden, it becomes more attractive to some people.

Why are narcotics usually not addictive when people take them for pain?

Addiction does not depend on the drug alone, but also on the reasons for taking it. Addicts use drugs to escape from the real world, but people living with chronic pain use some of the same drugs, including morphine, in order to function in the real world and do not become addicted.

Why are many clinicians and researchers skeptical about multiple personality disorder?

Skeptics worry that some clinicians may actually be creating the disorder in their clients through the power of suggestion and unreliable techniques like hypnosis. This does not mean that no legitimate cases exist, but great caution is warranted because of the epidemic of cases reported in the last two decades and because so many of those cases have turned out to be a result of therapists' suggestions.

Why did the number of "multiple personality disorder" cases jump from a handful to many thousands in only a decade?

Therapists who are looking for MPD reward such patients with attention and praise for revealing multiple personalities. Thus, therapists are creating the disorder in their clients through the power of suggestion and sometimes, outright intimidation.

What's the difference between schizophrenia and a "split personality"?

People with schizophrenia do not have a "split" or "multiple" personality. Schizophrenia is a fragmented condition in which words are split from meaning, actions from motives, and perceptions from reality. It is an example of a psychosis, which is a mental condition that involves distorted perceptions of reality and an inability to function in most aspects of life. "Split" or "multiple" personality, now called dissociative identity disorder, is a dissociative disorder and not a psychosis.

What are the five key signs of schizophrenia?

The signs of schizophrenia include bizarre delusions, hallucinations, disorganized and incoherent speech, disorganized and inappropriate behavior, and impaired cognitive abilities.

Is schizophrenia partly heritable?

There is evidence based on twin and adoption studies that schizophrenia is partly heritable. For example, a person has a much greater risk of developing schizophrenia if an identical twin develops the disorder, even if the twins are reared apart. Children with one schizophrenic parent have a lifetime risk of 12 percent, and children with two schizophrenic parents have a lifetime risk of 25-46 percent, compared to a risk in the general population of only 1-2 percent.

Could schizophrenia begin in the womb?

Evidence exists that damage to the fetal brain increases the likelihood of schizophrenia. This can occur if the pregnant woman suffers from malnutrition, or if she contracts an infectious virus during pregnancy. Thus, schizophrenia could begin in the womb.

KEY TERMS FILL-IN-THE-BLANKS PROGRESS TEST

Fill in the blanks with the key terms from the chapter that match the definitions provided. When you have finished this progress test, check your answers with those at the end of this chapter. You should review any key terms that you do not define correctly.

1. _____ Standardized objective questionnaires requiring written responses; they typically include scales on which people are asked to rate themselves.

2. _____ Psychological tests used to infer a person's motives, conflicts, and unconscious dynamics on the basis of the person's interpretations of ambiguous stimuli.

3. _____ Any behavior or emotional state that causes a person great suffering, is self-destructive, seriously impairs the person's ability to work or get along with others, or endangers others or the community.

4. _____ An anxiety disorder in which a person who has experienced a traumatic or life-threatening event has symptoms such as psychic numbing, reliving of the trauma, and increased physiological arousal.

5. _____ An exaggerated, unrealistic fear of a specific situation, activity, or object.

6. _____ A disabling fear of being trapped in a crowded public place and of being away from a safe place or person.

7. _____ An anxiety disorder in which a person feels trapped in repetitive, persistent thoughts and repetitive, ritualized behaviors designed to reduce anxiety.

8. _____ An anxiety disorder in which a person experiences recurring panic attacks, periods of intense fear, and feelings of impending doom or death, accompanied by physiological symptoms such as rapid heart rate and dizziness.

9. _____ A continuous state of anxiety marked by feelings of worry and dread, apprehension, difficulties in concentration, and signs of motor tension.

10. _____ Approaches that emphasize how individual vulnerabilities interact with external stresses or circumstances to produce mental disorders.

11. _____ A mood disorder in which episodes of both depression and mania (excessive euphoria) occur.

12. _____ A mood disorder involving disturbances in emotion, behavior, cognition, and body function.

13. _____ A disorder characterized by intense but unstable relationships, impulsiveness, self-mutilating behavior, feelings of emptiness, and a fear of abandonment by others.

14. _____ A disorder characterized by antisocial behavior such as lying, stealing, manipulating others, and sometimes violence; and a lack of guilt, shame, and empathy.

15. _____ A maladaptive pattern of substance use leading to clinically significant impairment or distress.

16. _____ A model that examines the role of the environment, learning, and culture in encouraging or discouraging drug abuse and addiction.

17. _____ A controversial disorder marked by the apparent appearance within one person of two or more distinct personalities, each with its own name and traits.

18. _____ An extreme mental disturbance involving distorted perceptions and irrational behavior.

19. _____ A condition in which the schizophrenic completely withdraws into a private world, sitting for hours without moving.

MULTIPLE-CHOICE PROGRESS TEST

Choose the single best answer for each of the following questions. When you have finished this progress test, check your answers with those at the end of this chapter. You should review the relevant pages in the text for the questions you do not answer correctly.

1. Which of the following is a criterion used by mental health professionals when defining mental disorder?
   a. Impairment of ability to work
   b. Self-destructive behavior
   c. Personal suffering
   d. All the above are criteria.

2. Which of the following statements about projective tests is TRUE?
   a. Projective tests have high reliability.
   b. Projective tests have high validity.
   c. Projective tests use ambiguous stimuli.
   d. None of the above is true.

3. Which of the following is a criticism of the DSM-IV?
   a. The danger of overdiagnosis
   b. The power of diagnostic labels
   c. The illusion of objectivity
   d. All the above are criticisms.

4. A _____ is an anxiety disorder in which a person experiences an exaggerated fear of a specific situation, activity, or object.
   a. generalized anxiety disorder
   b. posttraumatic stress disorder
   c. panic disorder
   d. phobia

5. Which part of the brain appears to be implicated in the development of posttraumatic stress disorder?
   a. The medulla
   b. The hypothalamus
   c. The hippocampus
   d. The amygdala

6. Repetitive thoughts of becoming contaminated by shaking hands constitutes a(n) _____, and repetitive hand washing is a(n) _____.
   a. obsession; obsession
   b. obsession; compulsion
   c. compulsion; obsession
   d. compulsion; compulsion

7. When people experience episodes of both depression and mania, they are said to have _____ disorder.
   a. obsessive-compulsive
   b. bipolar
   c. antisocial personality
   d. dissociative identity

8. Which of the following statements about depression is FALSE?
   a. Almost everywhere in the world, women are more likely to be diagnosed with depression.
   b. Typically, depressed people believe that their situation is dynamic and controllable.
   c. The more children they have, the more likely mothers are to become depressed.
   d. None of the above is false.

9. A _____ personality disorder is characterized by intense but unstable relationships.
   a. paranoid
   b. borderline
   c. antisocial
   d. dissociative

10. Which of the following statements about antisocial personality disorder is FALSE?
    a.   Antisocial personality disorder typically involves rule breaking at an early age.
    b.   Individuals with antisocial personality disorder do not respond to punishments that would make most people anxious.
    c.   Individuals with antisocial personality disorder lack empathy and have no regard for the rights of others.
    d.   None of the above is false.

11. Approaches that emphasize how individual vulnerabilities interact with external stresses or circumstances to produce mental disorders are called _____ models.
    a.   biological vulnerability
    b.   vulnerability-learning
    c.   vulnerability-stress
    d.   predisposition-stress

12. The more popular term for dissociative identity disorder is _____ disorder.
    a.   obsessive-compulsive
    b.   manic-depressive
    c.   multiple personality
    d.   antisocial personality

13. Which of the following is NOT an assumption of the biological model of addiction?
    a.   Addiction is a way of coping with stress.
    b.   Once an addict, always an addict.
    c.   A person is either addicted or not.
    d.   An addict must abstain forever.

14. Which of the following statements is FALSE?
    a.   Addiction patterns vary according to cultural practices and the social environment.
    b.   Policies of total abstinence tend to decrease rates of addiction rather than increase them.
    c.   Not all addicts have withdrawal symptoms when they stop taking a drug.
    d.   Addiction does not depend on the drug alone, but also on the reasons for taking it.

15. Going out on a date, eating in a restaurant, and speaking in front of a group of people probably would be the most difficult for someone with:
    a.   social phobia.
    b.   depression.
    c.   bipolar disorder.
    d.   generalized anxiety disorder.

16. _____ is a psychosis in which words are split from meaning, actions from motives, and perceptions from reality.
    a.   Dissociative identity disorder
    b.   Schizophrenia
    c.   Fugue state
    d.   Paranoid personality disorder

17. Active symptoms of schizophrenia involve an _____ of normal thinking processes; passive symptoms involve the _____ of normal traits and abilities.
    a.   exaggeration; exaggeration
    b.   exaggeration; absence
    c.   absence; exaggeration
    d.   absence; absence

18. The false belief of an individual with schizophrenia that he is Jesus or some other famous person is a (an) _____.
    a.   delusion
    b.   hallucination
    c.   compulsion
    d.   obsession

19. Which of the following is a negative
    symptom of schizophrenia?
    a. disorganized speech
    b. emotional flatness
    c. bizarre delusion
    d. hallucination

20. Which of the following statements about
    schizophrenia is FALSE?
    a. Neurotransmitter abnormalities are
       associated with schizophrenia.
    b. Nearly 90 percent of all persons with
       schizophrenia have a schizophrenic
       parent.
    c. There is a relationship between fetal
       brain damage and the onset of adult
       schizophrenia.
    d. None of the above is false.

Guided Study

1. Defining and Diagnosing Mental Disorders

1-1. mental
insane
harmful
dysfunction
evolutionary
suffer
self-destructive
work
endangers
community

1-2. Diagnostic
Statistical
Manual
Mental
symptoms
limitations
overdiagnosis
labels
normal
objectivity
culture-bound
syndromes

1-3. projective
unconscious
ambiguous
reliability
validity
Rorschach Inkblot
objective
Minnesota
Multiphasic
Personality
Inventory
inventories
questionnaires
scales
rate

2. Anxiety Disorders

2-1. anxiety
uncontrollable
generalized
six
physical
posttraumatic
stress
disorder
thoughts
detachment
arousal
neurological
panic
doom
heart attack

2-2. phobia
social
agoraphobia
safe
panic

2-3. obsessions
compulsions
obsessive-compulsive
repugnant
hand washing
checking

3. Mood Disorders

3-1. mood
mania
cognitive
severe
major
worthless
pleasure
twice
underdiagnosed

3-2. mania
exhilaration
trouble
mania
depression
bipolar
manic-depressive

3-3. vulnerability-stress model
genetic
abuse
neglect
relationships
cognitive
ruminate

4. Antisocial/Psychopathic Personality Disorder

4-1. distress
personality
Borderline
relationships
psychopathy

4-2. antisocial personality disorder
central nervous
frontal lobe
genetic
environmental

5. Drug Abuse and Addiction

5-1. maladaptive
impairment
biological
neurology
genetic
addictions
abuse
drugs
brains

5-2. learning
culture
cultural
alcoholism
abstinence
increase
decrease
withdrawal
addiction
reasons

5-3. learning
polarized
biological
always
learning
moderately

6. Dissociative Identity Disorder

6-1. Dissociative
multiple personality
personalities
name
childhood
traumatic
skeptical
creating
suggestion
sociocognitive
extreme
personalities

7. Schizophrenia

7-1. psychosis
   reality
   split
   multiple
   thinking
   delusions
   hallucinations
   speech
   salads
   disorganized
   behavior
   impaired
   catatonic

7-2. prefrontal
   temporal
   communication
   ventricles
   cerebrospinal
   genetic
   prenatal
   adolescence

Answers to Key Terms Progress Test

1. inventories
2. projective tests
3. mental disorder
4. posttraumatic stress disorder
5. phobia
6. agoraphobia
7. obsessive-compulsive disorder
8. panic disorder
9. generalized anxiety disorder
10. vulnerability-stress models
11. bipolar disorder
12. major depression
13. borderline personality disorder
14. antisocial personality disorder
15. substance abuse
16. learning model of addiction
17. dissociative identity disorder
18. psychosis
19. catatonic stupor

Item Number	Answers
1.	d. All the above are criteria.
2.	c. Projective tests use ambiguous stimuli
3.	d. All the above are criticisms.
4.	d. phobia
5.	c. the hippocampus
6.	b. obsession; compulsion
7.	b. bipolar
8.	b. Typically, depressed people believe that their situation is dynamic and controllable.
9.	b. borderline
10.	d. None of the above is false.
11.	c. vulnerability-stress
12.	c. multiple personality
13.	a. Addiction is a way of coping with stress.
14.	b. Policies of total abstinence tend to decrease rates of addiction rather than increase them.
15.	a. social phobia
16.	b. Schizophrenia
17.	b. exaggeration; absence
18.	a. delusion
19.	b. emotional flatness
20.	b. Nearly 90 percent of all persons with schizophrenia have a schizophrenic parent.

CHAPTER 12

Approaches to Treatment and Therapy

CHAPTER OVERVIEW

The chapter opens with a discussion of biological treatments. This includes various drug therapies such as antipsychotic drugs, antidepressant drugs, tranquilizers (which may be prescribed for anxiety disorders), and lithium carbonate (which is used for treating bipolar disorder). Limitations of drug treatments, such as the placebo effect, high dropout and relapse rates, disregard of effective non-medical treatments, dosage problems, unknown long-term risks, and untested off-label uses also are presented. Other biological treatments covered include prefrontal lobotomies, electroconvulsive therapy, transcranial magnetic stimulation, and deep brain stimulation.

The major schools of psychotherapy are explored next. First, psychodynamic therapies, such as Freud's psychoanalysis are described. Key aspects of psychoanalysis such as transference are identified and defined. An examination of behavioral and cognitive therapies including systematic desensitization, graduated exposure, flooding, behavioral self-monitoring, skills training, and rational emotive behavior therapy follows. Mindfulness and acceptance therapies, which focus on identification and acceptance of unwanted thoughts without attempts to control them, are mentioned next. Another major approach to psychotherapy that is mentioned is humanist and existential therapy, including client-centered therapy. Finally, the key components of family therapy and couples therapy are considered.

In order to evaluate psychotherapy, the therapeutic alliance and scientist-practitioner gap are discussed, as are results from controlled clinical trials on the effectiveness of psychotherapies. The various components of successful psychotherapy are presented, including a discussion of the therapeutic alliance. The chapter concludes with a look at when therapy helps and when therapy is harmful.

GUIDED STUDY

1. Biological Treatments for Mental Disorders

Read the section "Biological Treatments for Mental Disorders" and then answer the following questions. If you have trouble answering any of the questions, re-study the relevant material before going on to the review of key terms and the progress tests.

1-1. The most popular biological treatment for psychological disorders is

_____. _____ drugs, or neuroleptics, are used primarily in the treatment of _____ and other psychoses. These drugs block or reduce the sensitivity of brain receptors that respond to the neurotransmitter _____.

Some also increase levels of

_____. _____ drugs are used in the treatment of depression, anxiety, phobias, and obsessive-compulsive disorder. _____

_____ inhibitors elevate the level of norepinephrine and

_____. _____ antidepressants boost norepinephrine and serotonin by preventing reuptake of these substances. Drugs such as Prozac work on a similar principle, but only on the neurotransmitter, _____, and hence are called selective serotonin _____ inhibitors (SSRIs).

Drugs such as Valium and Xanax are _____ that increase the activity of the neurotransmitter gamma-aminobutyric acid (_____).

These drugs may assist people with

_____ disorder and those experiencing an acute _____ attack. A salt, _____ carbonate, is used to treat _____ disorder. Despite their popularity, there are several limitations with drug treatments. First, the _____ effect may be operating. That is, some will respond positively to new drugs because of their _____ or hopes rather than to the treatment itself. For example, some researchers believe that most of the effectiveness of _____ is due to this effect.

Second, there are high _____ and _____ rates associated with drug treatments. Third, the focus on drugs has often led to a _____ for effective, possibly better _____ treatments. Fourth, there is often a problem in determining the correct _____, due to the challenge of finding the _____ window.

And, drugs may be _____ differently in men versus women, the old versus the young, and different _____ groups. Fifth, the unknown _____ of taking these medications over time are not all known. Lastly, doctors often prescribe drugs for uses other than which it was originally tested, which is known as untested _____-_____ uses.

1-2. In the early 1900s, an early attempt to directly cure mental illness via the brain entailed destroying nerve fibers running from the prefrontal lobes to other brain areas, and was named _____ _____. Another controversial procedure is _____ therapy (ECT), which is used for the treatment of severe _____. It has been effective for people with crippling depression and _____ impulses who haven't responded to other treatments. However, the effect is _____-_____. A more recent and milder form of electrically stimulating the brains of severely depressed people is _____ _____ stimulation.

Terms for Review

The following is a list of the important terms from the section "Biological Treatments for Mental Disorders." Make sure you are familiar with each term before taking the progress test on these terms.

antipsychotic drugs
antidepressant drugs
monoamine oxidase inhibitors
tricyclic antidepressants
selective serotonin reuptake inhibitors
antianxiety drugs
lithium carbonate
placebo effect
prefrontal lobotomy
electroconvulsive therapy
transcranial magnetic stimulation

2. Major Schools of Psychotherapy

Read the section "Major Schools of Psychotherapy" and then answer the following questions. If you have trouble answering any of the questions, re-study the relevant material before going on to the review of key terms and the progress tests.

2-1. Sigmund Freud founded _____ in which patients gain _____ into the _____ reasons for their symptoms and unhappiness through talking. Clients who transfer _____ emotions or reactions, such as feelings about their _____, onto the therapist are said to be engaging in _____.

2-2. Behavioral and cognitive therapies focus on helping individuals to change their _____ and _____. Behavior therapy applies principles and techniques of classical and _____ conditioning to aid people to change their problematic behaviors. In _____ _____, clients are exposed to a fearful stimulus, but the amount of that exposure is controlled by the therapist and gradually increased. The most dramatic version of this is _____, in which clients are directly exposed to the maximum intensity of the fearful situation and remain there until the panic and anxiety decline. When this fearful exposure is combined with practicing the incompatible response of relaxation, it is called _____ _____, which is based on the classical conditioning procedure of _____. Another behavioral technique is behavioral _____-_____ where the person keeps track of the

_____ that are supporting their

problematic behaviors or situations. And,

behavioral therapists might engage in

_____ training, which involves

_____ and role-playing, to teach

clients abilities that they may not possess.

Cognitive techniques attempt to help

people identify the beliefs and

_____ that might be prolonging

their problems and teaches them to think

critically. A well-known contemporary

type of cognitive therapy is Ellis'

_____ _____

behavior therapy. In this therapy,

therapists directly challenge a client's

tendency to _____ and

catastrophize. Clients are forced to face

their unrealistic and irrational

_____.

2-3. Some therapists argue it is too difficult, if

not impossible, to get rid of unwanted

thoughts and feelings. Instead, they propose

_____ and _____, in

which the clients learn to explicitly

_____ and accept whatever

negative thoughts and feelings arise,

without trying to _____ them or

let them derail healthy behavior.

2-4. _____ therapies are based on the

assumption that human nature is basically

_____. Carl Rogers developed a

nondirective or _____ -

_____ therapy that utilized

_____ _____ regard

in an attempt to build the client's

_____-_____ and

sense of acceptance. According to Rogers,

it is critical that therapists feel

_____ toward their clients.

Existential therapists help clients explore

the meaning of _____ and

encourage them to take _____

for their situation in life.

2-5. Family therapists believe that their clients'

problems develop and are sustained in the

context of their _____. Family

members usually do not realize how they

_____ each other. Even when

the entire family is not treated, many

therapists treat individuals in a

_____-_____

perspective, which examines how each

family member forms part of a larger,

interacting system. A version of family

therapy is _____ therapy, which

is designed to manage conflicts that occur

in all relationships.

2-6. Many psychotherapists adopt an

_____ approach. They draw on

methods and ideas from various theories,

which allows them to be more

_____ in their treatment of their

clients. A key element of successful

therapy is that the therapist is able to

_____ the client into wanting to

_____.

221

Terms for Review

The following is a list of the important terms from the section "Major Schools of Psychotherapy." Make sure you are familiar with each term before taking the progress test on these terms.

psychoanalysis	cognitive therapy
psychodynamic therapy	rational emotive behavior
transference	therapy
behavior therapy	humanist therapy
graduated exposure	client-centered therapy
flooding	existential therapy
systematic desensitization	family-systems perspective
counterconditioning	integrative approach

3. Evaluating Psychotherapy

Read the section "Evaluating Psychotherapy" and then answer the following questions. If you have trouble answering any of the questions, re-study the relevant material before going on to the review of key terms and the progress tests.

3-1. Successful psychotherapy depends heavily upon a strong relationship between the therapist and client, termed the

_____ _____. For example, improvement is more likely when there is mutual _____ and agreement on the _____ of the therapy. Clients who do well in therapy are motivated to _____. It also is important that therapists distinguish normal _____ patterns from individual psychological problems. However, being aware of cultural differences should not lead to _____ clients.

3-2. The _____-_____ gap refers to the breach between scientists and therapists in psychology. The split between these two areas has been growing due to the increase in the number of

_____ schools that train their students only to do therapy. Also, the gap has widened because of the influx of _____ therapies in a crowded market. Many of the positive testimonials regarding the effectiveness of therapy may be a result of the _____ _____. Also, these testimonials may be due to the _____ of _____ effect, people who have put time, money, and effort into something will say that it was worth it. In an effort to circumvent these problems, clinical psychologists conduct _____ controlled trials, in which people with a specific disorder are randomly _____ to one or more treatment groups or to a _____ group.

3-3. Based on this research, it was found that for many problems and most emotional disorders, _____ and _____ therapies are the methods of choice. In fact, cognitive therapy's greatest success has been in the treatment of _____. Behavior and cognitive therapies also are particularly effective for _____ attempts, _____ disorders, _____ and impulsive violence, health problems, _____ and adolescent _____ problems, and reducing _____ in substance abuse.

3-4. Therapy can be harmful under the following conditions: 1) the therapist engages in _____ intimacies or other unethical behavior with the client; 2) the therapist is _____ or culturally ignorant; 3) the therapist uses inappropriate or coercive _____ on the client; 4) the therapist uses techniques that are not empirically supported and are potentially _____. Due to these potential risks, people in search of good, effective psychotherapy must become _____ consumers.

Terms for Review

The following is a list of the important terms from the section "Evaluating Psychotherapy." Make sure you are familiar with each term before taking the progress test on these terms.

therapeutic alliance
scientist-practitioner gap
randomized controlled trials

SAMPLE ANSWERS TO *YOU ARE ABOUT TO LEARN* QUESTIONS FROM TEXTBOOK

After you have read through the chapter, go back and review the "You Are About to Learn..." statements that precede each major section. Create your own answer to each question, then compare your answers to the following sample answers. If your answers are not similar to the sample answers, review the relevant sections of the chapter more carefully.

What kinds of drugs are used to treat psychological disorders?

The main classes of drugs employed to treat disorders are antipsychotic drugs used in the treatment of schizophrenia and other psychoses, antidepressant drugs used primarily in the treatment of depression, anxiety, phobias, and obsessive-compulsive disorder, tranquilizers for mild anxiety and panic disorder, and lithium carbonate for bipolar disorder.

What are important cautions about medications for emotional problems?

Drugs are often associated with improvements, but many times the improvement is due to a placebo effect rather than the drug itself. Drug treatments have very high relapse and dropout rates. The popularity of drugs has led to a neglect of nonmedical treatments, which are often effective and possibly better in many cases. Finding the appropriate dosage of a drug is very challenging and the risks associated with long-term drug use are frequently unknown, especially with untested combinations of drugs. Finally, even though drugs undergoes testing, in practice they are often prescribed for problems they were not originally tested, known as off-label prescriptions.

What are ways of electrically stimulating the brain and do they work?

Electroconvulsive therapy (ECT) has been effective with people who are suicidal and have not responded to medication or other treatments. Supporters of ECT cite research showing that when ECT is used properly, it is safe and effective and causes no long-term cognitive impairment, memory loss, or detectable brain damage. Critics reply that ECT often is used improperly and that it can indeed damage the brain. However, both sides agree that relapse rates are high with this treatment. Other techniques include transcranial magnetic stimulation and deep brain stimulation, both of which are lacking controlled studies at this time.

What are the major approaches to psychotherapy?

One major approach is psychoanalysis, which is based on Freud's beliefs in unconscious conflicts originating in childhood. Behavior therapy is the application of classical and operant conditioning principles to reduce undesirable behaviors and promote adaptive behaviors. Cognitive therapies focus on challenging unproductive thoughts and mental states. Mindfulness and acceptance therapies teach that people should identify and accept their negative thoughts and emotions, but not make attempts to eliminate such thoughts and emotions or allow them to interfere with functioning. Humanist therapy assumes that people are essentially good and just need non-judgmental support. Existential therapy explores the meaning of existence. Family and couples therapy attempts to cure disorders by correcting dysfunctional social interactions within families and couples.

How can behavior therapists help you change your bad habits?

Behavior therapies are based on the principles of classical and operant conditioning. A behavior therapist would strive to identify the reinforcers that are maintaining and supporting one's bad habits. One way to do this is to keep a record of the behaviors that one wishes to change. Once the unwanted habits and their corresponding reinforcers have been identified, a treatment program can be designed to change them.

How do cognitive therapists help people get rid of self-defeating thoughts?

Cognitive therapists help their clients get rid of self-defeating thoughts by having them identify their assumptions and biases, examine the evidence for their beliefs, consider other interpretations, and think critically. And, one type of cognitive therapy, rational emotive behavior therapy, uses rational arguments to challenge clients' unrealistic and irrational thoughts.

Why do humanist therapists focus on the "here and now" instead of the "why and how"?

Unlike psychodynamic therapies, humanist therapies generally do not delve into past conflicts, but aim instead to help people feel better about themselves and free themselves from self-imposed limits. Humanist therapists want to know how clients subjectively perceive their own situations, so that they can help them develop the will and confidence to bring about change. This is why they explore the "here and now" and not the "why and how."

Why do family therapists prefer to treat families rather than individuals?

Family therapists maintain that a person's problem developed in his or her family context and that it is sustained by this context. Thus, efforts to isolate and treat one member of the family without the others will fail because when one family member changes, each of the others must change as well. Even when it is not possible to treat the whole family, some therapists will treat individuals in a family systems perspective, taking into account how each family member forms part of a larger, interacting system.

What is the "scientist-practitioner gap"—and why has it been widening?

The "scientist-practitioner gap" refers to the gap between scientific psychologists and psychotherapists in their assessment of the value of empirical research to measure the effectiveness of therapy. Scientists are concerned that when therapists fail to keep up with empirical findings in the field (e.g., on the most beneficial methods for particular problems), their clients may suffer. Many psychotherapists, however, think that trying to evaluate psychotherapy using the standard methods of empirical research is futile, since psychotherapy is an art learned through clinical experience. The gap has widened because of the rise of professional schools that train their students only to do therapy, without much stress on research methods, and because of the proliferation of new therapies trying to survive in a crowded market. The gap may narrow since psychotherapists increasingly are being required to provide empirical assessments of therapy.

What form of psychotherapy is most likely to help if you are anxious or depressed?

Behavior and cognitive therapies work best for anxiety disorders and depression. Exposure techniques are more effective than any other treatment for posttraumatic stress disorder and agoraphobia. Systematic desensitization effectively treats specific phobias. Cognitive-behavior therapy often is more effective than medication for panic disorder, generalized anxiety disorder, and obsessive-compulsive disorder. Cognitive therapy has been successful in the treatment of mood disorders, especially depression.

Under what conditions can psychotherapy be harmful?

Psychotherapy can be harmful when therapists engage in sexual intimacies or other unethical behavior with their clients, when they are prejudiced or culturally ignorant, when they use inappropriate or coercive influence on their clients, and when they use potentially dangerous techniques that are not scientifically supported.

KEY TERMS FILL-IN-THE-BLANKS PROGRESS TEST

Fill in the blanks with the key terms from the chapter that match the definitions provided. When you have finished this progress test, check your answers with those at the end of this chapter. You should review any key terms that you do not define correctly.

1. _____ Drugs commonly, but often inappropriately, prescribed for patients who complain of unhappiness, anxiety, or worry.

2. _____ Drugs used primarily in the treatment of schizophrenia and other psychotic disorders.

3. _____ A procedure used in cases of prolonged and severe major depression in which a brief brain seizure is induced.

4. _____ Antidepressants that elevate the level of norepinephrine and serotonin in the brain by blocking or inhibiting an enzyme that deactivates these neurotransmitters.

5. _____ Antidepressants that boost serotonin levels by preventing the reuptake of serotonin.

6. _____ A drug frequently given to people suffering from bipolar disorder.

7. _____ The apparent success of a medication or treatment that is due to the patient's expectations or hopes rather than to the drug or treatment itself.

8. _____ In behavior therapy, a step-by-step process of desensitizing a client to a feared object or experience.

9. _____ In behavior therapy, a method in which the client is taken directly into the feared situation until the anxiety subsides.

10. _____ In psychodynamic therapies, a critical process in which the client transfers unconscious emotions or reactions, such as emotional feelings about his or her parents, onto the therapist.

11. _____ A form of therapy designed to identify and change irrational, unproductive ways of thinking and hence to reduce negative emotions and their behavioral consequences.

12. _____ A form of cognitive therapy devised by Albert Ellis, designed to challenge the client's unrealistic or irrational thoughts.

13. _____ A humanist approach to therapy devised by Carl Rogers which emphasizes the therapist's empathy with the client and the use of unconditional positive regard.

14. _____ An approach to doing therapy with individuals or families from the standpoint of seeing how each member forms part of a larger, interacting system.

15. _____ In psychoanalysis, the process of saying freely whatever comes to mind in connection with dreams, memories, fantasies, or conflicts.

16. _____ Research designed to determine the effectiveness of a new medication or form of therapy, in which people with a given problem or disorder are randomly assigned to one or more treatment groups or to a control group.

17. _____ The bond of confidence and mutual understanding established between therapist and client, which allows them to work together to solve the client's problems.

MULTIPLE-CHOICE PROGRESS TEST

Choose the single best answer for each of the following questions. When you have finished this progress test, check your answers with those at the end of this chapter. You should review the relevant pages in the text for the questions you do not answer correctly.

1. Many _____ block or reduce the sensitivity of brain receptors that respond to dopamine.
   a. antipsychotic drugs
   b. tricyclic antidepressants
   c. MAO inhibitors
   d. tranquilizers

2. Which of the following drugs is prescribed for depression?
   a. Antipsychotic drugs
   b. MAO inhibitors
   c. Tranquilizers
   d. None of the above is an answer.

3. _____ increase the activity of GABA.
   a. Antipsychotic drugs
   b. Tricyclic antidepressants
   c. MAO inhibitors
   d. Tranquilizers

4. Jack's mood varies from severe depression to manic states. Which of the following drugs should he take for his disorder?
   a. Prozac
   b. Valium
   c. Clozapine
   d. Lithium carbonate

5. Which of the following is NOT a side effect of antidepressant drugs?
   a. Weight loss
   b. Decreased sexual desire
   c. Headaches
   d. Dry mouth

6. Electroconvulsive therapy is used for the treatment of _____.
   a. severe depression
   b. schizophrenia
   c. obsessive-compulsive disorder
   d. antisocial personality disorder

7. Which of the following types of psychotherapists would be most likely to use transference?
   a. Rational emotive therapist
   b. Behavioral therapist
   c. Psychodynamic therapist
   d. Client-centered therapist

8. Systematic desensitization and flooding are _____ therapies.
   a. psychodynamic
   b. cognitive
   c. behavioral
   d. humanist

9. Which of the following pairings of therapist and therapy is NOT correct?
   a. Albert Ellis and cognitive therapy
   b. Carl Rogers and psychodynamic therapy
   c. Aaron Beck and cognitive therapy
   d. Sigmund Freud and psychoanalysis

10. In _____ therapy, the therapist uses logical arguments to challenge a client's unrealistic beliefs or expectations.
    a. client-centered
    b. rational emotive behavior
    c. existential
    d. aversive conditioning

11. _____ therapies start from the assumption that people seek self-actualization and self-fulfillment.
    a. Humanist
    b. Cognitive
    c. Behavioral
    d. Psychodynamic

12. _____ therapy helps clients face with courage the great questions of life, such as death, freedom, and alienation.
    a. Rational emotive
    b. Existential
    c. Psychodynamic
    d. Family

13. Which of the following is FALSE regarding family therapy?
    a. Family therapists believe that people's problems develop in the context of their families.
    b. Family members usually are aware of how they influence one another.
    c. Each family member is seen as forming part of a larger, interacting system.
    d. When one family member changes, each of the others must change, as well.

14. The resolution of conflicts and breaking out of destructive habits are the primary goals of:
    a. family therapy.
    b. existential therapy.
    c. psychodynamic therapy.
    d. couples therapy.

15. The apparent success of a treatment that is due to the patient's expectation or hopes rather than the treatment itself is called _____.
    a. the placebo effect
    b. the justification of effort effect
    c. the therapeutic window
    d. an empirically validated treatment

16. The disagreement between scientific psychologists and psychotherapists regarding the value of using standard empirical methods to evaluate psychotherapy is referred to as the _____.
    a. therapeutic alliance
    b. scientist-practitioner gap
    c. clubhouse model
    d. narrative method

17. The bond of confidence and mutual understanding established between therapist and client is called the _____.
    a. therapeutic window
    b. therapeutic alliance
    c. clubhouse model
    d. family systems approach

18. Which of the following pairings of problem and the most successful therapy for that problem is INCORRECT?
    a. Childhood behavior problems and humanist therapy
    b. Specific phobias and systematic desensitization
    c. Depression and cognitive therapy
    d. Panic disorder and cognitive-behavior therapy

19. Therapy clients can be harmed by:
    a. the use of unreliable methods, like hypnosis to retrieve old memories.
    b. therapist-induced disorders resulting from a therapist's coercive influence.
    c. bias on the part of the therapist who does not understand the client's culture.
    d. All the above are answers.

Guided Study

1. Biological Treatments for Mental Disorders

1-1. medication
Antipsychotic
schizophrenia
dopamine
serotonin
Antidepressant
Monoamine oxidase
serotonin
Tricyclic
serotonin
reuptake
tranquilizers
GABA
panic
anxiety
lithium
bipolar
placebo
expectations
antidepressants
relapse
dropout
disregard
nonmedical
dosage
therapeutic
metabolized
ethnic
risks
off-label

1-2. prefrontal lobotomy
electroconvulsive
depression
suicidal
short-lived
transcranial magnetic

2. Major Schools of Psychotherapy

2-1. psychoanalysis
insight
unconscious
unconscious
parents
transference

2-2. behavior
beliefs
operant
graduated exposure
flooding
systematic desensitization
counterconditioning
self-monitoring
records
reinforcers
skills
modeling
expectations
rational emotive
overgeneralize
thoughts

2-3. mindfulness
acceptance
identify
eradicate

2-4. Humanist
good
client-centered
unconditional positive
self-esteem
empathy
existence
responsibility

2-5. families
influence
family-systems
couples

2-6. integrative
flexible
motivate
change

3. Evaluating Psychotherapy

3-1. therapeutic alliance
respect
goals
improve
cultural
stereotyping

3-2. scientist-practitioner
professional
unvalidated
placebo effect
justification
effort
randomized
assigned
control

3-3. behavior
cognitive
depression
suicide
anxiety
anger
child
behavior
relapse

3-4. sexual
prejudiced
influence
dangerous
educated

Answers to Key Terms Progress Test

1. tranquilizers
2. antipsychotic drugs
3. electroconvulsive therapy
4. monoamine oxidase inhibitors
5. selective serotonin reuptake inhibitors
6. lithium carbonate
7. placebo effect
8. systematic desensitization
9. exposure (flooding)
10. transference
11. cognitive therapy
12. rational emotive behavior therapy
13. client-centered (nondirective) therapy
14. family-systems perspective
15. free association
16. randomized controlled trials
17. therapeutic alliance

Item Number	Answers
1.	a. antipsychotic drugs
2.	b. MAO inhibitors
3.	d. Tranquilizers
4.	d. lithium carbonate
5.	a. weight loss
6.	a. severe depression
7.	c. psychodynamic therapist
8.	c. behavioral
9.	b. Carl Rogers and psychodynamic therapy
10.	b. rational emotive behavior
11.	a. Humanist
12.	b. Existential
13.	b. Family members usually are aware of how they influence one another.
14.	d. couples therapy
15.	a. a placebo effect
16.	b. scientist-practitioner gap
17.	b. therapeutic alliance
18.	a. childhood behavior problems and humanist therapy
19.	d. All the above are answers.

CHAPTER 13

Emotion, Stress, and Health

CHAPTER OVERVIEW   The chapter opens with a discussion of the nature of emotion.   This includes a description of the relationship between facial expressions and emotion, the structures in the brain responsible for the components of emotion, hormones that help to produce emotion, and how thoughts affect emotional experience.   The effect of culture on emotion is addressed next through an exploration of the varieties of emotion in different cultures and the ways that culture influences how people communicate their emotions. Then, the topic of gender and emotion is examined.

The effects of stress on the body and the mind are identified.   Coverage includes Selye's general adaptation syndrome, the relationship between stress and illness, and how optimism and pessimism and one's sense of control affect health.   Next the effects of the emotions of hostility, which involves the Type A personality, and depression on people's health are discussed.   The chapter also examines how emotional inhibition can influence one's health.   Finally, ways to cope with various emotions and stress are offered.   These include cooling off, solving the problem, rethinking the problem, and drawing on and giving social support.

GUIDED STUDY

1. The Nature of Emotion

Read the section "The Nature of Emotion" and then answer the following questions. If you have trouble answering any of the questions, re-study the relevant material before going on to the review of key terms and the progress tests.

1-1. Psychologists focus on three main components to emotion: _____ changes in the face, brain, and body; _____ processes such as _____ of events; and _____ influences that shape the experience and _____ of emotion. Research on the physiological factors of emotion has identified certain basic or _____ emotions, which generally include fear, anger, sadness, joy, surprise, disgust, and contempt. However, _____ emotions are those that are specific to certain cultures. Paul Ekman and his colleagues have found much evidence that supports the _____ of seven basic facial _____ of emotion. Facial expressions reflect people's emotions but they also can _____ them. According to the process of _____ _____, facial muscles send messages to the _____ regarding the basic emotion being expressed. For example, when people contract the muscles associated with _____, their positive emotions increase. According to Darwin, facial expressions evolved to help

people _____ their emotional states to others and provoke a response from them. This is supported by the study of babies, who seem primed to respond to _____ expressions of emotions. Other researchers examine the parts of the _____ that are involved in specific emotions or that are responsible for different aspects of emotional experience. For example, the _____ regions of the brain are involved in the impulses to approach or withdraw from a person or situation. Another brain structure that plays a key role in emotion, especially anger and _____, is the _____, which is located in the limbic system. This structure is responsible for making the initial decision to either _____ or _____ from a person or situation. Scientists have also discovered brain cells that fire when a person or animal observes others carrying out an action, which are called _____ _____. These are involved in imitation and reading emotions and play a role in _____, which explain why emotion seem to spread easily among people, a phenomenon known as _____ _____. Other research focuses on how hormones are involved with emotion. Stress or intense emotion leads the _____ nervous system to command the adrenal glands to release two hormones involved in emotion, _____ and

235

_____. These hormones produce a state of _____ and alertness and are released during many emotional states. However, emotions do differ from each other _____ and are associated with different patterns of brain activity. The use of physiological responses to detect deception is the idea behind the _____ _____, also known as a lie detector. Most psychological scientists regard these tests as _____.

1-2. Researchers have studied how emotions are created or influenced by beliefs, _____ of the situation, expectations, and _____, which are the explanations that people make of their own and other people's behavior. Some emotions are not experienced until certain cognitive capacities have _____. For example, _____ and guilt do not occur until a child is _____ or _____ years old.

Terms for Review

The following is a list of the important terms from the section "The Nature of Emotion." Make sure you are familiar with each term before taking the progress test on these terms.

emotion	facial feedback
primary emotions	mirror neurons
secondary emotions	mood contagion

2. Emotion and Culture

Read the section "Emotion and Culture" and then answer the following questions. If you have trouble answering any of the questions, re-study the relevant material before going on to the review of key terms and the progress tests.

2-1. Many psychologists agree that all humans are capable of feeling the _____, hardwired emotions, but individuals may differ in their abilities to experience the _____ emotions that reflect their culture. Throughout the world, the distinction between primary emotions and more complex _____ variations is reflected in _____. And, as _____ develop, they come to experience the cultural nuances of emotional experience. Other psychologists argue, however, that there is no aspect of emotion that is not affected by _____. Both sides of this debate agree that cultures determine much about which people feel emotional _____. For example, disgust is universal, but the _____ of what produces disgust changes as humans mature and varies across cultures.

2-2. Emotions also are expressed differently depending on a culture's _____ _____ for emotion. For example, even the smile has many _____ and uses that are not universal. Display rules also influence _____ language, which involves _____ signals of body movement, _____, gesture, and gaze. Display rules dictate not only what to do when people are feeling an emotion, but

236

also how and when to show an emotion that they do _____ feel. When acting out an emotion that people do not really feel, they are engaging in _____ _____.

2-3. Regarding gender and emotion, there is little evidence that one sex _____ any of the everyday emotions more often than the other does. The major difference between the sexes has less to do with whether they feel emotions than with how and when their emotions are _____ and how they are _____ by others. For example, _____ in North America smile more often than _____ do, gaze at their listeners more, have more emotionally _____ faces, use more expressive hand and _____ movements, and _____ others more. Women also talk about their _____ more than men do. In contrast, the only emotion that most men in North America express more freely than women do is _____ toward strangers, especially other _____. However, the influence of a particular situation often overrides _____ rules. For example, an important factor in the situation for both men and women is the _____ of the participants. And, North American _____ differences in emotional expression are by no means universal. Therefore, whether men or women are more emotional depends on the circumstances and their _____.

Terms for Review

The following is a list of the important terms from the section "Emotion and Culture." Make sure you are familiar with each term before taking the progress test on these terms.

display rules
body language
emotion work

3. The Nature of Stress

Read the section "The Nature of Stress" and then answer the following questions. If you have trouble answering any of the questions, re-study the relevant material before going on to the review of key terms and the progress tests.

3-1. According to Hans Selye, the body's response to external stressors consists of physiological responses that occur in three phases, (1) the _____ phase, (2) the _____ phase, and (3) the _____ phase, all of which comprise the _____ _____ syndrome. Current approaches focus on other physiological structures and mechanisms involved with _____. For example, when someone is under stress, the _____ sends messages to the _____ glands which active the _____ division of the autonomic nervous system. Also, hormones from the hypothalamus result in the release of _____ from the adrenal glands. One of the bodily systems that stress affects is the _____ system. The field

237

of _____ is dedicated to how psychology, the nervous and endocrine systems, and the immune systems are related to one another. The white blood cells of the immune system are designed to recognize and destroy foreign substances called _____, such as viruses and bacteria.

3-2. The responses made by individuals to negative life events fall into two categories: the optimistic explanatory style and the pessimistic explanatory style. Overall, _____ is associated with better health and well-being. Optimists may have better health because they take better _____ of themselves. Pessimists often do _____ things, like _____ too much and refuse to take _____ for illness. Optimists are more likely than pessimists are to be active _____ solvers, get _____ from friends, and to seek _____ that can help them. Optimism also is related to having an _____ locus of control. Feeling in control affects the _____ system. However regarding health, there are limits to how much control over events people should feel. Health and well-being are not enhanced by _____-_____. In addition, cultural differences show that control in a Western culture, referred to as _____ control, involves people trying to influence events by attempting to exert control over

them. On the other hand, control in an Eastern culture, referred to as_____ control, involves people trying to accommodate to a bad situation by changing their own aspirations or desires.

Terms for Review

The following is a list of the important terms from the section "The Nature of Stress." Make sure you are familiar with each term before taking the progress test on these terms.

general adaptation syndrome   antigens
alarm phase   locus of control
resistance phase   internal locus of control
exhaustion phase   external locus of control
HPA axis   primary control
psychoneuroimmunology   secondary control

4. Stress and Emotion

Read the section "Stress and Emotion" and then answer the following questions. If you have trouble answering any of the questions, re-study the relevant material before going on to the review of key terms and the progress tests.

4-1. There is evidence that once a person already has a virus or medical condition, _____ emotions can increase the risk of illness and affect the speed of _____. Emotion and illness were first linked through research on _____ personalities. These individuals are _____, impatient, angry, hard _____, and have high _____ for themselves. Being a Type A personality alone does not place one at greater risk of heart disease; being Type A and having _____ or antagonistic _____ does seem to place one at greater risk. Proneness to anger is a significant risk factor for impairments of the _____ system, elevated _____ _____, _____ disease, and even slower healing of _____. In addition, clinical _____ appears to be a risk factor for heart disease.

4-2. When studying the emotional content of writing by nuns, researchers found a strong correlation between _____ emotions described and _____ six decades later. People who express positive feelings are also more likely to attract _____ and _____ than are people who are bitter and brooding. This is important because _____ support contributes to good health.

4-3. Individuals who have the personality trait of emotional _____ constantly try to deny feelings of anxiety, anger, or fear and pretend that everything is fine. These suppressors are at _____ risk of becoming ill versus those who can acknowledge their fears. One explanation for this is that prolonged inhibition of thoughts and emotions requires _____ effort that is stressful to the body. The benefits of _____ occur only when the revelation produces _____ and understanding, thereby ending the repetition of _____ thoughts and unresolved

_____. Another important tool to get rid of negative emotions is to let go of _____, since _____ is the antidote to anger.

Terms for Review

The following is a list of the important terms from the section "Stress and Emotion." Make sure you are familiar with each term before taking the progress test on these terms.

cynical/antagonistic hostility

5. Coping with Stress

Read the section "Coping with Stress" and then answer the following questions. If you have trouble answering any of the questions, re-study the relevant material before going on to the review of key terms and the progress tests.

5-1. The most immediate way to deal with stress and negative emotions is to take time out and reduce the body's physical _____. For example, one effective way to cope with stress is to use relaxation techniques such as _____ meditation.

5-2. One type of coping, _____-_____ coping, concentrates on the emotions the problem has caused. _____-_____ coping, on the other hand, focuses on identifying the problem and learning as much about it as possible. Becoming informed increases feelings of _____ and can speed _____.

5-3. Another way of coping with stress is to _____ the problem. Even when a stressful problem cannot be solved, people can change the way they _____ about it. This involves (1) _____ the situation, (2) learning from the _____, and (3) making social _____.

5-4. One last coping strategy is drawing on _____ _____, by reaching out to others. Having friends can improve one's _____. Research has found that people who have more friends and relations are likely to _____ longer than are people who have few. Unfortunately, friends and family members can be _____

of stress and negative emotions. And, they may be _____ in times of trouble due simply to _____ or awkwardness. Finally, _____ support has health benefits since it encourages people to solve problems, helps them _____ the situation, and fosters _____.

Terms for Review

The following is a list of the important terms from the section "Coping with Stress." Make sure you are familiar with each term before taking the progress test on these terms.

mindfulness meditation   problem-focused coping
emotion-focused coping   reappraisal

SAMPLE ANSWERS TO *YOU ARE ABOUT TO LEARN* QUESTIONS FROM TEXTBOOK

After you have read through the chapter, go back and review the "You Are About to Learn..." statements that precede each major section. Create your own answer to each question, then compare your answers to the following sample answers. If your answers are not similar to the sample answers, review the relevant sections of the chapter more carefully.

Which facial expressions of emotion do most people recognize the world over?

Paul Ekman and his colleagues collected much evidence for the universality of seven basic facial expressions of emotion: anger, happiness, fear, surprise, disgust, sadness, and contempt.

Which parts of the brain are involved with different aspects of emotion?

The prefrontal regions of the brain are involved in emotional impulses to either approach or withdraw from a person or situation, as well as the regulation of emotion. The amygdala, a small structure in the brain's limbic system, is responsible for evaluating sensory information, quickly determining its emotional importance, and making the initial decision to approach or withdraw from a person or situation.

How do mirror neurons generate empathy, mood contagion, and synchrony?

When you observe another person experience something, mirror neurons in your own brain are firing in a similar manner. As such, you begin to feel as the people around you feel.

Which two hormones provide the energy and excitement of emotion?

Under stress and intense emotion, the adrenal glands will send out the hormones epinephrine and norepinephrine. These chemicals help produce arousal and alertness, allowing your body the energy to take necessary action.

How do thoughts create emotions and why can't an infant feel shame or guilt?

Emotions are often created or influenced by beliefs, perceptions of the situation, expectations, and the attributions that people make. Infants cannot feel shame or guilt because these emotions require a sense of self and the ability to perceive that one has behaved badly or let down another person. Infants are not mature enough cognitively to have a sense of self or such perceptions of the situation. The ability to feel shame or guilt does not occur until children are about 2 or 3 years old.

Why do people from different cultures disagree on what makes them angry, jealous, or disgusted?

Although these emotions are universal and occur across cultures, the specific content that evokes such emotions varies and is highly influenced by learning and the rules of cultures.

Why do psychologists debate whether there are primary and secondary emotions?

Some psychologists believe that the distinctions between primary and secondary emotions don't make sense. They argue that there is no aspect of emotion that is not influenced by culture or context.

How do cultural rules affect the way people display or suppress their emotions?

The display of emotion can have many meanings and uses that are not universal and that depend on a culture's display rules, which are social and cultural rules that regulate when, how, and where a person may express or suppress emotions. For example, Americans tend to smile more frequently than Germans do; this does not mean that Americans are friendlier than Germans are, but that they differ in their notions of when a smile is appropriate. The Japanese smile even more than Americans do, to disguise embarrassment, anger, or other negative emotions whose public display is considered rude and incorrect.

Why do people engage in "emotion work" to convey emotions they currently aren't experiencing?

The rules of society sometimes demand that we regulate our emotions when in the presence of others. Occasionally this requires us to show emotional states that we do not feel, such as when we are in our job roles.

Are women really more "emotional" than men?

There is little evidence that one sex feels emotions more often than the other does. The major difference between the sexes has less to do with whether they feel emotions than with how and when their emotions are expressed. Gender roles greatly affect the expression of emotions. Compared to North American men, North American women are encouraged to be more emotionally expressive, smile more, gaze at their listeners more, have more emotionally expressive faces, use more expressive hand and body movements, and touch other people more. In contrast, most North American men express only one emotion, anger toward strangers, more often than women do. Otherwise, they are expected to control and mask negative feelings. Differing display rules for communicating emotion help explain why many people in Western cultures think women are more emotional than men are. These North American gender differences, however, are not universal. In addition, even within a culture, the influence of a particular situation, for example the status of the participants, often overrides gender rules.

How does the body respond to physical, emotional, and environmental stressors?

The first stage of the body's reaction to stress is the alarm phase, in which the body prepares to meet the immediate threat by releasing hormones and other physiological changes. The second stage is the resistance phase, in which the body continues to resist or cope with an unavoidable stressor. The final stage is the exhaustion stage, which occurs when the body's resources are too depleted to continuing resistance.

Why does being "stressed out" increase the risk of illness in some people but not others?

Some people's responses to stress vary due to learning history, gender, preexisting medical conditions, and genetic predisposition for high blood pressure, heart disease, obesity, diabetes, or other health problems.

How can psychological factors affect the immune system?

Noise, bereavement and loss, work-related problems, and poverty and powerlessness are all stressors that are especially likely to affect the immune system, and thus increase the risk of illness or poor health.

When is a sense of control good for

The kind of control that is related to better health is an

242

you, and when is it not?

internal locus of control—the belief that one is basically in charge of one's life and well-being and that if one becomes sick one can take steps to get better. However, there are limits to how much control someone should feel. It is not beneficial for people to believe they can control every aspect of their lives. Health is not enhanced by self-blame or the belief that all diseases can be prevented by doing the right thing.

Which emotion may be most hazardous to your heart?

People who are chronically angry and resentful are significantly more likely than non-hostile people are to get heart disease, even when other risk factors, such as smoking and a poor diet, are taken into account. These people tend to have the toxic kind of hostility, cynical or antagonistic hostility, which characterizes people who are mistrustful of others and ready to provoke mean, furious arguments.

Does chronic depression lead to physical illness?

Chronic depression appears to be a significant risk factor for heart disease, though probably not in a direct way. Depressed people may fail to take care of themselves, reducing the body's ability to recover.

Why is confession often as healthy for the body as it is for the soul?

Confession often produces insight and understanding, which helps end the stressful repetition of obsessive thoughts and unresolved feelings.

When you're feeling overwhelmed, what are some ways to calm yourself?

One of the best ways to calm oneself is to use relaxation techniques, such as progressive relaxation training. Another way is exercise. Other methods include getting a soothing massage, listening to music, and writing in a journal. Such activities give the body a chance to recover from the intensity of the initial stress response and the corresponding negative emotions.

Why is it important to move beyond the emotions caused by a problem and deal with the problem itself?

Although most people engage in emotion-focused coping after any tragedy or disaster, eventually they become ready to concentrate on solving the problem itself. Problem-focused coping tends to increase one's sense of control and can speed recovery.

How can you learn to rethink and reappraise your problems?

Some of the most effective "rethinking" strategies are: reappraising the situation, learning from the experience, making social comparisons, and cultivating a sense of humor. Even when people cannot fix a problem, they can change the way they think about it. Problems can be turned into challenges, losses into unexpected gains. People who cope successfully often compare themselves to others who are, they feel, less fortunate. And, humor is a good way to cope, especially if it allows people to see the ridiculous aspects of the problem and gain a sense of distance from it or control over it.

What is the importance and limitations of social support?

Friends can help someone cope by offering concern and affection. They can help evaluate problems and plan a course of action. They can offer resources and services. Most importantly, they are sources of attachment and connection, which everyone needs throughout life. Consequently, having friends can improve people's health. Of course, sometimes friends are not helpful. They themselves may be sources of unhappiness, stress, and anger. In addition to instigating conflicts, they may not be supportive in times of trouble due to ignorance or awkwardness. They may abandon their friend or say something stupid and hurtful. Sometimes they block their friend's efforts to change bad health habits. And, they may offer the wrong kind of support because they have never been in the same situation.

KEY TERMS FILL-IN-THE-BLANKS PROGRESS TEST

Fill in the blanks with the key terms from the chapter that match the definitions provided. When you have finished this progress test, check your answers with those at the end of this chapter. You should review any key terms that you do not define correctly.

1. _____ Emotions that are specific to certain cultures.

2. _____ A state of arousal involving facial and bodily changes, brain activation, cognitive appraisals, subjective feelings, and tendencies toward action.

3. _____ The process by which the facial muscles send messages to the brain about the basic emotion being expressed.

4. _____ A small structure in the brain's limbic system that plays a key role in emotion.

5. _____ Emotions that are considered to be universal and biologically based.

6. _____ Expression of an emotion, often because of a role requirement, that a person does not really feel.

7. _____ Social and cultural rules that regulate when, how, and where a person may express (or suppress) emotions.

8. _____ An effort to modify reality by changing other people, the situation, or events.

9. _____ According to Hans Seyle, a series of physiological responses to stressors that occur in three phases: alarm, resistance, and exhaustion.

10. _____ The stage of the general adaptation syndrome in which persistent stress depletes the body of energy and therefore increases vulnerability to physical problems and eventually illness.

11. _____ A general expectation about whether the results of your actions are under your own control (internal locus) or beyond your control (external locus).

12. _____ An effort to accept reality by changing your own attitudes, goals, or emotions.

13. _____ People who are ambitious, have a sense of time urgency, are irritable, respond physiologically to threat and challenge very quickly, and are impatient with anyone who gets in their way.

14. _____ The type of hostility characterized by people who are mistrustful of others and ready to provoke mean, furious arguments.

15. _____ The process of choosing to think differently about a situation.

16. _____ Coping that concentrates on the emotions the problem caused.

17. _____ Learning to alternately tense and relax the muscles, from toes to head, and to meditate by clearing your mind.

MULTIPLE-CHOICE PROGRESS TEST

Choose the single best answer for each of the following questions. When you have finished this progress test, check your answers with those at the end of this chapter. You should review the relevant pages in the text for the questions you do not answer correctly.

1. Which of the following statements is FALSE?
   a. The facial expressions associated with anger and happiness are universal.
   b. Authentic smiles last longer than false smiles do.
   c. There are culture-specific variations in the expression of emotion.
   d. None of the above is false.

2. According to _____, a smile tells people they are happy, and a frown that they are angry or perplexed.
   a. mood contagion
   b. display rules
   c. facial feedback
   d. culture-specific hypothesis

3. Regions of the _____ prefrontal cortex are specialized for the motivation to _____ others; regions of the _____ prefrontal cortex are specialized for the motivation to _____ others.
   a. right, approach; left, escape
   b. right, escape; left, escape
   c. left, approach; right, escape
   d. left, approach; right, approach

4. The _____, a small structure in the brain's limbic system, plays a key role in emotion.
   a. amygdala
   b. cerebellum
   c. hypothalamus
   d. thalamus

5. Which of the following is NOT a response of the sympathetic division of the autonomic nervous system to arousal?
   a. Pupils dilate.
   b. Heart beats faster.
   c. Digestion speeds up.
   d. Breathing speeds up.

6. Based on the research on attributions and grades, which of the following students is most likely to feel angry?
   a. Students who believe they did well because of their own efforts
   b. Students who believe they did well because of a lucky fluke or chance
   c. Students who believe their failures were their own fault
   d. Students who blame others for their failures

7. Which of the following is FALSE?
   a. Secondary emotions are the emotions that are specific to certain cultures.
   b. Display rules regulate when, how, and where a person may express or suppress emotions.
   c. There is little evidence that one sex feels emotion more often than the other does.
   d. None of the above is false.

8. Which of the following is the correct order of the three phases in Selye's general adaptation syndrome?
   a. Alarm, resistance, exhaustion
   b. Alarm, exhaustion, resistance
   c. Exhaustion, alarm, resistance
   d. Exhaustion, resistance, alarm

9. Which of the following disorders appears to be associated with a high risk of heart disease?
   a. Clinical depression
   b. Personality disorder
   c. Social phobia
   d. Generalized anxiety disorder

10. Which of the following is NOT associated with a pessimistic explanatory style?
    a. Self-destructive behavior
    b. More illness
    c. More achievement
    d. Slower recovery from setbacks

11. People who are optimistic and have "positive illusions":
    a. do not deny their problems.
    b. are more likely than pessimists to be active problem solvers.
    c. take better care of themselves when they are sick.
    d. All the above are answers.

12. An internal locus of control helps to:
    a. make people more likely to take action to improve their health when necessary.
    b. speed recovery from surgery and some diseases.
    c. resist infection by cold viruses.
    d. All the above are answers.

13. A personality trait that involves suppressing one's feelings almost all the time is _____.
    a. reappraisal
    b. emotional inhibition
    c. primary control
    d. secondary control

14. _____ cultures emphasize _____ control in which people try to influence existing reality by changing other people, other events, or circumstances.
    a. Western; primary
    b. Western; secondary
    c. Eastern; primary
    d. Eastern; secondary

15. Which of the following is the characteristic of some Type A people that is dangerous to their health?
    a. Determination
    b. Hostility
    c. Impatience
    d. Intensity

16. Expressing happiness at the news of a friend's promotion despite wanting the job for oneself and feeling disappointment and sadness is an example of:
    a. a display rule.
    b. emotion work.
    c. a secondary emotion.
    d. mood contagion.

17. Eventually most people move from _____-focused coping to _____-focused coping when faced with stressful problems.
    a. problem; emotion
    b. emotion; problem
    c. relaxation; reappraisal
    d. reappraisal; relaxation

18. Which of the following statements is FALSE?
    a. People who have good social support live longer than do those who do not.
    b. Hostile arguments in married couples impair their immune systems.
    c. Having friends can improve people's health.
    d. None of the above is false.

Guided Study

1. The Nature of Emotion

1-1. physiological
cognitive
interpretations
cultural
expression
primary
secondary
universality
expressions
influence
facial feedback
brain
smiling
communicate
adults'
brain
prefrontal
fear
amygdala
approach
withdraw
mirror neurons
empathy
mood contagion
sympathetic
epinephrine
norepinephrine
arousal
physiologically
polygraph machine
invalid

1-2. perceptions
attributions
matured
shame
2
3

2. Emotion and Culture

2-1. primary
secondary
cultural
language
children
culture
about
content

2-2. display rules
meanings
body
nonverbal
posture
not
emotion
work

2-3. feels
expressed
perceived
women
men
expressive
body
touch
emotions
anger
men
gender
status
gender
culture

3. The Nature of Stress

3-1. alarm
resistance
exhaustion
general adaptation
stress
hypothalamus
endocrine
sympathetic
cortisol
immune
psychoneuroimmunology
antigens

3-2. optimism
self-destructive
drink
medication
problem
support
information
internal
immune
self-blame
primary
secondary

4. Stress and Emotion

4-1. negative
recovery
Type A
ambitious
workers
standards
cynical
hostility
immune
blood pressure
heart
wounds
depression

4-2. positive
longevity
friends
supporters
social

4-3. inhibition
greater
physical
confession
insight
obsessive
feelings
grievances
forgiveness

5. Coping with Stress

5-1. arousal
mindfulness

5-2. emotion-focused
Problem-focused
control
recovery

5-3. rethink
think
reappraising
experience
comparisons

5-4. social support
health
live
sources
unsupportive
ignorance
giving
reappraise
forgiveness

Answers to Key Terms Progress Test

1. secondary emotions
2. emotion
3. facial feedback
4. amygdala
5. primary emotions
6. emotion work
7. display rules
8. primary control
9. general adaptation syndrome
10. exhaustion phase
11. locus of control
12. secondary control
13. Type A personality
14. cynical/antagonistic hostility
15. reappraisal
16. emotion-focused coping
17. progressive relaxation

Item Number	Answers
1.	b. Authentic smiles last longer than false smiles do.
2.	c. facial feedback
3.	c. left, approach; right, escape
4.	a. amygdala
5.	c. digestion speeds up
6.	d. students who blame others for their failures
7.	d. None of the above is false.
8.	a. alarm, resistance, exhaustion
9.	a. clinical depression
10.	c. more achievement
11.	d. All the above are answers.
12.	d. All the above are answers.
13.	b. emotional inhibition
14.	a. Western; primary
15.	b. hostility
16.	b. emotion work.
17.	b. emotion; problem
18.	d. None of the above is false.

CHAPTER 14

The Major Motives of Life: Food, Love, Sex, and Work

CHAPTER OVERVIEW

The chapter opens with definitions of motivation, both intrinsic and extrinsic, and continues with discussions of many motives that are important to people: food, love, sex, and achievement. Next, a discussion of the motive to eat is presented. Topics include the biology of weight, environmental and cultural influences on weight and eating, and eating disorders. The section on the motive to love describes theories of love and how biology, attachment, gender, and culture affect love.

The third motive explored is the motive for sex. This presentation encompasses biological aspects of sexuality, including how hormones affect sexual behavior and an evolutionary view of sex. Also, the psychological viewpoint is presented, which includes the motives for sex and a section on sexual coercion and rape. Cultural and gender variations in sexuality and types of sexual orientations are identified.

The last motive discussed is the motive to achieve. The questions of how motivation affects work and how work affects motivation are addressed. The need for achievement and how it is measured, as well as different goals involved with achievement motivation are considered. The influences of self-efficacy and the self-fulfilling prophecy are explained. The chapter ends with a discussion of motivational conflicts, as in approach-avoidance situations, and how they may be resolved.

GUIDED STUDY

1. The Hungry Animal: Motives to Eat

Read the section "The Hungry Animal: Motives to Eat" and then answer the following questions. If you have trouble answering any of the questions, re-study the relevant material before going on to the review of key terms and the progress tests.

1-1. _____ is defined as an inferred process within a person or animal which causes that organism to move toward a goal or away from an unpleasant situation. When people are motivated to do something for its own sake, they are being motivated by _____ motivation and when they are motivated to do something because of external rewards, the motivation is _____. It was originally believed that being overweight was a sign of _____ _____. Results of controlled _____ revealed that this was not the case. Also, studies showed that heaviness is not always caused by _____. The leading explanation for these research findings is that a biological mechanism keeps a person's body weight at a genetically influenced _____ _____. This is the weight a person stays at when neither trying to _____ or _____ weight. In addition, people each have a genetically programmed rate at which they burn calories, _____ _____ rate, and a fixed number of _____

cells. Set-point theory predicts that the _____ of weight and body fat is high, and the results from twin and _____ studies show that it is. In addition, genetic research on obesity has isolated a gene, which causes fat cells to secrete a protein, _____, which travels through the blood to an area in the _____ that regulates appetite.

1-2. The role of genetics in weight and body shape cannot account for the recent increase in rates of weight-gain epidemic. Instead, environmental influences must be considered, including the increased abundance of fast food and _____ foods; the widespread consumption of high-sugar, high-calorie _____ _____; the sharp decline in _____ and other expenditures of energy; increased _____ sizes of food and drink; and the abundance of highly _____ foods. Also, a _____ customs and standards of what the _____ body should look like influence eating habits and activity levels. Ironically, while people of all _____ and social classes have been getting fatter, the cultural ideal for a woman's body size in the United States, Canada, and _____ has been getting _____. And, pressures have increased for men to be _____ and muscular. Today's _____ but otherwise

_____ female ideal may reflect cultural _____ about whether women's proper role is domestic or _____. And, for men, having a strong, muscular body is now a sign of _____, rather than _____.

1-3. The battle between biology and culture can cause physical and emotional problems, such as eating disorders. Two common eating disorders are _____ nervosa, which involves episodes of excessive eating followed by forced vomiting or use of laxatives, and _____ nervosa, characterized by a radically reduced consumption of food and emaciation. These eating disorders are much more common in _____ than in _____.

Terms for Review

The following is a list of the important terms from the section "The Hungry Animal: Motives to Eat." Make sure you are familiar with each term before taking the progress test on these terms.

motivation	basal metabolism rate
intrinsic motivation	leptin
extrinsic motivation	bulimia nervosa
set point	anorexia nervosa

2. The Social Animal: Motives for Love

Read the section "The Social Animal: Motives for Love" and then answer the following questions. If you have trouble answering any of the questions, re-study the relevant material before going on to the review of key terms and the progress tests.

2-1. One distinction made between different types of love is that between _____ love, characterized by intense emotions and sexual passion, and _____ love, characterized by affection and trust. Social bonding depends on a number of factors, including hormones such as _____ and _____. When animals experience attachment, it stimulates the release of _____ in the brain.

2-2. Love can be predicted by social factors as well. One major predictor is _____, which refers to how close others are to you. Another major predictor is _____ because we tend to prefer people with the same looks, attitudes, beliefs, values, personality, and interests as ourselves. According to Shaver and Hazan, adults, just like babies, can have attachments that are _____, _____, or _____. According to the _____ theory of love, people acquire their attachment styles mainly from how their _____ cared for them. One of the factors that diminishes happiness between couples is _____, constant thinking and worrying about the loved one and the relationship.

2-3. Although both sexes become equally attached and suffer equally when a love relationship _____, women and men do differ in terms of how they _____ love. In contemporary Western society, many women express love in _____, whereas many men express love in _____. Today, in every developed nation, only very small numbers of women and men would consider marrying someone they did not _____.

Terms for Review

The following is a list of the important terms from the section "The Social Animal: Motives for Love." Make sure you are familiar with each term before taking the progress test on these terms.

passionate love	anxious attachment
companionate love	avoidant attachment
vasopressin	attachment theory of love
oxytocin	obsessiveness
secure attachment	

3. The Erotic Animal: Motives for Sex

Read the section "The Erotic Animal: Motives for Sex" and then answer the following questions. If you have trouble answering any of the questions, re-study the relevant material before going on to the review of key terms and the progress tests.

3-1. Psychologists consider human sexuality a blend of _____, psychological, and _____ factors. One of the first researchers of sexual behavior to promote the idea that males and females are alike in their basic anatomy and physiology was _____. Laboratory research by _____ and Johnson in the 1960s confirmed Kinsey's assertions regarding the similarities between females and males. Masters and Johnson did, however, disagree with Kinsey's assertion that women have a _____ sexual capacity compared to men. One biological factor that promotes sexual desire is the hormone _____. Some have tried to use testosterone to enhance sexual desire, but there have been three significant problems: (1) There is no _____ on the difference between normally low and abnormally deficient levels, (2) it is easy to _____ the symptoms of a biological deficiency because those are also symptoms of _____ and _____ problems, and (3) the _____ _____ of androgen such as testosterone can range from unpleasant to harmful. The question of whether the biologically based _____ _____ of men and women are alike or different continues to be debated. _____ psychologists have promoted a biological approach to sexuality. According to this view, it is evolutionarily _____ for males to compete with other males for access to young and fertile females and to try to win and then _____ as many females as possible. Females, on the other hand, need to shop for the best _____ deal. Critics have challenged this viewpoint on a number of conceptual and methodological grounds. For example, much of the evolutionary view may be based on _____ of sexual behavior rather than actual behavior. Further, there a great deal of cultural _____ of sexual behavior across times and places. Much of the data that evolutionary psychologists have relied on have come from questionnaires and interviews, which may reflect what people _____ instead of what they actually _____.

3-2. Psychologists have observed that the sexiest sex organ is the _____, where perceptions begin. For most individuals, the primary reasons for sex are to enjoy it, express _____ and intimacy, or to make _____. Men and women differ in their perceptions of, and experiences with, sexual coercion. In one study, nearly _____-_____ of the women claimed that men had forced them to do something sexually that they did not want to do but only _____ percent of the men said they had ever forced a woman into a sexual act. The most extreme example of sexual coercion is _____. Men who rape have several motivations: _____ and _____ toward women; a desire to dominate, _____, or punish the victim; and _____.

3-3. There are many _____ variations in sexuality. The rules and requirements about sex are transmitted via

sexual _____, which are sets of _____ rules that specify proper sexual behavior for a person and vary with the person's age, culture, and, gender.

3-4. Research has shown that _____ is not a result of having a smothering mother, an absent father, or emotional problems. This has led researchers to turn to biological explanations for _____ _____. Many have tried to use _____ exposure to _____ to explain brain organization and partner preference, but results have been inconclusive. The basic problem with trying to find a single origin of sexual orientation is that sexual _____ and behavior take different _____, and they don't _____ strongly.

Terms for Review

The following is a list of the important terms from the section "The Erotic Animal: Motives for Sex." Make sure you are familiar with each term before taking the progress test on these terms.

sexual scripts

4. The Competent Animal: Motives to Achieve

Read the section "The Competent Animal: Motives to Achieve" and then answer the following questions. If you have trouble answering any of the questions, re-study the relevant material before going on to the review of key terms and the progress tests.

4-1. _____/_____ psychologists have measured the qualities

that spur _____ and success and also the environmental conditions that affect _____ and satisfaction. McClelland proposed that people have an inner _____, which he measured with the _____ _____ _____ (TAT). The empirical evidence for the TAT shows that it does not have strong test-retest _____. Today, the study of achievement _____ emphasizes _____ rather than inner drives. A goal is most likely to improve motivation and performance when it is _____, _____ but achievable, and is _____ in terms of what is wanted rather than what is to be avoided. For example, _____ goals are positive experiences that are sought directly while _____ goals involve the effort to avoid unpleasant experiences. In addition to defining _____, people need to know what to do when setbacks occur. People who are motivated by _____ goals may stop trying to improve when they fail. In contrast, people who are motivated by _____, or learning, goals regard failure as a source of information that will help them improve. In fact, children praised for their _____ rather than their intelligence and ability are less likely to give up when faced with failure. How hard people work to achieve their goals also depends on their _____, which

can create a _____-_____ prophecy. Another consideration is _____-_____, which is the belief that one is capable of producing desired results. A strong sense of _____-_____ has a positive effect on goal achievement.

4-2. Many psychologists want to know how the work we do, and the _____ under which we do it, influences our motivation to succeed. For example, achievement depends on having the _____ to achieve. It is also important that the work feels meaningful and _____ to employees; employees have _____ over many aspects of their work; tasks are _____ rather than _____; employees have _____ relationships with superiors and co-workers; employees receive useful _____ about their work; and the company offers opportunities to learn and _____.

Terms for Review

The following is a list of the important terms from the section "The Competent Animal: Motives to Achieve." Make sure you are familiar with each term before taking the progress test on these terms.

industrial/organizational psychology   avoidance goals
Thematic Apperception Test   performance goals
self-fulfilling prophecy   mastery goals
approach goals   self-efficacy

5. Motives, Values, and the Pursuit of Happiness

Read the section "Motives, Values, and the Pursuit of Happiness" and then answer the following questions. If you have trouble answering any of the questions, re-study the relevant material before going on to the review of key terms and the progress tests.

5-1. Generally, people who are motivated by the _____ satisfaction of an activity are happier and more satisfied than those motivated solely by _____ rewards. American culture puts a high value on accumulating _____. However, people who are motivated primarily to get rich have poorer _____ adjustment and lower _____ than do people whose primary values are self-acceptance, _____ with others, or wanting to make the _____ a better place. And, conflicts between values and goals can lead to emotional stress and _____. Researchers have identified three kinds of motivational _____. _____-_____ conflicts occur when people are equally attracted to two or more possible activities or goals.

_____-_____ conflicts occur when people have to choose between alternatives that are disliked.

_____-_____ conflicts occur when a single activity or goal has both positive and negative aspects. If conflicts remain unresolved, they can take an _____ toll. Another viewpoint on psychological motives is offered by _____ who referred to people's motives as forming a pyramid. The bottom of the pyramid contains _____ survival needs, whereas the top of the hierarchy represents _____-_____ and self-transcendence. Although this theory is very popular, it has little _____ support. Instead, it appears more common for people to have _____ needs that they are trying to satisfy.

Terms for Review

The following is a list of the important terms from the section "Motives, Values, and the Pursuit of Happiness." Make sure you are familiar with each term before taking the progress test on these terms.

approach-approach conflicts
avoidance-avoidance conflicts
approach-avoidance conflicts

SAMPLE ANSWERS TO *YOU ARE ABOUT TO LEARN* QUESTIONS FROM TEXTBOOK

After you have read through the chapter, go back and review the "You Are About to Learn..." statements that precede each major section. Create your own answer to each question, then compare your answers to the following sample answers. If your answers are not similar to the sample answers, review the relevant sections of the chapter more carefully.

What biological mechanisms make it difficult for obese people to lose weight and keep it off?

The leading explanation of such phenomena is that a biological mechanism keeps a person's body weight at a genetically influenced set point—the weight the person stays at when not trying to gain or lose. Everyone has a genetically programmed basal metabolism rate and a fixed number of fat cells. A complex interaction of metabolism, fat cells, and hormones keeps people at the weight their bodies are designed to be. Thus, when a heavy person diets, the body's metabolism slows down to conserve energy and fat reserves. When a thin person overeats, metabolism speeds up, burning energy.

How do notions of the ideal male and female body change over time and across cultures?

The notions of what is attractive have often changed as the cultural symbols of status have changed. For example, being a heavily muscled man used to be considered unattractive because it indicated that the man was probably a laborer, farmer, and someone else of low status. However, today it is considered attractive because it indicates a man has the money and time to join a gym and work out. Similarly, the curvy, big-breasted female body is associated with femininity, nurturance, and motherhood. However, many whites associate femininity with incompetence. And, professionally ambitious women may feel pressured to look boyishly thin and muscular in order to avoid appearing "soft," feminine, and dumb. Also, women who have eating disorders have internalized the unrealistic body ideal, and tend to be depressed, perfectionist, and more self-critical than are healthy eaters.

Why are people all over the world getting fatter?

This is due to environmental changes. The leading culprits are the increased abundance of low-cost, high-calorie foods; the habit of eating high-calorie food on the run rather than leisurely meals; the rise in energy-saving devices; the convenience of driving over walking or biking; and the preference for watching television rather than doing anything active.

What are the major forms of eating disorders, and why are they increasing among both sexes?

Bulimia nervosa is one of the major eating disorders, in which the person typically binges and then purges. Anorexia nervosa is another major eating disorder, which involves the person becoming dangerously thin. The rates have been increasing because current cultural factors frequently create dissatisfaction with one's body.

259

How does biology affect attachment and love?

Certain neurotransmitters and hormones play a key role in the development of attachment and love. For example, the hormones vasopressin and oxytocin influence feelings and expressions of love, caring, and trust between mothers and babies, between friends, and between lovers.

What are some key psychological influences on whom and how you love?

Proximity and similarity are two major predictors of whom we love. That is, we tend to choose friends and lovers from the set of people who live close by and who share our looks, attitudes, beliefs, values, personality, and interest.

What are the three basic styles of attachment and how do they affect relationships?

The three basic styles are secure, anxious, or avoidant attachments. Securely attached lovers are rarely jealous or worried about being abandoned and tend to be more compassionate and helpful. Anxious lovers are always agitated about their relationships. They tend to worry about being left and therefore are often clingy. Avoidant people distrust and avoid intimate attachments.

How do economic concerns influence love and marriage?

In developed nations only tiny numbers of men and women would consider marrying someone they did not love. Pragmatic (income) reasons for marriage, with romantic love being a remote luxury, persist only in underdeveloped countries and in other cultures in which the extended family still controls female sexuality and the terms of marriage.

Which part of the anatomy is the "sexist sex organ?"

Researchers have shown repeatedly that the sexiest sex organ is actually the brain, where perceptions begin. People's values, fantasies, and beliefs profoundly affect sexual desire and behavior.

Why is pleasure only one of the many motives for having sex?

People have sex for many reasons, including common factors such as expressing love and intimacy, making babies, money or perks, duty or feelings of obligation, rebellion, power over the partner, and submission to the partner to avoid anger or rejection.

How does culture affect sexual practice?

Culture influences the use of sexual scripts, which are sets of implicit rules that specify proper sexual behavior for a person in a given situation. These vary according to the person's gender, age, religion, social status, and peer group.

What are the puzzling origins of sexual orientation?

Researchers have long struggled to identify the determining factors in sexual orientation. They have discovered that homosexuality is not the result of having a smothering mother, an absent father, or emotional problems. Androgens, especially during the prenatal stage, may play a role. Ultimately, it is very difficult to pinpoint an origin because sexual identity and behavior take different forms and they don't correlate strongly.

What are the three kinds of goals that are most likely to improve the

Goals that are the most motivating are ones that are specific, challenging but achievable, and are framed in terms of gains

motivation to succeed?

rather than avoiding loss.

What is the important difference between mastery goals and performance goals?

With mastery goals, a person is motivated to increase their skill or competence in a given area. This is contrasted with performance goals, where the focus is on performing well for other people and thereby being judged favorably and avoiding criticism.

How is the desire to achieve affected by the opportunity to achieve?

The opportunity to achieve is an important working condition that affects achievement. Once in a career, people may become more motivated to advance up the ladder or less so, depending on how many rungs they are permitted to climb. Also, when someone does not do well at work, others may say that it is the individual's own fault because he or she lacks the internal drive to perform. But what the person may really lack is a fair chance to make it, and this is especially true for those who have been subjected to systematic discrimination, such as women and ethnic minorities. Women and members of minority groups often face a "glass ceiling," a barrier to promotion that prevents advancement.

Which aspects of a job are more important than money in increasing satisfaction with work?

Aspects of the work environment known to increase work satisfaction and involvement are: a) the work is meaningful; b) employees have control over many aspects of their work; c) tasks are varied; d) the company maintains clear and consistent rules; e) employees have supportive relationships with their superiors and co-workers; f) employees receive useful feedback; and, g) the company offers opportunities to learn and advance.

Why are people poor at predicting what will make them happy or miserable?

People tend to adjust to new experiences, both good and bad, more quickly than they realize. As such, when these positive and negative events do occur, they do not have the long-lasting effect that people had originally predicted.

Why can't money buy happiness-- and what does?

When individuals do achieve increased wealth, they quickly adjust to the new level of income and begin to once again imagine that even more money will make them happy. As such, money rarely sustains long-term happiness. Finding and doing activities and experiences that are intrinsically motivating is more likely to produce happiness than having things or wealth.

What are the three basic kinds of motivational conflicts?

Approach-approach conflicts occur when an individual is confronted with two equally motivating activities or goals and now must make a choice between two desirable outcomes. Avoidance-avoidance conflicts are those in which the individual is forced to choose between two equally undesirable activities or goals and is unable to avoid both. In approach-avoidance conflicts, there is only one activity or goal, but it produces conflict because that activity or goal has both positive and negative qualities.

KEY TERMS FILL-IN-THE-BLANKS PROGRESS TEST

Fill in the blanks with the key terms from the chapter that match the definitions provided. When you have finished this progress test, check your answers with those at the end of this chapter. You should review any key terms that you do not define correctly.

1. _____ A theory in which people's motives form a pyramid.

2. _____ The desire to do something for its own sake and for the internal pleasure it provides.

3. _____ The motive to associate with other people, as by seeking friends, companionship, or love.

4. _____ The desire to do something for the sake of external rewards, such as money or fame.

5. _____ Sets of implicit rules that specify proper sexual behavior for a person in a given situation, varying with the person's age, culture, and gender.

6. _____ Collections of rules that determine the proper attitudes and behavior for men and women, sexual and otherwise.

7. _____ A protein that travels through the blood to the hypothalamus, which is involved in the regulation of appetite.

8. _____ The rate at which the body burns calories for energy.

9. _____ The genetically influenced weight range for an individual, maintained by biological mechanisms that regulate food intake, fat reserves, and metabolism.

10. _____ An eating disorder characterized by fear of being fat, a distorted body image, radically reduced consumption of food, and emaciation.

11. _____ An eating disorder characterized by episodes of excessive eating followed by forced vomiting or use of laxatives.

12. _____ A person's belief that he or she is capable of producing desired results, such as mastering new skills and reaching goals.

13. _____ An expectation that is fulfilled because of the tendency of the person holding it to act in ways that bring it about.

14. _____ A learned motive to meet personal standards of success and excellence in a chosen area.

15. _____ A projective test that asks respondents to interpret a series of drawings showing scenes of people; usually scored for unconscious personality traits and motives, such as the need for achievement, power, or affiliation.

16. _____ Goals framed in terms of desired outcomes or experiences.

17. _____ Goals framed in terms of increasing one's competence and skills.

18. _____ Goals framed in terms of performing well in front of others, being judged favorably, and avoiding criticism.

19. _____ Conflicts that require one to choose between the lesser of two evils.

20. _____ Conflicts that occur when a single activity or goal has both a positive and a negative aspect.

MULTIPLE-CHOICE PROGRESS TEST

Choose the single best answer for each of the following questions. When you have finished this progress test, check your answers with those at the end of this chapter. You should review the relevant pages in the text for the questions you do not answer correctly.

1. Passionate love involves _____ while companionate love involves _____.
   a. sexual passion; emotional intensity
   b. sexual passion; infatuation
   c. affection and trust; sexual passion
   d. emotional intensity; affection and trust

2. According to the attachment theory of love, _____ lovers are rarely jealous or worried about being abandoned.
   a. securely attached
   b. anxious
   c. ambivalent
   d. avoidant

3. Which of the following statements about Maslow's pyramid of needs theory is TRUE?
   a. Basic survival needs are at the top level of the pyramid.
   b. Social needs for belonging and affection are below security needs in the pyramid.
   c. This theory has not been supported by research.
   d. None of the above is true.

4. Which of the following is TRUE regarding Masters and Johnson's research on human sexuality?
   a. Their sample consisted of people from various age groups.
   b. Their research confirmed that male and female orgasms are remarkably similar.
   c. Their findings showed that orgasms are physiologically different depending on the source of stimulation.
   d. Their findings were collected using the naturalistic observation method.

5. Which of the following statements about gender and love is FALSE?
   a. Men and women differ, on average, in how they express love.
   b. Neither sex loves more than the other in terms of "love at first sight," or

companionate love.
   c. Both sexes suffer when a love relationship ends if they did not want it to end.
   d. None of the above is false.

6. Based on the national survey described in the text, nearly _____ of the women said that a man, usually a husband or boyfriend, had forced them to do something sexually that they did not want to do. But only about _____ of men said they had ever forced a woman into a sexual act.
   a. 25 percent; 3 percent
   b. 50 percent; 33 percent
   c. 33 percent; 25 percent
   d. 3 percent; 1 percent

7. Which of the following findings would NOT support the evolutionary view of sexuality?
   a. Men reporting more interest than women do in the youth and beauty of their sexual partners
   b. Men being quicker than women are to have sex with partners that they do not know well
   c. Men being more inclined than women are toward polygamy and promiscuity
   d. Men being more inclined than women are to emphasize the financial resources or prospects of a potential mate

8. Which of the following statements about cultural variations and sexuality is TRUE?
   a. Cultures differ in what parts of the body are erotic.
   b. Cultures differ in the sexual acts that are considered erotic.
   c. Cultures differ in whether sex is seen as something joyful and beautiful or as something ugly and dirty.
   d. All the above are true.

9. Which of the following statements about sexual orientation is FALSE?
   a. The overwhelming majority of children of gay parents do not become gay.
   b. Females with a history of prenatal exposure to high levels of androgens are more likely than are other females to become bisexual or lesbian.
   c. Homosexuality is unrelated to smothering mothers and absent fathers.
   d. The vast majority of homosexual men and lesbians have a close gay relative.

10. According to the set point theory of weight:
    a. everyone has a fixed number of fat cells.
    b. when a heavy person diets, the body's metabolism slows down to conserve energy.
    c. when a thin person overeats, metabolism speeds up, burning energy.
    d. All the above are answers.

11. Compared to the role leptin plays in the obesity of mice, its role in human obesity is:
    a. simpler.
    b. more complicated.
    c. about the same.
    d. minor.

12. Which of the following nongenetic influences on weight boosts the body's metabolic rate and may lower its set point?
    a. Watching television
    b. Eating high-calorie food
    c. Exercise
    d. Driving

13. In _____, the sufferer typically binges and then purges by vomiting or using laxatives. This disorder and other eating disorders are more common in _____.
    a. bulimia; men
    b. bulimia; women
    c. anorexia nervosa; men
    d. anorexia nervosa; women

14. A goal is most likely to improve performance when:
    a. one defines the goal as "doing one's best."
    b. one gives oneself an indefinite amount of time to achieve it.
    c. the goal is challenging but achievable.
    d. All the above are answers.

15. People who are motivated by _____ are concerned with increasing their competence and skills and _____ discouraged by criticism and failure.
    a. mastery goals; are
    b. mastery goals; are not
    c. performance goals; are
    d. performance goals; are not

16. A person's belief that he or she is capable of producing desired results is called _____.
    a. self-fulfilling prophecy
    b. self-efficacy
    c. need for achievement
    d. approach-approach conflict

17. Novice parachute jumpers must choose between the fear of jumping and the fear of losing face if they do not jump. This is an example of an _____ conflict.
    a. approach-approach
    b. avoidance-avoidance
    c. approach-avoidance
    d. avoidance-approach

Guided Study

1. The Hungry Animal: Motives to Eat

1-1. Motivation
intrinsic
extrinsic
emotional disturbance
experiments
overeating
set point
gain
lose
basal metabolism
fat
heritability
adoption
leptin
hypothalamus

1-2. processed
soft drinks
exercise
portion
varied
culture's
ideal
ethnicities
Europe
thinner
strong
big-breasted
skinny
ambivalence
professional
affluence
poverty

1-3. bulimia
anorexia
women
men

2. The Social Animal: Motives for Love

2-1. passionate
passion
companionate
vasopressin
oxytocin
endorphins

2-2. proximity
similarity
secure
avoidant
anxious
attachment
parents
obsessiveness

2-3. ends
express
words
actions
love

3. The Erotic Animal: Motives for Sex

3-1. biological
cultural
Kinsey
Masters
lesser
testosterone
consensus
misdiagnose
depression
relationship
side effects
sex drive
Evolutionary
adaptive
inseminate
genetic
stereotypes
variation
say
do

3-2. brain
love
babies

one-fourth
3
rape
narcissism
hostility
humiliate
sadism

3-3. cultural
scripts
implicit

3-4. homosexuality
sexual orientation
prenatal
androgens
identity
forms
correlate

---

4. The Competent Animal: Motives to Achieve

4-1. Industrial/organizational
achievement
productivity
drive
Thematic Apperception Test
reliability
motivation
goals
specific
challenging
framed
approach
avoidance
goals
performance
mastery
efforts
expectations
self-fulfilling
self-efficacy
self-efficacy

4-2. conditions
opportunity
important
control
varied
repetitive
supportive
feedback
advance

---

5. Motives, Values, and the Pursuit of Happiness

5-1. intrinsic
extrinsic
wealth
psychological
well-being
affiliation
world
unhappiness
conflicts
Approach-approach
Avoidance-avoidance
Approach-avoidance
emotional
Maslow
basic
self-actualization
empirical
simultaneous

Answers to Key Terms Progress Test

1. Maslow's hierarchy of needs
2. intrinsic motivation
3. need for affiliation
4. extrinsic motivation
5. sexual scripts
6. gender roles
7. leptin
8. basal metabolism rate
9. set point
10. anorexia
11. bulimia
12. self-efficacy
13. self-fulfilling prophecy
14. need for achievement
15. Thematic Apperception Test (TAT)
16. approach goals
17. mastery (learning goals)
18. performance goals
19. avoidance-avoidance conflicts
20. approach-avoidance conflicts

Answers to Multiple-Choice Progress Test

Item Number	Answers
1.	d. emotional intensity; affection and trust
2.	a. securely attached
3.	c. This theory has not been supported by research.
4.	b. Their research confirmed that male and female orgasms are remarkably similar.
5.	d. None of the above is false.
6.	a. 25 percent; 3 percent
7.	d. Men being more inclined than women are to emphasize the financial resources or prospects of a potential mate
8.	d. All the above are true.
9.	d. The vast majority of homosexual men and lesbians have a close gay relative.
10.	d. All the above are answers.
11.	b. is more complicated.
12.	c. exercise
13.	b. bulimia; women
14.	c. the goal is challenging but achievable.
15.	b. mastery goals; are not
16.	b. self-efficacy
17.	b. avoidance-avoidance